$500

Studies in the
NEW TESTAMENT

Studies in the
NEW TESTAMENT

by
Frederic L. Godet

KREGEL PUBLICATIONS
Grand Rapids, Michigan 49501

Studies in the New Testament by Frederic L. Godet.
Copyright ©1984 by Kregel Publications, a
division of Kregel, Inc. All rights reserved.

Library of Congress Cataloging in Publication Data

Godet, Frederic Louis, 1812-1900.
  Studies in the New Testament.

  Translated from French.
  Reprint. Originally published: Studies on the New
Testament. London: Hodder and Stoughton, 1876.
  1. Bible. N.T.—Criticism, interpretation, etc.—Ad-
dresses, essays, lectures. 2. Jesus Christ—Person and
offices—Addresses, essays, lectures. I. Title.
BS2395.G63 1984   225.6   84-7137
ISBN 0-8254-2722-3

Published in the United States of America

CONTENTS

PUBLISHER'S PREFACE

Frederic L. Godet is known for his firm defense of the orthodox Christian position. He withstood the growing theological liberalism in Protestant theology and schools of his day. He is remembered as one of the most influential Swiss Protestant Reformed scholars of his generation.

Of him, it was written, "Unquestionably, Frederic L. Godet is one of the first, if not the very first, of contemporary commentators on the Scriptures. His portraits and his descriptions are projected upon the canvas with the brilliancy of the fluorescent light as compared with the oil lamp of ordinary comprehension." Godet's writings belong to the select and limited class of books which touch the common things with a freshness, penetration, and harmony of view, which, in the highest degree of it, we call genius.

He took his undergraduate work at the University of Neuchatel and studied theology at Bonn and Berlin under Johann A. Neander. He was ordained to the Christian ministry in 1836 and served as Professor of Biblical Exegesis and Critical Theology. In 1873, he was one of the founders of the Evangelical Free Church of Neuchatel and Professor of New Testament Exegesis in the Free Evangelical Theological School. His extensive training in and use of the original languages (Hebrew and Greek) of the Scriptures became a reservoir of understanding and truth from which flowed, through his pen, the originality and beauty of his commentaries.

Seldom does one find a book more striking, interesting, and instructive. In this work, *Studies in the New Testament*, covering the whole of the New Testament, Godet's insight is profound and his teaching is weighty and suggestive.

Dr. F.B. Meyer said of this commentary, "to an immense erudition, to a living piety, Godet unites a profound feeling of reality; there is an ardent love for the Savior, which helps the believer to comprehend the work, the acts, and the words of his Divine Master."

Topics dealt with in *Studies in the New Testament* are: "The Origin of the Four Gospels," Matthew, Mark, Luke and John; "The Person of Jesus Christ" as the Son of Man, the Son of God, the God-Man; "The Work of Jesus Christ," His Work for Me and His Work in Me; "The Four Principal Apostles," Peter, James, Paul and John, and "The Book of Revelation." What a treasury of help is offered here for the student of the New Testament who will find the expressions of Godet so laden with truth and so artistically offered.

1

THE ORIGIN OF THE FOUR GOSPELS

OF all the important events which took place in the world before the advent of Jesus Christ, there is not one which has been recorded in four narratives,—much less in four narratives nearly contemporaneous with the event and simultaneous with each other. The appearance of Jesus on earth has been alone the object of this signal distinction. Before the end of the century in which Jesus Christ was born, four original histories of His life and works were in circulation among the Churches, and in the world.

These four pictures resemble one another in certain respects to such a degree that, to the eye of an ordinary reader, they appear to be only copies of one another. Put into the hands of the generality of Christians the four gospels, or four copies of any one amongst them, and the majority will discover scarcely any difference between the two. But this apparent uniformity vanishes at once on a more careful reading. To the eyes of a discerning reader the differences manifest themselves in as marked and decided a manner as the difference of features amongst four brothers in whose faces one had at first only noticed the family likeness.   Ultimately the differences appear so striking that it becomes a little difficult to recognise in these documents that amount of agreement which cannot fail to exist between four true accounts of the same event.

The first contrast which the thoughtful reader detects is that which exists between the gospel of St. John and the three others.   The course of the ministry of Jesus, though with some differences, is, speaking generally, the same in these latter ; so that it is easy to harmonise their narratives.   It is for this reason that they are called " the Synoptics."[1]   St. John's gospel does not lend itself so easily to such a process. The course of the ministry of Jesus is traced in lines so different as to render it difficult to make this narrative agree with the three others.

But when we look deeper still, we discover, even in the synoptics themselves, differences so marked that we may compare them to various species in the same genus ; and thus we are led to ask how this diversity is compatible with the accuracy of the three narratives.

No doubt faith is independent of the solution of this problem.   She perceives by direct intuition the divine character, not only of the event narrated, but

---

[1] From the Greek *synopsis*, which signifies a view comprehending in one a number of distinct histories arranged side by side.

even of the manner in which it is recorded. The remark " This is not the style of an inventor " applies both to the substance and to the form of our gospel narratives : to the substance,—for the phenomenon described is too miraculously holy to be the creation of a human imagination ; to the form,—for such sobriety, such unwavering objectivity in the narration of so sublime a fact, can be the effect only of the complete self-suppression of the writer in presence of the divine reality. . . . Faith—that organ with which we are endowed for the perception of divine things, just as, by means of the eye, we perceive the light— seizes at once on these characteristics, and appropriates without hesitation the object which, in her eyes, possesses them. But if faith is not dependent upon the solution of the difficulty indicated, she seeks for it, nevertheless.

That which saves us is faith, and faith alone ; but that which satisfies is a faith which has arrived at perfect harmony with herself.

Such satisfaction is a lawful object of desire ; and our wish is by this essay to help to procure it for our readers. We wish to show them that if the unity of our four gospel narratives constitutes the *certainty* of the knowledge we have of Christ, we are indebted to their diversity for the *richness*, the fulness of this knowledge.

To attain this end it is necessary to go back to the origin of these narratives, which alone will enable us to explain their diversity without impeaching their credibility.

In the various domains of literature we possess two classes of instruments for ascertaining the origin of any ancient document : first, the records transmitted from ancient times respecting its composition, and especially its authorship, together with the traces which its existence and its use have left upon contemporaneous or subsequent writings; secondly, the indications which the work itself contains on the various questions relating to its origin—indications easily discovered by a careful study of its contents.

When these two kinds of *criteria* [1] lead to the same result, as great a degree of certainty is reached as is attainable by science. If the results do not agree, the student is compelled to suspend his judgment.

Let us follow the same course. Science offers us no other. Let us first consult the accounts transmitted by the most ancient teachers of the Church, respecting the composition of our gospels. Amongst these venerable witnesses were to be found some men, as we shall see, who were personally acquainted with the apostles. Their accounts of the origin of the apostolic writings are generally marked by a character of simplicity, as contrasted with the pious exaggerations noticeable in the reports of subsequent writers.

---

[1] A Greek word which signifies means of judging and estimating.

Let us listen then, first of all, to those voices which reach us, as it were, from the very threshold of the apostolic times. Then let us confront the words of these ancient witnesses with such indications as study will enable us to gather from the gospels themselves.

For us faith is not to be called in question, but only to be enlightened. She possesses Him whose life is the subject of our four gospel narratives. But she undertakes to account for the diversity between the four portraits which have been preserved to us of His Person ; for she would fain raise her intuition of the Christ to the level of that of those who beheld Him, agreeably to the words of one of these : " That which we have seen and heard declare we unto you, that ye also may have fellowship with us,"[1]—that is to say, that you may see and hear Him in spirit, as we have seen and heard Him with our bodily eyes and ears.

1

THE GOSPEL OF MATTHEW

We find this treatise placed, in all ancient documents, at the head of the gospel records, and of the whole canon of the New Testament, as constituting the connecting link between the Old and the New

---

[1] 1 John i. 3.

Covenant ; we will ourselves give reasons to justify this way of viewing it.

I. We have two very ancient accounts of its origin, —one given by Papias, bishop of Hierapolis, in Phrygia, in the first half of the second century, who died probably about the year 160 ; the other by Irenæus, presbyter, afterwards bishop of Lyons, who lived in the second half of the same century, and died about the year 200. The former had been, according to ancient testimony, a hearer of the apostle John; the latter a disciple of Polycarp, the friend and companion of the same apostle during his sojourn in Asia Minor in the latter part of his life.

The words of the former are : " Matthew composed the discourses in the Hebrew tongue, and every one translated them as he was able." What are we to understand by this expression, *the discourses ?* Does it mean the sermons of Jesus ? If so, the Hebrew document composed by Matthew would not have been a gospel, properly so called, but simply an account of the teachings of Jesus. Or, are we to understand by *the discourses* the revelation of God in Jesus Christ ? [1] If we take this to be the meaning, we might consider the object of Matthew's treatise to be the whole history of the ministry of Jesus, and there would be no difference between our canonical Greek gospel, which

---

[1] This is quite an admissible rendering of the Greek. In fact, the word used by Papias (*Logia*) signifies *oracles*—divine discourses. *Cf.* Rom. iii. 2.

bears the name of this apostle, and the document attributed to him by Papias, except that of language. As to the last words of this account, they signify, no doubt, that before the publication of the Greek translation of Matthew's Hebrew work, the wandering preachers, or *evangelists*, who made use of it in the Churches in which only Greek was spoken, and who made it the text of their addresses, were obliged to translate it *vivâ voce*.

Irenæus expresses himself as follows, on the same subject : " Matthew also published the Gospel among the Jews in writing, in their own language, while Peter and Paul were preaching at Rome and founding the Church there." The apostle in this case must have written in Palestine, and about the year 63 ; for that is the only date at which Peter and Paul could have been present together in the capital of the world. Against the soundness of this reasoning it has been objected that the Church was not founded in Rome by either the one or the other ; for it has been proved that it existed many years before their arrival in that city.[1] But it must be remembered that from the standpoint of the second century, —the date of Irenæus' writing,—the whole of the

---

[1] The unquestionable fact that the epistle to the Romans was composed in the winter of the year 58-59, whilst the arrival of St. Paul in Rome did not take place till 61 (Acts xxviii.), would of itself be sufficient proof of this as far as that apostle is concerned.

apostolic period appeared as an age of laying foundations.

To these two ancient testimonies we add a third, of
rather later date, but important as summing up all
that is told us by the fathers : it is that of Eusebius,
bishop of Cesaræa, at the close of the third and beginning of the fourth century.   He expresses himself
as follows : " Matthew wishing, after having begun
by preaching to the Jews, to go and preach also
to other nations, put his gospel into writing, in the
language of the fathers (Hebrew), and thus filled up
the void about to be made by his absence."   It would
seem that the apostles left Jerusalem about the year
60.   Even in A.D. 59, at the time of his last visit to
that city, Paul seems to have found there, as rulers of
the Church, only James, the *brother of Jesus*, who
was not an apostle, and the council of presbyters over
whom he presided.[1]   The date indicated by Eusebius
coincides, then, very nearly with that given by Irenæus.
Putting them together, we should say that it was
between the years 60 and 63 that, according to the
oldest traditions, Matthew composed his written
gospel in Palestine.

Finally, a collective testimony of the highest
importance is that contained in the title which our
canonical gospel has borne ever since the second
century—" the gospel according to Matthew."

---

[1] Acts xxi. 18 sqq.

In this title the word *gospel* means, not the book itself, but, according to the original sense of the word, the contents of the book: the gospel, that is, the *good news* of salvation, *according to the version* of Matthew.[1]

In this title was expressed, not the opinion of a few theologians only, but that of the Churches of that age.

Accordingly, our gospel is constantly used by the fathers from the middle of the second century. Justin Martyr ranks it amongst those *memoirs* of the apostles, and of their fellow-labourers, from which he draws all his information upon the life of Jesus. We even find our gospel quoted at a still earlier date. The so-called epistle of Barnabas, which dates from the end of the first century or the beginning of the second, not only extracts from it a saying of Jesus, but in so doing makes use of the form of quotation which is only usual with regard to books considered by the Church to have a divine authority—"*as it is written.*"[2]

To sum up the result of these testimonies. Our first canonical gospel was regarded and used, in the

---

[1] See my commentaries on the gospels of John (vol. i., pp. 140—142) and of Luke (vol. i., pp. 63, 64, 2nd edit.)

[2] Hilgenfeld, a critic belonging to the rationalistic school, candidly admits, in speaking of this quotation, that "we have here the earliest trace—dating from the end of the first century —of the application of the notion of *Holy Scripture* to a statement in the Gospel." (*Der Kanon*, p. 10.)

second century of the Church, as the reproduction in Greek of a document composed by Matthew in Hebrew, about the year 60, or from that to 63, and which contained either an account of the ministry of Jesus in general, or else of His teachings only.

II. Now let us put out of our minds all that has been said ; let us put out of sight even the title of the book we are studying ; and let us look in its own pages for traces of its origin.

The *object* with which it was composed cannot be for a moment doubtful. The author, recounting a history, purposes, while doing so, to lay the foundations of faith in the Person who is the subject of it. With this view he introduces Him as the Messiah promised *to the Jews*, and brings into special prominence through the whole of his narrative that harmony between the events and the prophecies by which Jesus is marked out as *the Christ*.

This object is evident from its opening words : "The book of the generation of Jesus Christ, the son of David, the son of Abraham" (Matt. i. 1). He is that descendant from Abraham "in whom," according to Moses, "all the families of the earth were to be blessed." He is that Son of David who, according to Isaiah, was to "establish His kingdom for ever."[1] He is, then, the expected Messiah, the King of Israel, and consequently also the Saviour of the world. The last

---

[1] Gen. xii. 3 ; Isa. ix. 7.

words of the book correspond with this preamble, and exhibit this programme fulfilled in Jesus, as the result of all His conflicts and apparent defeats : "All power is given unto me in heaven and in earth. Go ye therefore, and teach all nations, baptizing them in the name of the Father, and of the Son, and of the Holy Ghost : teaching them to observe all things what-soever I have commanded you." (Matt. xxviii. 18—20.)

The whole history which leads us onwards from these first to these last words, is stamped with the same Messianic seal.

The formula, "*that it might be fulfilled,*" is like a *refrain* repeated in every page of the book. In the two first chapters we find five detached incidents of the childhood of Jesus, connected with five prophetic sayings. At the opening of the ministry, in chap. iv., is a prophecy of Isaiah which forms as it were its general text or motto, and announces that Galilee is to be the theatre of the Messianic work. In chap. viii., as the central point of a collection of miraculous incidents, we have a saying of the same prophet, revealing the moral significance of all these wonders : "Himself took our infirmities and bare our sicknesses." The series of teachings given in chap. xii. is also con-nected with a prophetic saying : "Behold my servant whom I have chosen . . . . he shall not strive nor cry . . . . a bruised reed shall he not break." And so on, up to the account of the Passion, of which every feature is in some way designated as the fulfilment of a prophecy.

The ruling thought of such a narrative as this is evident. This gospel is the demonstration of the rights of sovereignty of Jesus over Israel as their Messiah. This treatise is addressed in the first place to the ancient people of God. And if Israel will not understand and believe, it will be for the world to profit by it. For the King of Israel is also King of the world.

It is not so easy to see clearly the *manner of composition*, as the object, of this treatise. This task, however, it does not seem to us impossible to fulfil.

On a closer study of the first gospel, we are struck with a salient feature which may help to put us on the right track. Interwoven into the text of the narrative we meet at intervals with certain grand discourses, or sets of discourses, fitted into the framework of the history. These discourses are five in number :

1. The sermon of Jesus commonly called the *Sermon on the Mount* (v.—vii.), which forms in our gospel the opening scene of the ministry of Jesus in Galilee. This is the new code of the kingdom of God, proclaimed as from the top of another Sinai ; the formula of a higher righteousness, before which that of the Scribes and Pharisees was to pale.

2. An instruction addressed to the twelve apostles upon the subject of their ministry, at the moment

when Jesus for the first time commits to them an independent mission (x.) This is the normal instruction upon the apostolate.

3. A collection of parables on the kingdom of heaven (xiii.) This constitutes a series of pictures, representing in a rational order the different aspects of the great fact of the kingdom of God upon earth : its foundation—in the parable of the sower ; its development, abnormal in appearance but divine nevertheless—in that of the tares ; its power, considered first in its intensity, then in its extent—in those of the leaven and of the mustard seed ; its supreme value, in virtue of which it more than indemnifies man for all the sacrifices he makes to gain possession of it—in those of the hidden treasure and the pearl of great price; finally its consummation—in the parable of the net.

4. An instruction on discipline given to the Church mainly with reference to the line of conduct she is to adopt towards her erring members xviii.)

5. An important group of discourses connected together by the one idea of the judgment exercised by Jesus Christ (xxiii.—xxv.) ; comprehending these three principal acts : the condemnation of the then existing theocratic authorities; the destruction of Jerusalem and the end of the world ; and the universal judgment. This fifth group answers to the first and third, as the office of *judge* is the complement of those of *lawgiver* and of *king*. Had not Isaiah said

(xxxiii. 22), "The Lord is our judge, the Lord is our lawgiver, the Lord is our king; He will save us"?

These five discourses certainly form the salient feature in the physiognomy of the first gospel. They are distinguished from the narrative in which they are imbedded by the nearly identical form of words with which they all five terminate : "And when Jesus had ended these sayings" (vii. 28) ; "And it came to pass when Jesus had made an end of commanding His twelve disciples" (xi. 1). Compare, besides, xiii. 53 ; xix. 1 ; xxvi. 1. Does it not seem as if, before they belonged to the narrative of which they are now a part, these five discourses had formed one whole, which the author of our story had thought fit to take to pieces in order to set each of these jewels in some place which he had marked in the history of our Lord's ministry. Add to this fact the following less noticeable feature : that in the discourses of Jesus the passages from the Old Testament are generally quoted from the ancient Greek translation called the Septuagint, while in the narrative portions the quotations are more often from the Hebrew text. Must we not here recall the words of the aged Papias respecting the original document of Matthew: "Matthew composed *the discourses*"? In fact, if we cut away from our gospel all the narrative framework, the purely historical portions, what have we left? These five great discourses ; in other words, the document of

St. Matthew exactly as Papias describes it, if we take his word *discourse* in its strict sense.

We must here call to mind that Papias had himself composed a work entitled " An Explanation of the Discourses of the Lord," and that this work was divided into five books. May not each of these books have had for its subject one of the five great discourses comprised in the document of the apostle ?

If such was in reality the primitive work of Matthew, we should conclude from this that its character was didactic and not historical. It was exclusively an exposition of our Lord's teaching. And in that case it is natural to admit that the plan of such a work ought to be systematic. All the instructions of the Master would be there grouped under some principal heads, of which it is not difficult even now to trace the titles, and of which we can easily see the connection : 1st, *the new law ;* 2nd, *the apostolate ;* 3rd, *the kingdom of heaven ;* 4th, *the Church ;* 5th, *the consummation of all things.*

In such a work as this, of which the historical side was almost completely effaced, it might happen that the author, in order to set forth with greater clearness and fulness the mind of the Lord on each of these five subjects, put together words spoken by Jesus on different occasions, and grouped into one whole the parables which His wisdom as a Teacher would not have allowed Him to accumulate in this way in preaching to the people ; and this explains quite naturally how it is that the elements, combined together in these discourses of Matthew, are found in Luke scattered among five, six, and even ten different sets of circumstances.[1] It does not appear to me that, in the majority of these cases, a thorough student of the subject could refuse to give the preference to the position indicated by the third gospel.[2] Luke is in each case like a botanist who prefers to contemplate a flower in the very place of its birth, and in the midst of its natural surroundings. Matthew is like the gardener who, with a view to some special object, puts together large and magnificent bouquets.

Assuredly there was delivered a "Sermon on the Mount"; Luke confirms it. There was delivered an instruction to the Twelve; Mark and Luke bear witness to it. There was a certain day in the ministry of Jesus on which He first introduced the system of teaching by parables. But to the discourses really belonging to these decisive moments, Matthew has added many words spoken by the Lord on other

---

[1] It occurs no less than nine times that words grouped together by Matthew in the Sermon on the Mount, are found in Luke referred to particular and very different occasions.

[2] Compare, for example, the manner in which the Lord's Prayer is placed, Matt. vi. 9—13 and Luke xi. 1—4 ; and in the same way the precepts on prayer, Matt. vii. 7, 8, and Luke xi. 9, 10 (at the close of the parable of the Friend at midnight); and the precept on faith, Matt. vi. 26—30 and Luke xii. 24—29 (in connection with the parable of the Rich Fool).

occasions on the same subjects. Certainly there was nothing to prevent his adopting this system, if his book, instead of having an historical aim and plan, was arranged in the order of subjects. We owe it to his legitimate adoption of this method that he has succeeded in so marvellous a manner in reproducing the unique impression which was produced upon the multitude by the sermons of the Master, and that we can even now form an idea of the effect described in these words : "And the people were astonished at His doctrine, for He taught them as one having authority, and not as the scribes."

We ask ourselves in the third place, and as if tradition told us nothing on the subject, who could have been the *author* of the more ancient document which forms the foundation of our canonical gospel, and who was the *compiler* of this latter ?

As to the first question, the principal fact fitted to throw light upon our researches is this : none but a witness of the teachings of Jesus Christ could have represented in so striking a manner their majesty, holiness, and force. He must have felt their power himself, to succeed in giving them so much power over others. To this fact we must add another, which is being more and more recognised by all critics worthy of the name : it is that the preaching of Jesus, as reported in the first gospel, transports us in an especially vivid manner into the midst of the historic circumstances of Israelitish life at that time.

It is, then, impossible that this account should not have proceeded from a man who had himself *lived through* these scenes. Now this man—this eye-witness—who is he?

Among the twelve apostles there was one, and perhaps only one, whose previous occupation had accustomed him to the use of the pen,—he who had once been collector of taxes, Levi, surnamed Matthew. Might we not expect that he, first, would have felt himself called upon, or have been asked by his colleagues, to stereotype in writing the most important part, but also that which it would be the most difficult to preserve in its purity, of the Master's legacy to the world—His instructions?

The supposition that it was so—probable in itself—is confirmed by two facts, sufficiently trifling, it is true, in appearance, but perhaps in a case such as this really so much the more significant.

1. The first gospel alone appends to the name of Matthew, in the list of the twelve apostles, that epithet, of little honour in the world's estimation, but dear to the heart of him to whose thoughts it recalled the love of which he had been the object—*the publican*.[1]

2. In the list of the twelve apostles contained in the gospels and in the Acts, they are generally divided into pairs, perhaps the very same which the Lord Himself formed when He first sent them out to

---

[1] Matt. x. 3.

preach; and the fourth pair is always composed, except in the Acts, of Matthew and Thomas. Now, in the other synoptists, Matthew is placed the first, while in the gospel we are considering he occupies the second place in relation to his associate.[1]

If, on the one hand, these indications naturally direct our thoughts to the apostle Matthew, it must be said, on the other hand, that, when we consider attentively the narrative portions of the first gospel, it is difficult to attribute them to an apostle. They are all given in so compendious a form. The intuitive descriptive character is altogether wanting. Comparing these narratives with those of the other two synoptists, we should even sometimes charge them with inaccuracy,[2] were it not evident that the author is hastening on to the word of Jesus at the end, which in his eyes is its soul, and which alone is, in fact, essential to the object he has in view—that of setting forth the Messianic dignity of Jesus.

How, then, are we to reconcile these contradictory criteria? By acknowledging that the discourses in our canonical gospel are indeed the reproduction of the Hebrew apostolic document, and that the historical portions, although founded upon the oral

---

[1] Matt. x. 3, compared with Mark iii. 18 ; Luke vi. 15 (Acts i. 13).

[2] Compare the account of the healing of the centurion's servant, Matt. viii. 5—13, with Luke vii. 1—10 ; and the raising of Jairus' daughter, Matt. ix. 18 sqq., with Mark v. 22 sqq. and Luke viii. 41 sqq.

narrations of the apostle, were not written by his own hand. No doubt some coadjutor of Matthew, who had helped him in his work of evangelisation, undertook the labour of translating into Greek *the discourses* which had been drawn up by him in their original language, and to complete this work by distributing their contents through an evangelical narrative, complete in itself, and conformable to the type of Christian instruction adopted by the apostles.

Such a document, whoever may have been the compiler, certainly deserved the name of *the Gospel according to Matthew,* given to it by Christian antiquity.

Lastly, we inquire to what date these two works belong—that of the apostle, and that of the translator and second editor.

An answer may be drawn from chap. xxiv., particularly verse 15. This chapter contains a discourse of Jesus, in which the two events of the destruction of Jerusalem and the end of the world are completely amalgamated into one. According to Luke, these two future events were announced by our Lord in two distinct instructions.[1] The fusion of the two catastrophes into one, in Matthew and Mark, leaves no room to doubt that these gospels were written *before* the first of the two events so closely united in the prophecy. But verse 15 especially has a great import-

---

[1] Luke xvii. (the end of the world), and xxi. (the destruction of Jerusalem).

ance in the question now before us. Jesus wishes to
warn the Jewish disciples living in Palestine against
joining in the revolt, and in the war which will issue
in the destruction of Jerusalem. He persuades them
to retire in time to the mountain country on the other
side of Jordan, and gives as a signal for their flight
the moment when the pagan standards shall be planted
on the soil of the Holy Land. Here—an instance
unparalleled in our gospel records—the writer suddenly interrupts the discourse of the Saviour with this
remark of his own: "Whoso readeth let him understand."[1] This parenthesis proves that the writer drew
up this discourse before the fulfilment of the sign which
had been announced. For of what use would have been
this striking *nota-bene,* after the event had happened?
As this warning is found in the Greek version—we
cannot say whether it had previously existed in the
original Hebrew—we must hence conclude that this
translation appeared just at the time when the storm
was seen approaching, a little before the year 66, when
this long-threatened war actually broke out, therefore
about 64 or 65 A.D.; and as some time must have
intervened between the publication of the Greek
version and that of the apostolic document, we shall

---

[1] This remark has been sometimes attributed to Jesus Himself, as if it referred to the prophecy of Daniel which He had just
been quoting. But this explanation cannot be applied to the
parallel passage, Mark xiii. 14, where the quotation from Daniel
should be omitted, according to the MSS., as an interpolation
from Matthew.

not be far wrong in placing the latter about the year
60 A.D.

This is the date to which, after innumerable vaga-
ries,[1] rationalistic criticism itself has returned, as witness Holtzmann, who places the composition of St.
Matthew's document about the year 60, and that of
the Greek version about 68.

In this manner, like the prodigal son, does criticism
quietly re-enter the paternal home. After having
disdainfully rejected the assertions of tradition, it ends
by rendering them a deliberate homage.

It is not only on this chronological question that
criticism is brought to recognise the harmony between
internal evidence and primitive tradition; but—as
we have just shown—on all the questions relating
to the somewhat complex origin of the first gospel.

The use of each of the two kinds of criteria has led
us on all the important points to the same results,
which we will formulate thus :

The document which forms the basis of the first
gospel—the Hebrew work containing the *discourses*
of Jesus, was composed by the apostle Matthew
about the year 60 A.D., thirty years after the ascension of our Lord. Our canonical gospel, which
includes this document, and completes it with regard
to the history, bears traces of the evangelising work

---

[1] It is not long since Baur brought down the composition of
St. Matthew's gospel to the second century, about the year
130 !

of the same apostle, and was composed about the year 65.

These dates themselves give a clue to the real object of this document. It had a theocratic mission to fulfil. It was the *ultimatum* of Jehovah to His ancient people. Believe, or prepare to perish! Recognise Jesus as the Messiah, or await Him as your Judge! The book which contains this final summons is the close of the Old Testament as well as the opening of the New. It has just that place marked out for it in the archives of the kingdom of God on earth—the Bible—which has been assigned to it by the feeling of the Church.

2

THE GOSPEL OF MARK

This work does not at first sight possess the august stamp of a book written under a Divine commission which characterises that which precedes it. It produces upon us the effect of a narrative containing simply some personal recollections put together without any systematic aim or plan; it is the work of one who, having his mind full of the great scenes he has contemplated, burns with the desire to make all those who have not witnessed them share with him his feelings of wonder and adoration.

We will endeavour to bring into definite shape this first and vague impression. And for that purpose let us try to clear up the origin of this document.

I. We possess, with reference to this gospel, two accounts of great antiquity, and very strongly authenticated: the testimony of Papias, of which the value is in this case enhanced by the fact that it rests upon that of an ancient presbyter, an immediate disciple of Jesus; and that of Clement of Alexandria, a contemporary of Irenæus. This latter, according to the declaration of its author, only reproduces a tradition handed down from one to another by the *presbyters who succeeded each other from the beginning*.

The following are the words in which the presbyter, a native of Palestine, who instructed Papias, narrated to him the origin of the second gospel: " Mark, having become the amanuensis of Peter,[1] wrote down exactly all that he remembered of things either said or done by Christ; but without order.[2] For he had not himself heard the Lord, nor actually accompanied Him; but had only, as I have just said, accompanied Peter at a later time. Now this latter gave his instructions as occasion called for them, and not as a complete exposition of the discourses of the Lord; so that Mark is not to be blamed for writing down a

---

[1] This might be also translated the *interpreter*.

[2] It is possible that the testimony of the aged presbyter extends only to this point, and that the rest is an explanation added by Papias.

certain number of detached facts, just as he remembered them. For he only aimed at one object : not to omit anything he had heard, nor to alter it in any point." The essential fact attested by this account is that the gospel of Mark is simply a compilation of the narratives that used to be given by St. Peter in the Churches through which he passed, preaching the Gospel.

Mark had at first accompanied Paul, then Barnabas; it was only therefore at a later period, during the latter journeys of Peter, that he joined him in order to give him help in his mission. Now Peter, journeying from place to place, used to recount the acts or the teachings of Jesus according to the needs of his auditors. He did not give, as Matthew had done in his document, a connected and complete exposition of the teaching of Jesus ; and Mark, drawing up by degrees what he had heard from his lips, could not, when he came to put together these detached narratives, give them so much order as might have been desirable. Hence arises, according to Papias, the fragmentary, abrupt, and incomplete character of his gospel, which we must attribute, not to the negligence of its author, but to the circumstances of its origin.

Papias does not tell us where and on what occasion Mark devoted himself to this work of compilation ; or, at all events, Eusebius, to whom we owe the preservation of the passage just quoted, has not trans-

mitted to us anything more respecting the testimony
of this father.   But the following account of Clement
may serve to complete that of Papias : " When Peter
was publicly preaching the Word in Rome, and in the
might of the Spirit proclaiming the Gospel, his auditors entreated Mark, who had for some time accompanied him, and who remembered all that Peter had
said, to write down the things related by him, and
then, when he had written the Gospel, to send it to
those who had asked him for it ;[1] which request, when
Peter heard of it, he neither opposed nor supported."

It was, then, in Rome, in the latter part of the life
of Peter, about 64 A.D.—if Peter really fell a victim
to the persecution of Nero—that Mark drew up this
work.   He did so at the request of the Church, which
had not heard Peter during so long a time as he who
had been his travelling companion.   Peter, on his
part, took up a position altogether passive with
reference to this work.   And, on due reflection, we
shall understand his motive for so doing ; it would
not be right for him to hinder the work, if it might
prove a source of any blessings to the Church ;
neither, on the other hand, would he encourage it, for
if this work was to be really what it ought to be, was
it not necessary that it should originate in an impulse

---

[1] This passage is usually translated thus : " And that Mark,
having written the Gospel, gave it to those who had asked him
for it," but the words which follow cannot be naturally explained
in this sense.

from a higher source ? This account of the facts, though it has been treated with scorn, bears upon its face a striking look of truthfulness.

After two such explicit testimonies, we shall only cite in addition that contained in the title : *the Gospel according to Mark.* These words give expression to the belief of the whole primitive Church ; and they evidently mean, not that we have here a document compiled *after the manner* or according to the mode of preaching of Mark (it could only have been expressed so if Mark had been an apostle), but that it is the Gospel of Jesus Christ *as set forth* by Mark.

If, then, we are to attribute any value to these testimonies, we shall be disposed to consider our second canonical gospel as having been composed in Rome for the Christians in that city, and at their request, by Mark, the companion of Peter, and conformably to the oral deliverances of that apostle, a little before the persecution of Nero, to which he fell a victim in August 64.

II. Hitherto we have listened to others ; let us now proceed to the work of research and discovery for ourselves. The book into whose origin we are searching lies before us ; we should be very wanting in skill if we could not detect in it some indications of the secret of its composition.

And first, let us inquire who may have been the readers for whom this gospel was intended ? Were they, like those of the first gospel, either Jews or disciples of Jewish origin, who were to be led to Jesus or to be confirmed in the faith? Assuredly not. The second gospel quotes scarcely any prophecy.[1] And as he gives long explanations of Jewish customs— explanations which Matthew abstains from altogether in the parallel passages [2]—we must admit that it is for Christians of Gentile origin that the author of this gospel is writing. Where were such readers to be found? In Asia Minor? In Greece? In Italy? This question, it seems to us, will best be answered by the help of the following indications:

The author has a marked preference for words of Latin origin, whether he substitutes them for the corresponding Greek words used by the other sacred writers (as *speculator* instead of *stratiotes*, as the term for a soldier; *centurion* instead of *hecaton tarchos*, for a captain; *xestes* from *sextarius*, for a vessel of six gallons), or appends them as an explanation to the Greek word ("*aule*, that is to say *prætorium*"). This fact shows that the author is writing under the influence of a Latin atmosphere. Once even he is led to describe in Roman money the worth of a Jewish coin: "two mites, which make a *codrantes*" (the Roman *quadrant*).

A very significant indication of this document having

---

[1] The only prophetic citation in the narrative is that in i. 2, 3; that from Daniel xiii. 14 is not, according to the MSS., authentic. It is an interpolation drawn from Matthew—the result of a marginal note.

[2] Compare especially Mark vii. 1—4 with Matt. xv. 1, 2.

been composed, not only in the Latin-speaking world, but especially for the Church in Rome, occurs in the account of the Passion. Simon of Cyrene, the bearer of the cross of Jesus, is described as the *father of Alexander and Rufus*. This indication evidently pre-supposes that the two sons of Simon were persons well known to, and of consideration in, the Church for which the author was writing : there is no similar instance in the other gospels. If, then, we can ascertain where these men lived, we shall know the place from which the author wrote. The epistle to the Romans here comes to our aid. " Salute," says Paul to the Church in Rome, " Rufus, chosen in the Lord, and his mother and mine" (Romans xvi. 13). The family of Simon had therefore migrated to Rome. Paul, who had known them in the East, sends his greeting to them in that city. And the author of our second gospel, having the surviving members of the family before his eyes at the time he was writing, felt constrained to do honour to the unique part which its head had played in the drama of the Cross. These indications seem to me clear enough.

The second question is this : What is the source from which the facts related in this document have been drawn ? Do they proceed from some legendary tradition of a much later date than the lifetime of Jesus Christ, or do they emanate from one of the eye-witnesses of the ministry of Jesus ?

The answer to this question forces itself upon the

critical student with ever-increasing definiteness. If there exists anywhere a narrative which bears upon its face the stamp of *autopsy*, of the style of an actual eye-witness, it is that of our second gospel. It is marked with the vividness of local colouring, and the freshness of directly personal recollection. Either it is a mere imitation,—and the tone of candour and of almost naïve simplicity which marks the whole of it forbids that supposition,—or else we are forced to recognise in it the work of an eye-witness. Let us recall a few of these graphic touches : " And He was in the hinder part of the ship asleep on a pillow" (iv. 38) ; " and he, casting away his garment, rose and came to Jesus" (x. 50) ; " there were many coming and going, and they had no leisure so much as to eat " (vi. 31) ; " and looking up to heaven, He sighed " (vii. 34). In other places we have the record of the moral impressions produced upon our Lord : " And when He had looked round about Him with anger . . . " (iii. 5) ; " then Jesus beholding him, loved him " (x. 21) ; "and Jesus went before them, and they were amazed ; and as they followed they were afraid " (x. 32), etc. Who then was it who caught these fleeting expressions of anger or of love in the eye of the Master ? who could have thus pictured for us the secret emotions of the disciples at certain important moments ? The whole of this gospel is full of touches of this kind, which, like jewels upon a dress, impart to its pictures an incomparable brilliancy.

Again, we must draw attention to the narrator's habit of preserving the Aramaic expressions used by our Lord while translating them into Greek—*Talitha cumi* (v. 41), *Ephphatha* (vii. 34), *Abba* (xiv. 36). It is as if he still heard the very sound of the voice of Jesus, and felt constrained to report His words in their original form.

It is therefore amongst those who formed the circle of the habitual companions of Jesus that we are driven to look for the writer of a narrative such as this. Which of them shall we conjecture it to be ?

The feeling which inspires the whole of the second gospel, from beginning to end, is that of wonder and admiration for the Lord. I use the word admiration rather than love, not that I would exclude the latter sentiment, but the former predominates. It expresses itself in the very first words of the book : " The beginning of the Gospel of Jesus Christ, the Son of God : "[1] that is to say, Here begins the portrait of the life of a being whose every word and every act is stamped with the seal of Divinity. This feeling of astonishment and admiration overflows in every part of the narrative. The author loves to paint the expression of that feeling in the multitudes, because he was so filled with it himself. " And they were all

---

[1] The omission of the words *Son of God* in the MS. *Sinaïticus*, and in that alone, cannot at all shake their authority. Such omissions are common in that document, which is written with astonishing carelessness.

amazed" (i. 27) ; " and all the city was gathered together at the door " (i. 33) ; " insomuch that Jesus could
no more openly enter into the city " (i. 45) ; " insomuch that they were all amazed " (ii. 12) ; "and they
were astonished with a great astonishment " (v. 42),
etc., etc. [1]

Now amongst those who lived in the closest intercourse with Jesus, who is that one who experienced
in the highest degree this feeling—which gives the
ruling inspiration to the second gospel? and who on
all occasions expressed it with the greatest energy in
the name of all his comrades? It is Peter. If perhaps this disciple was not the one who had the most
love of the Lord, he certainly had the most admiration for Him.

Some characteristics of a more special kind lead us
equally to recognise in Peter that one among the
disciples whose testimony fills the pages of the book
before us.

Assuredly it is no accident that, in the scene at
Cesaræa Philippi, the second gospel records the crush-
ing answer of Jesus to Peter : " Get thee behind me,
Satan ; " while it omits those grand words which
precede it in Matthew : " Thou art Peter, and upon
this rock I will build my Church." [2]   It is not without
some motive that in the account of the storm on the

---

[1] Compare also i. 37 ; ii. 2 ; iii. 9, 20 ; iv. 1 ; v. 24 ; vi. 2, 51,
55 ; vii. 22, 37 ; ix. 14.

[2] Compare Mark viii. 27—33 with Matt. xvi. 13—23.

lake, Mark omits the fact, so glorious for Peter, of his miraculous walk upon the water to meet Jesus.[1] And are we to account it a mere chance that Mark alone mentions, both in the prophecy and in the history of Peter's denial, the *two* warnings given to him by the two cock-crowings, which made the fall of the disciple the more inexcusable ?[2]

In all these instances we can only explain the difference between Mark's account and that of Matthew, which agree in all other points, by allowing that Peter omitted, in the narrations he gave to the Churches, and which were collected by Mark, all circumstances which told in his favour, and brought into notice only those which tended to his humiliation. Otherwise we should have to assume that the second gospel was the work of a determined enemy of Peter.

A distinguished critic, in a work just published, has made a very sagacious analysis of Mark's gospel,[3] and has arrived at this interesting conclusion, that very often the text can only be explained by admitting that we have in it the narrative of Peter preserved literally, but modified only in this respect, that the personal pronoun—the *we* of Peter—has been changed to *they*, which alone suits the written narrative.

---

[1] Compare Mark vi. 50, 51, with Matt. xiv. 28—33.

[2] Compare Mark xiv. 30, and 68—72, with the three parallel accounts.

[3] Klostermann, *Das Marcus-Evangelium*, 1867.

We will quote two examples.   Mark relates (iii. 13 —19) the account of the appointment of the Twelve. But the election of Peter is not mentioned : only the surname of *Peter* which Jesus gave him ; while the appointment of John and James is expressly mentioned, and that together with the surname which Jesus also conferred upon them.   How are we to explain this omission with regard to Peter ?   There is but one way.   Mark relates the fact thus : " And He ordained twelve that they should be with Him. . . . And Simon He surnamed Peter."   Have we not here the literal reproduction of Peter's own account : " And he chose *us* twelve, and *me* he surnamed Peter " ?   The election of the narrator being already included in the *us*, there was no need to repeat it. On coming out from the synagogue at Capernaum (i. 29), Jesus goes with His four disciples, Peter, Andrew, James, and John (who had been mentioned before in verses 16—20), into Peter's house.   Mark expresses it in this way : " And forthwith, when they were come out of the synagogue, they entered into the house of Simon and Andrew with James and John." " They entered " . . . who ?   According to the preceding verses it must have been Jesus and His four disciples.   But then the expression " with James and John " has no meaning, since they were both included in *they*.   All is explained if we *re*-translate Mark's account into that of Peter : " And *we* entered (Jesus, Andrew, and I) into *our* house with James and John."

Let people dispute as they may as to the justness of this refined analysis, which to my mind is quite undeniable. The following is a fact of a more general kind upon which there can be no disagreement; it is that our gospel of Mark is only a development of Peter's preaching to Cornelius (Acts x.), and that the latter has with good reason been called the gospel of Mark *in nuce*.

Such are the many traces of some kind of participation of Peter in the composition of the narratives preserved in the second gospel. Must we then conclude that Peter himself composed this book? By no means.

In the first place, we possess an epistle by this apostle, generally held to be authentic; and the style of it has nothing in common with that of this gospel. Besides, we can scarcely imagine the apostle Peter, the former Galilean fisherman, who later in life had become a man, not of contemplation and study, like John, but of action and missionary enterprise, taking up his pen to draw up a work of such length.

If, then, the narratives which we have here are his, and yet are not by his own hand, there remains but one possibility: one of his hearers must have drawn them up. Who then is this anonymous author?

Even if tradition had not mentioned him, the first epistle of Peter would have given us a clue to his name. The apostle there sends greetings from Mark, *his son*, taking this word evidently in the spiritual

sense in which Paul also applies it to Titus and
Timothy,—that of his son in the faith. John, surnamed
Mark, was the son of a mother living in Jerusalem,
and at whose house Peter was so well known that the
servant, even without seeing him, recognised him by
the sound of his voice.[1] It is then natural to suppose
that it was this apostle who had sown the seeds of
faith in the young man's mind. For this reason he
calls him *his son,* and by this title designates him, in
a manner, as his spiritual heir, the depository of
his sole treasure—the knowledge of Jesus Christ, his
Lord. We cannot then attribute to any other person,
with greater probability, the putting together of the
narratives of Peter. And, once arrived at this point,
shall we not be tempted to ask whether the young
man mentioned in the scene at Gethsemane, and who
there plays a strange and mysterious part,[2] was not
himself Mark, who, after the manner of painters, has
thus affixed his signature to his picture, as Matthew
had done to his in the account of the call of the publican from the receipt of custom?

The date at which the second gospel was composed
may be argued from the following facts. The two
sons of Simon of Cyrene, of whom one at least, according to Rom. xvi. 13, held an influential position
in the Church of Rome, were still living. The apostolic age was, therefore, not very far advanced. And
since the warning to the disciples in Palestine to take

---

[1] Acts xii. 12—17.   [2] Mark xiv. 51, 52.

heed to the sign given them by Jesus for the time of their flight, is found in Mark (xiii. 14) as well as in Matthew, the fated hour of the destruction of Jerusalem (in 70), and even that of the beginning of the war (in 66), had not yet struck. Thus it would be about the year 64 or 65 that we must date the composition of this document. Holtzmann also considers the work of Mark, which formed the basis of the second gospel, to have been anterior to the destruction of Jerusalem.

Here a comparison suggests itself which, if well founded, would not be without weight. It is well known that the end of the second gospel, from xvi. 9, is missing in some of the most ancient MSS.; in others it is found in a different form; and in some others an altogether different conclusion takes its place. How are we to account for this phenomenon? Mark cannot have concluded his narrative at ver. 8. An appearance of the risen Jesus had been promised by the angel to the women, in the first part of the chapter; the author could not close his narrative without first giving an account of it. It has been conjectured that the last leaves of the book were accidentally lost. We have an instance of the kind in the loss of the end of the MS. *Sinaïticus*. But then we shall have to suppose that there existed only one copy of Mark's document in the Church. However little this work may have been made use of up to that time, still, would not some means have been

devised of filling up this accidental lacuna ? Is it not
much more likely that the author was interrupted in
his work at the moment when he had reached this
point in the narrative, and that he was obliged to
leave it unfinished ? In this way two kinds of documents came to be circulated in the Church : the one
reproducing the original copy left in its incomplete
state ; the other, copies finished in various manners
at a later date. If this was the fact, it may be asked
what could have been the incident which so suddenly
interrupted Mark in his work. As we know that
this evangelist wrote in Rome in the latter part of
the life of Peter, it is natural to suppose that the
breaking out of the terrible persecution which befell
this Church, and put an end to the life of the apostle
in 64, was the cause of the interruption. If this
was so, the date of our gospel would be fixed very
exactly.

However that may be, the gospel of Mark presents
itself to us, according to the evidence of tradition, as
well as of the indications furnished by the book itself,
as a collection, more or less complete, of the narratives which Peter used to give of his Master's ministry
—narratives intended, not like Matthew's gospel, to
give a final warning to God's people, but to reproduce,
as in a series of pictures, the unparalleled scenes which
had been witnessed by the actual spectators of our
Lord's life. This document, then, deserves more than
any other the name of *Apostolic Memoirs*.

3

THE GOSPEL OF LUKE

I. The records handed down to us by ecclesiastical history with regard to the origin of the third gospel are both fewer and shorter than those it has preserved for us respecting the composition of the two first. One reason of this probably is that the evangelist has himself given us, in a remarkable preamble (i. 1—4), all the information we need upon the origin and the nature of his work.

Here are a few words from the pen of Irenæus : "Luke, the companion of Paul, put into writing the gospel preached by the latter."

In the so-called *Muratori* fragment, which seems to have been written about the same time (near 180 A.D.), and which contains more especially the tradition of the Italian Churches respecting the books of the New Testament, we find the following passage relating to Luke : "In the third place, the book of the gospel according to Luke, Luke the Physician, whom Paul had associated with himself, as one zealous for righteousness, to be his companion, wrote in his own name as he thought good. Now he had not himself seen the Lord in the flesh ; but having carried his inquiries as far back as possible, he began his history with the birth of John." It is difficult to distinguish in this passage how much belongs really to tradition, and how much is only a reproduction of the ideas contained in Luke's own preamble.

Clement of Alexandria reports, following the ancient presbyters, "that the two gospels which contain the genealogies (those of Matthew and Luke) were written the first,"—consequently, before Mark and John. It is impossible to explain this declaration otherwise than by an actual tradition. How can we suppose it argued from exegesis?

It appears from a passage in Tertullian that it was an opinion received by many in his time, that "the work of Luke was to be attributed to Paul himself." This represents, roughly speaking, a fact of which we shall establish the substantial truth.

Lastly, we find in St. Jerome the following passage : " Luke, a Syrian physician, a native of Antioch, and a disciple of the apostle Paul, composed his book in the countries of Achaia and Bœotia." From whence has this father drawn his information ? As he relates that Luke was buried at Constantinople, to which place his ashes were removed, together with those of Andrew the apostle, in the twentieth year of the reign of Constantius, he probably knew that it was from the countries he mentions that the remains of these two servants of Christ had been brought.

We gather from these brief notices that Luke's work was composed in Greece, a little earlier than that of Mark, consequently between the years 60 and 64, at the same time as that of Matthew ; and that that document stands to St. Paul's apostolate in a relation analogous to that which we have shown to exist between the second gospel and Peter's ministry, or between the first gospel and the ministry of Matthew.

II. Do these results agree with those to which we are led by the study of the gospel itself?

As to the *destination* of this book, it was certainly written by one who had before his mind the Greek world, and probably by one who lived within its limits. We see an indication of this, first in the preamble, in which the author gives an account of his plan and of the object he has in view. This prologue precisely resembles those of the great Greek historians, particularly Herodotus and Thucydides. There is nothing like it in the two other synoptics. The person, in some high position, to whom the work is dedicated, is called *Theophilus*. This name, of Grecian origin, though it is sometimes used by the Jews, leads us to suppose that the noble person who bore it was a Greek. We must add that, in dedicating this work to him, St. Luke was probably not thinking only of the use he would personally make of it. The publication of a book was at that time a much more costly undertaking than it is now, since every copy had to be made by hand. By accepting the manuscript which was dedicated to him, the wealthy Theophilus became what was called the *patron*, or, as we should now say, the *sponsor* of the book. He undertook to make it known, to have copies made of it, and to circulate these amongst those about him, and who belonged to the same nation as himself.[1]

Lastly, the character of the narrative agrees wonderfully with the Greek turn of mind. "The Jews," says St. Paul, "require a sign, and the Greeks seek after wisdom." A work well shaped into an artistic whole, a history advancing by well-marked steps, and systematically progressive, an interconnection easily perceptible of causes and effects,—these for a Greek mind constituted the best material for carrying conviction. Now it is precisely this kind of evidence which is to be drawn from the third gospel. And the preamble leads us even to think that such was the deliberate intention of the author. "It seemed good to me also, having had perfect understanding of all things from the very first, *to write unto thee in order*, most excellent Theophilus, *that thou mightest know the certainty* of those things wherein thou hast been instructed." He alone carries us back to the first beginnings of this divine history, to the two births— those of John and of Jesus. He pictures for us, as no other evangelist does, the thoroughly human development, first of the infancy and then of the youth of Jesus. Even in the most miraculous events of His life, such as the Baptism and the Transfiguration, he

---

[1] The ancient Judæo-Christian romance entitled "The Clementines," of about the year 160, makes Theophilus a man of high position in Antioch, who after having listened to the preaching of Peter, gave up his palace to be used as a church.

brings out carefully the human, or, as we might say, natural element in the story—the prayer of Jesus. From the day on which Jesus calls His four first disciples (v.) to that on which He appoints the twelve apostles (vi.), from this latter to the day He sends them out on their first mission (ix.), and again to that on which He organises a mission on a still larger scale —that of the seventy disciples (x.), one sees in this gospel the work of Jesus enlarging gradually, as He Himself had "increased in wisdom and stature." This organic growth of the Person and of the work, constitutes at the same time the preparation for the birth and development of the spiritual body of the Church which the Lord is forming for Himself here below. And it is in this way that the book of the Acts has the appearance of a necessary continuation of our third gospel. From Nazareth to Capernaum, from Capernaum to Jerusalem, in the gospel,—from Jerusalem to Antioch, from Antioch to Rome, in the Acts,—we observe in the history an unbroken progress such as satisfies the intelligence of the reader who wishes to picture clearly to himself the progress of the working of Christianity. This continuity consti- tutes the unity of the two parts of the work of Luke. In this way it has come to pass that this author, writing for a people gifted above all others with the historic sense, has become the *true historian* of the life and work of Jesus Christ.

It is not less evident that this author was one of

the friends and fellow-labourers of the apostle of the
Gentiles. He classes himself, in the preamble, not
with the apostles, but amongst those who owe their
knowledge of the Gospel to the tradition derived
from the first witnesses and ministers of the Word.
And which of these was to him the centre of
attraction ?

The analogy which is so remarkable between his
account of the institution of the Last Supper and that
of Paul (1 Cor. xi.) is in itself a significant indication.
The relation in which the appearances of the risen
Jesus, recorded in Luke xxiv., stand to those enumerated by Paul in 1 Cor. xv., is a no less evident
indication of the connection which existed between
Paul and the author of our narrative.

What, then, is the third gospel, in its entirety, but a
firm groundwork of historic fact, of which the purpose
is to serve as a foundation for the edifice raised by
Paul ? There were two key-notes of that apostle's
preaching : the complete *gratuitousness* of the salvation offered by Jesus, and the *universality* of its
intended scope. Now, what is the significance of
those features and of those words of the life and
teaching of Jesus which have been specially preserved
for us by St. Luke ? Angels salute Him at His
nativity, not only with the name of *Christ*, but with
that of *Saviour*. They celebrate the good-will of
God, not towards the Jews, but towards *men*. The
genealogy of Jesus, in chap. iii., is traced up not only

to Abraham, but to Adam, the father of all mankind. In chap. iv. Jesus proclaims Himself, according to the words of Isaiah, as He who comes to heal the *broken-hearted.* " My son, my daughter, thy sins are forgiven thee ; thy faith hath saved thee." Such is His language, whether He addresses the paralytic laid at His feet, or the sinner who bathes them with her tears, or the sick woman who has taken courage to touch the hem of His garment. The parables which Luke specially loves to relate are not those in which we see unfolded the grand historic development of the kingdom of heaven on earth, but rather those which picture to us the domestic scenes wherein the Divine compassions are seen to meet the faith of the sinner ; the lost sheep sought out by the shepherd, and carried home upon his shoulders ; the lost piece of money, searched for by the woman even to sweeping the house; the penitent son, whom paternal love restores without delay or condition to his filial position ; or, once more, the publican, the whole of whose worship consists in striking his breast, and who returns from it *justified* to his house. Amongst the words of Jesus on the cross, Luke relates His prayer for His murderers, and His merciful reply to the prayer of the penitent thief. The last picture given us by the evangelist is that of the blessing given by Jesus to His apostles as He ascends to Heaven, lifting up His hands, as does a priest in blessing the people.

What is the lesson taught by all these distinguish-

ing traits which make up the peculiar heritage of
Luke? It is this one : that salvation "*by grace* through
faith," [1] such as was proclaimed by Paul, corresponded
perfectly to the thought of Christ ; and that the work
of that apostle was but the continuation of the line of
which the Master's Hand had traced the beginning.

If the first gospel may be considered as a treatise
upon the Messianic sovereignty of Jesus over Israel,
the third is not less evidently that which sets forth
the right of the Gentiles to share in the salvation
marked out by Christ. A gospel such as this could
only originate in the circle which surrounded St. Paul
in his missionary life. It was only necessary to transform its facts into doctrine, to obtain what Paul calls
his gospel.

It would be possible, even apart from all tradition,
to discover the one among St. Paul's fellow-workers
to whom this work should be attributed ; and that by
the help of the following indications : 1. The author
of the Acts having adopted the expression "*we*" in
those cases in which he wishes to indicate that he was
present without mentioning himself by name, it follows
that he could not have been one of the companions of
Paul designated *by name* in the history (Barnabas,
Silas, Timotheus, etc. ; compare particularly xx. 4, 5).
2. Paul gives Luke the title of physician (Col. iv. 14) ;
and this profession demanded then, no less than it
does now, some scientific and literary study; this

---

[1] Eph. ii. 8.

quality also is precisely that which characterises, in a
remarkable manner, the author of the third gospel.

But have we not here an artifical composition, put
together expressly with the object of furnishing a
foundation for the preaching and labours of the
apostle? Not so; one fact is enough to indicate the
true manner of composition of this document—that is,
the complete difference of style between the four first
verses (i. 1—4) and the remainder of the gospel from
ver. 5 onwards. The preamble (ver. 1—4) exhibits
the purest and most classical Greek style; but this
style does not recur again till the end of the book of
Acts. In the remainder of the gospel, from ver. 5,
and in the first part of the Acts, the language is more
or less tinctured with Aramaisms.[1] This difference of
style can only be accounted for in one way—that is,
by supposing that in the preamble to the gospel, and
in the latter half of the Acts, the author wrote in his
own style and language; while in all the rest of the
gospel, and in the first part of the Acts, he has
consulted or reproduced written documents, either
Aramaic or translated from that language. This is,
besides, the conclusion we should draw from his own
declaration (i. 1, 2), from which it appears that at the
time at which he was writing, there were already in
existence a large number of written documents relating

---

[1] That is, with words and terms of language borrowed from
Aramaic, akin to the Hebrew, which the Jews at that time
spoke.

to the ministry of Jesus. It is quite clear that he had before him more than one of these works, and that he made use of them in composing his own. And as these documents contained, according to Luke himself, the results of traditions received from the apostles, they would naturally have been written either in the language of the Twelve, or under the influence of that language. Even had they been already translated into Greek, they could not fail still to bear the stamp of the language of the original tradition. We observe here for the first time, in one of the evangelists, evidence of the use of written documents. It is not, however, impossible that here and there Luke may have put together his history solely from information which he had collected orally; and that would explain why it is that in many passages his style has a much less decided Aramaic stamp than in others.

What was the *date* of Luke's work? The majority of the critics of our day, grounding themselves upon the distinction so clearly drawn in this gospel between the date of the destruction of Jerusalem and that of the end of the world, and upon the fact that our author interposes between these two events a whole period which he calls "*the times of the Gentiles*," place the composition of this gospel some time after the destruction of the Jewish nation, between the years 70 and 80. Others bring it down to the year 100 or 110, and even later. It would be impossible in the latter case to account for the wonderful purity of the traditions contained in this book, which contrast so strongly with the legendary and already dubious character of many of those relating to the life of Jesus which have been transmitted to us by the fathers of the second century—even by a Papias and an Irenæus. It would be still more difficult to explain how, at so late a date, any author could have reproduced so exactly the circumstances which gave occasion to certain words of Jesus, and which bring out in so striking a manner their wonderful appropriateness. Even written documents, in the hands only of private individuals, would scarcely through so long a time have escaped the alterations which very soon after the death of the apostles began to sully oral tradition.

Neither does it appear to me that the distinction, which Luke marks so clearly in our Lord's discourses, between the time of the destruction of Jerusalem and that of the end of the world, gives sufficient reason for thinking that this gospel must necessarily have been written some time *after* the former of these events. For, in fact, we have in many words of Jesus a proof that He Himself clearly distinguished between these two future events. He places the destruction of Jerusalem in the time of the generation then living ; while as to the end of the world, He announces that *that day* is not known " by the angels, neither by the Son, but by the Father only." He seems even to relegate it to a distant future, when he says that "the

Gospel must first be preached in all the world," that "the bridegroom will not come till midnight, when he is no longer expected, or even in the morning," etc. What, then, forbids our supposing that Jesus in His discourses distinguished between these two events, just in the way we find them actually kept distinct in Luke? And may we not see in this a fresh instance of a truth which a comparison between Matthew and Luke brings continually into notice—that the latter separates and refers to their original context of circumstances the various elements which the former has massed together and combined into a whole; and for this reason, that the one was aiming at historical accuracy, while the other only applied himself to didactic teaching.

If, as we have elsewhere endeavoured to prove,[1] Luke had before him neither our canonical Matthew nor Mark's manuscript, his work must have appeared at nearly the same date as the two others. Otherwise he would assuredly have known and have made use of these more ancient documents. This circumstance leads us to place the composition of the third gospel in the years 63, 64, at the same date as Matthew, and a little before that of Mark, which agrees with the traditions of the fathers.

Nevertheless we should have no difficulty—were there sufficient evidence for it—in accepting Holtz-

---

[1] See my Commentary on St. Luke, vol. ii., pp. 531—538, 2nd edit. Now complete in one volume, *Kregel Publications*, 1981.

mann's conclusion, who, after having said, "Matthew wrote immediately before the destruction of Jerusalem," adds, "Few years can have elapsed between Matthew's composition and that of Luke." This writer seems astonished to find that he has thus arrived at results which agree so entirely with the data furnished by tradition. There is in this fact, indeed, a good lesson for modern criticism, which, after having rejected with contempt the assertions of the fathers, ends in discovering that they agree in nearly every point with the results of its own investigations. The fathers were but men, no doubt— sometimes even men of small intelligence or education ; but they were men of gravity, sincerity, and holiness, and who, for the most part, (such is the case with Polycarp, Papias, Justin Martyr, etc.,) gave up their lives for their faith. They may have been mistaken or deceived ; but they did not speak lightly, or without having some strong reason for the things they affirmed, on matters which were so precious to their hearts.

Putting together all these indications, we can form a tolerably clear idea, and one probably not far from the truth, of the origin of this gospel. We know from the Acts that in the year 59, when Paul arrived in Jerusalem, immediately before his arrest, Luke arrived there with him. We know also that when, two years later, he left Cæsarea for Rome, Luke was his fellow-traveller, and shared with him the dangers

of the shipwreck in which that voyage terminated.[1]
It is therefore probable that Luke passed the two years
which intervened between this arrival and this departure, with Paul in Palestine, and that it was then that
he had the opportunity of gathering information and
collecting the materials which enabled him to compose
such a work as this. From Cæsarea, where the apostle
was a prisoner, it was only a two days' journey to the
places which had been the principal scenes of the
ministry of Jesus—the borders of the lake of Gennesa-
reth. Like a bee which goes forth to forage in the
meadow, and returns to elaborate in its hive the honey
it has thus obtained, so, no doubt, he used to gather
in his travels the facts which it was his purpose to
utilise at a later time,[2] and to prepare, together with
the help perhaps of the apostle himself, that admirable
work to which he only put the finishing touches at a
later date, probably in Greece, during the latter part
of the apostle's captivity in Rome in 63.[3]

Having thus inquired into the origin of each of the
synoptics separately, we must now endeavour further
to gain a view of the relations in which they stand to

---

[1] Acts xxi. 17 : "And when *we* were come to Jerusalem, the
brethren received *us* gladly." xxvii. 1 : "And when it was
determined that *we* should sail into Italy. . . ."

[2] Luke i. 3 : "Having had perfect understanding of these things
from the very first."

[3] The apostle does not append a personal salutation from himself in the epistle to the Philippians, as he does in those of a
slightly earlier date, addressed to the Colossians and to Philemon.

each other. Many links connect them together. In all we observe the same general division : the ministry in Galilee,—the Passion in Jerusalem. The same series of narratives recur in a considerable number of cases. We will give but two instances : the connection which is established by these three gospels between the journey to Gadara, the healing of the woman with an issue of blood, and the raising of Jairus' daughter ;[1] and the almost complete parallelism between them with reference to the facts relating to the latter part of the Galilean ministry.[2] And, lastly, the same turn of the sentences, the same selection of forms of expression, in innumerable passages.

It has been often thought that these striking resemblances are to be accounted for by the use which the later evangelist made of the documents of one or other of his predecessors. But how could such a process of copying, pushed sometimes to the extent of a literalism the most servile, have given place on a sudden to an independence in regard to both substance and manner, carried almost to contradiction, or, one might say, to total rebellion ? Why is it that, side by side with these almost identical passages, we find transpositions, suppressions or additions of facts, which would indicate in the later evangelist a singular

---

[1] Matt. viii. 23 to ix. 26 ; Mark iv. 36 to v. 43 ; Luke viii. 22-56.

[2] Matt. xvi. 13 to xviii. 35 ; Mark viii. 27 to ix. 51 ; Luke ix. 18-50.

defiance of the authority of his predecessor's narrative, if he had it before him at the time? Or how, again, are we to account for so important a modification of the general plan as the interpolation by Luke, between the ministry in Galilee and that in Jerusalem, of a complete history of a journey, comprehending ten chapters—that is, nearly half of his whole work—and which has nothing analogous to it in the two other gospels?

The question has consequently been raised whether, instead of accounting for the points of resemblance by the direct influence of one of these documents upon the others, it would not be better to admit that they have all three been drawn from other documents closely resembling each other, and which were in circulation in the Church at the time of their composition. But if these more ancient writings, which the three evangelists made use of, so much resembled each other that we can by this means account for the identity even of a great number of expressions and constructions in our three gospels, how can we account in the same way for the points of difference, so numerous and sometimes so grave, which distinguish them from each other? And if these earlier writings were themselves marked by differences so considerable, how can we explain by their use the employment by our evangelists, in common, of the most trifling words? Evidently the difficulty is only removed a step further.

For our own part, we are quite convinced that there is but one way of accounting for this combination of points of literal resemblance, with differences sometimes considerable, which makes of our three gospels a phenomenon unique in the history of literature. St. Luke, in enumerating the principles upon which rested the unity with each other of the members of the Church in Jerusalem, and which made this whole multitude to be of one mind and one spirit, specially mentions *the apostles' doctrine.*[1]　Evidently the point in question was the witness which they bore to Jesus Christ, the account which they gave of the events of His life, the exposition of His teachings grouped together more or less systematically : all this, it must be understood, by word of mouth only.　This daily teaching was the Church's nourishment, her New Testament—at that time no other existed—and, as has been said, her Heaven.　Certain cycles of narratives, more or less fixed, must at that time have formed themselves, consisting of a series of facts which they loved to relate in one course of instruction. This whole exposition was governed by the sense of a great contrast—that between the active ministry which Jesus had carried on in Galilee, and by which He had founded the Church, and the tragic end of His earthly life in Judea.　These narratives being continually reproduced, first by the apostles, then by the evangelists who had been taught in their school, soon

---

[1] Acts ii. 42.

assumed, as any history does which is frequently repeated by the same person, a more or less fixed and stereotyped form ; and notwithstanding the variations which necessarily resulted from the individuality of the narrators and the diversity of their personal recollections, the primitive apostolic type marked with its strong and indelible stamp the whole of the narratives which constituted the *oral tradition* circulated in the Churches.

This type assumed a character still more fixed when the traditions, after having been for some time in circulation in their Aramaic form, were cast into the mould of the Greek language, for the benefit of the numerous Jews in Jerusalem and in Palestine who could only speak this latter language, and who from the first had joined the Church in great numbers.[1] The general distribution of the materials, the interconnection of the several narratives which had been already formed, were preserved. Certain Greek phrases were selected and adopted once for all as the established equivalents for Aramaic words hard to translate, which Jesus had made use of.[2]

This is, to our mind, the sole method of accounting for the mysterious relation which exists between the Synoptists, and which has for so long a time

---

[1] Acts vi. 1—6.

[2] For instance, the Greek word *epiousios*, which we translate *daily* in the fourth petition of the Lord's Prayer.

obstinately defied the efforts of criticism.[1] The oral tradition thus reduced to shape, first in Aramaic and then in Greek, possessed on the one hand enough of consistency to make it possible for us to account by its aid for the resemblances in respect of general character and of points of detail which we notice even to this day in its threefold canonical form, and on the other hand for the flexibility and elasticity which are required if the points of disagreement are to appear as the result of involuntary accident rather than of a deliberate protest of one of the narratives against another.

The transition from the oral teaching to its present written form was only gradually brought about. Probably the first step of the process was the reduction to writing of certain special narratives or discourses. It might be some evangelist who wished to fix in his memory the tenour of one of our Lord's instructions, or some hearer who desired to preserve accurately the memory of some feature in His life of which he had heard an account.

The time arrived when these fragmentary documents, having become numerous, were put together in such a manner as to form *collections of anecdotes*. Such were probably the writings alluded to by St. Luke in the two first verses of his preamble.[2]

---

[1] The historian Gieseler has the merit of having been the first to bring into prominent notice this way of solving the difficulty.

[2] The Greek expression used by St. Luke ($\dot{a}\nu a\tau\dot{a}\xi a\sigma\theta a\iota\ \delta\iota\dot{\eta}\gamma\eta\sigma\iota\nu$) is precisely fitted for describing compositions of this kind.

To these rudimentary gospels before long succeeded those we now possess, which are distinguished
from the former by a more definite plan, and by the
preponderance of a central idea or dominant thought,
which constitutes the unity of the narrative. Let
any one now turn to the preamble in Luke, and say
whether the hypothesis we have just submitted of
the probable course of events does not correspond with
the order traced by the evangelist himself in this remarkable passage : 1st, an oral tradition, proceeding
immediately from the apostles, as the original source
of all the narratives which were in circulation in the
Church ; 2nd, the putting together of these into a
number of documents, none of which were adequate
to the greatness of their subject ; and, 3rd, the drawing
up of our canonical gospels.

This study of the Synoptists leads us to the following result :

The first gospel contains the primitive apostolic
tradition, worked up and put together in that particular form in which the apostle Matthew used to
state it.   This form was characterised, first, by the five
great courses of instruction into which the publican-
apostle had gathered up the teaching of his Master ;
and, secondly, by the tendency to demonstrate His
Messianic dignity by bringing into relief the relation
between the prophecies and His history.

The contents of the second gospel consist of the
same apostolic tradition, which was current from the

beginning in Jerusalem and in Palestine ; but here it takes the form in which St. Peter used to relate it in the churches, allowing himself the free and spontaneous insertion into it of a number of little points of detail, as they were brought to his mind at the moment by his personal recollection, and which Mark, his companion, and the compiler of his narratives, used eagerly to take down.

What could be more natural, from this point of view, than, on the one hand, the striking points of resemblance noticeable in these two writings, which both reproduce the same sacred tradition, and, on the other, all those disagreements on secondary points which result from differences of individual character and of circumstances in the narrators ?

The gospel of Luke is a third branch growing out of the same stem of primitive apostolic teaching, but diverging much further from the other two than those do from one another. The reason of this is that the compilation of Luke does not proceed directly from the oral tradition. There intervenes another working up of the materials—namely, those collections of anecdotes of which we have spoken, and which have left their Aramaic stamp strongly impressed upon the narratives of the third gospel. Further, Luke has used a twofold liberty of criticism with respect to the tradition received in the Church : first, in endeavouring to complete it with reference to particular events which it had omitted ; and, secondly, in trying to replace into their original context a number of our Lord's sayings which tradition had incorporated into large groups of His discourses. This is affirmed by Luke himself in ver. 3 and 4 of his preamble; and the whole of his gospel confirms it.

Thus, then, the first gospel is a work of an essentially *liturgical* character, conformably to the didactic tendency of Matthew's document which has been inserted into it, and which will always form the salient feature of its physiognomy.

The second has more of an *anecdotical* character; that is to say, it is at once more familiar and more picturesque, befitting the narrative of such a man as Peter, with his sure and ready judgment and vivid impressions, but a mind that had never undergone the effects of a high intellectual culture.

The third, and the third alone, really deserves the name of *history*, in the sense which had come to attach to that word among the Greeks, trained in the higher efforts of the intellect. It consists of an orderly and critical exposition of the facts, well adapted to set them in their clearest light, and just such as we might expect from such an author as Luke, whose profession as a physician had initiated him into the methods of procedure of the literary and scientific culture of his time.

The date which we have assigned to the composition of these three writings—between 60 and 65—agrees perfectly with the circumstances of the Church at that

time. It was just the time when the first generation
of Christians were beginning to come to a clear understanding with themselves, and when its great representatives were being dispersed among the nations,
soon to disappear one after another from the stage
of this world. How would it be possible for them
not to endeavour at that time to stereotype, in written
records, the great and sacred memories of which
they were in a sense the official depositaries? "If
the art of writing had not existed before," says
Lange, "men would have invented it at that time,
and for that purpose."

4

THE GOSPEL OF JOHN

St. Matthew had set forth the life of Jesus from the
point of view of its relation with the sacred Israelitish
past. St. Mark had described it simply as it appeared
to the first eye-witnesses, without comparing the
Christ with anything but Himself. St. Luke had
seen opening before men, by means of it, a whole
new *future*—the conquest of the pagan world by the
Gospel.

All aspects of it seemed exhausted;—past, present,
and future,—are not these all the possible dimensions
of time? If there was to be a fourth gospel, and it
was not to be, at least as to its fundamental idea, a

repetition of one of those which preceded it, it must find its occasion and point of view in a sphere superior to time—in eternity. This is, in fact, the special characteristic of John's gospel.

I. Let us first recall to mind the accounts transmitted to us by Christian antiquity respecting the origin of this document, as well as the facts, borrowed from the literature of the second century, which may throw light upon this question.

Irenæus, who had lived in his youth with the friend and disciple of St. John, Polycarp, bishop of Smyrna, writes as follows: "After that, John, the disciple of the Lord who had leaned on His bosom, himself also published a gospel while he was living at Ephesus in Asia." Irenæus mentions in several places this sojourn of John in Asia, of which many attempts have been made in modern times to question the reality.[1] "All the presbyters who met with John, the disciple of the Lord, in Asia, declare that it is he who communicated these things to them; for he lived there with them up to the time of Trajan." We know that this emperor came to the throne in the year 98. Irenæus adds that the principal object of John in writing this gospel was to combat certain false doctrines which were beginning to arise among the Asiatic churches.

We find in the Muratorian fragment, already quoted, the following passage: "The fourth gospel is by John. John, one of the disciples, being solicited by

---

[1] Lützelberger, Keim.

his fellow-disciples and bishops, said to them, ' Let us fast together for the next three days, and then communicate to each other the revelations which each shall have received.' The following night it was revealed to Andrew, one of the apostles, that John should write the whole in his own name, and that all the others should criticise what he had written. . . . What is there, then, surprising in the fact that John should say in his epistles, speaking of himself, ' That which we have heard, which we have seen with our eyes, and our hands have handled . . . . declare we unto you.' He thus proclaims himself to be not only an eye and ear witness, but also the narrator of all the wonderful events of the Lord's life." The part which some of the other apostles play in this history, especially Andrew, is very remarkable. It must have been tradition which furnished these facts.

Clement of Alexandria relates that which follows, in accordance once more with the tradition which the presbyters had handed down to one another up to his time : " John, the last, having noticed that the *bodily things* (the external events of our Lord's life) were recorded in the gospels (our three synoptics of which Clement had just been narrating the origin), at the instigation of the men of note, and moved by the Spirit, composed a *spiritual gospel* (one suited to the purpose of initiating the Church into the spirit of these events)."

I omit the less original accounts of Eusebius and of Jerome; but I cannot refrain from quoting one more testimony, more ancient than any of the preceding, if it is authentic. It is drawn from a preface to John's gospel, transcribed in a Latin manuscript of the gospels which exists in the Vatican. In this fragment, which, according to Tischendorf, dates from a time anterior to that of Jerome, we read as follows: "The gospel of John was published and given to the Church by that apostle while he was still living; as Papias of Hierapolis, his beloved disciple, relates, at the end of his five exegetical books."[1] A quotation so direct is a fact of importance, which will make it impossible any longer to plead, with the boldness which has been common hitherto, the pretended silence of the aged Papias as an argument against the authenticity of the fourth gospel.

To these sufficiently detailed accounts, we must add a series of facts belonging to the ecclesiastical history of the second century, and which all corroborate our belief in the wide diffusion and in the truly apostolic authority of this gospel at that time.

---

[1] In the fragment, the word is *exoteric*, which is clearly a misreading of *exegetic*, an epithet drawn from the title of Papias' work, "An *Exegesis* of the Discourses of the Lord." We have already seen that this document was divided into five books (see p. 15). The remainder of this fragment gives some other details of much more doubtful character, and which do not appear to rest on the same authority.

Thus it is that we trace indications, more or less distinct, of its influence, in the so-called epistle of Barnabas, in the best authenticated letters of Ignatius, in the epistle to Diognetes, in the Shepherd of Hermas, and above all in the writings of Justin Martyr. All these works belong to the orthodox Church.[1] But this influence appears still more evident amongst the sects of the most opposite tendencies, as in the Gnostic, Basilides, whose works contain many express quotations from John; in his successor Valentine, whose whole system, as M. Bunsen has said, was built of materials borrowed from John's prologue, and whose principal disciple, Heraclion, even wrote a complete commentary upon this gospel; in Marcion, a Gnostic heretic of quite another kind, who opposed the law to the gospel, and whose letters, according to the report of Tertullian, attested that he recognised our gospel as the work of John, without, however, attributing to it any authority, just for this reason, that he considered its author tainted with Judaism; in the Judæo-Christian or Essene party, from which proceeded the famous *Clementine Homilies*, a book in which our fourth gospel is more than once quoted; and yet this party constituted the ecclesiastical antipodes of Marcion. One small sect alone seems to have disputed the authenticity of this gospel—that

---

[1] Keim thinks it impossible to deny the traces of the use of the fourth gospel in all these documents, succeeding one another in the first half of the second century.

which in later times received from Epiphanius the
name of *Alogi*. But its rejection by them contains in
itself an indirect testimony in favour of this gospel;
for they attributed it to Cerinthus, the well-known
adversary of John in Ephesus, which proves that in
their belief it had been really composed in that town,
and in the time of the apostle.

It would be difficult to understand how all these
detailed accounts could have been fabricated and
adopted without dispute by the whole Church, and
how so many authors, orthodox and heretical, and
of the most opposite tendencies, could have given
such entire credence to this gospel, had not a very
well-founded tradition been the source of the idea
which men had formed for themselves of its apostolic
origin.

The result of this summing up of the evidence is:
(1) that the fourth gospel was written by the apostle
John; (2) that this took place in Asia Minor during
the latter part of that apostle's life, in the midst of
the numerous churches founded there by St. Paul,
and with the object of lifting these former heathens
to an elevation of faith worthy of the divine object
of Christian worship; (3) that it was written at the
instigation of the bishops of these churches, and even
of some of John's colleagues in the apostolate—
particularly Andrew, who was living then in those
countries; (4) that John, while composing this
narrative of Christ's ministry, had before him the

three earlier gospels already in circulation in the Church.

II. We have now to ascertain, by the study of the gospel itself, how far we may trust these data furnished by ecclesiastical history.

That the fourth gospel was intended for the use of churches which had already made some progress in the Christian life, and were well instructed in the events of our Lord's ministry, it is not difficult to prove. How came the narrator to speak of *the Twelve*, as he does in vi. 70, as well-known persons, without having said a word of their election? How should he have left out between the return of Jesus into Galilee (iv. 43) and His sojourn in Judæa (v. 1) two whole months; and again, between this sojourn and the miracle of the multiplying of the loaves (vi. 1), one whole month; and yet again, between this last event and the departure for Jerusalem (vii. 1), nearly eight months; and lastly, between this journey and the following one to the Feast of Dedication, an interval of more than two months,— had he not supposed his readers to be well acquainted with all the events of the Galilean ministry with which the synoptic narratives are filled? How could he have described Bethany (xi. 1) as *the town of Mary and her sister Martha*, when he had never even mentioned these two persons? How should he describe Mary (xi. 2) as the woman *which anointed the Lord with ointment*, not having yet related that incident? We see from one end of the book to the other, indications that the author supposes his readers well acquainted with the history of Jesus, and that he wishes only to bring into notice certain events which had either been omitted by tradition, or not sufficiently comprehended.

The churches for which this gospel was intended belonged to the Gentile world. For not only is the author moved to bring into special prominence the part played by the Greeks in our Lord's ministry,[1] but he also gives explanations of Jewish customs;[2] and twice he translates the Hebrew word *Messiah* into the Greek *Christ*.[3]

Lastly, it is in Asia Minor, and not in Greece, properly so called, that we have to look for these Greeks. For it was in Asia that the speculations were current to which the evangelist alludes in his prologue, when he calls upon his readers to see in Jesus the revelation of the *Logos* or Divine Word. Was it not in the same way to the churches in that country that Paul, in his epistles to the Ephesians and to the Colossians, set forth more especially the divinity of the Christ, because it was in that portion of the Church that the questions relating to this great subject were already being agitated? So then the fact of this gospel having been written for the churches of Asia Minor cannot be called in question.

The *object* which the author had in view we find

---

[1] vii. 35 ; xii. 20.　　　　　[3] i. 41; iv. 25.
[2] ii. 6 ; iv. 9 ; xix. 40.

expressly stated by himself in xx. 30, 31. It was his
wish, by the help of these few incidents selected out
of the history of his Master, to bring his readers to
perfect faith in Him as the Christ the Son of God,
and to enable them to have life through Him. For
this purpose, the gospels already in circulation did
not seem to him sufficient. Even with regard to the
history, he found some points in them which needed
filling up : nearly a whole year of His active life in
Judæa, before the time when that Galilean ministry
began, to narrate which was almost the sole object of
the synoptic gospels ; also four residences in Jerusalem
and one visit to Bethany, before His last sojourn in
the capital—journeys which the synoptists had altogether omitted. These were historical lacunæ which
he wished to fill up ; and connected with them were
some still more important omissions. It had been
nearly always on occasion of the great national festi-
vals that Jesus had spoken those weighty discourses
about Himself in which He spiritualised the symbols
of the Old Testament, so as to apply them to Himself.
Now, if we except the great discourse on the *bread
of life*, delivered in Galilee on occasion of a Passover
celebrated in that province (vi.), it was in Jerusalem
that He had made these great assertions of His
Messianic character.[1] Oral tradition had preserved

---

[1] The conversation with Nicodemus (iii.) at the feast of the
Passover ; the discourse on His relation to the Father (v.) at
the feast of Purim ; the discourse on the fountain of living water

but feeble traces of them, as well as of these sojourns in Jerusalem. It had naturally preserved with greater care the memory of the popular preaching and familiar intercourse which had marked the ministry of Jesus in the small towns and villages of Galilee. It was of great importance, therefore, to restore to the Church those treasures which she was in danger of losing for ever, and to reproduce in a permanent manner those manifestations of the inner consciousness of Christ in the way in which they had impressed themselves deeply upon the mind of the beloved disciple. So only could all believers be brought to re-echo that full profession of faith uttered by Thomas, and which sums up the teaching of the fourth gospel: " My Lord and my God !"

This then is the direct object of our gospel. And by this means the author at the same time overthrew indirectly all the errors which began to arise in Asia respecting the Person of our Lord : that of John the Baptist's disciples, who placed their master above Jesus ; of Cerinthus, who made of Jesus a mere man to whom at a certain period of his life the heavenly Christ had united Himself ; of the heretics called the *Docetæ*, who maintained that our Lord's body was nothing but a mere apparition ; of the Ebionites, who saw in Jesus only the son of Joseph and Mary raised to the dignity of Messiah. All these false systems

---

vii.—x.[a]) at the feast of Tabernacles ; the discourse on the subject, " *I and my Father,*" at the feast of Dedication (x.[b]).

fell to pieces before these words, of which our whole gospel is the exhibition—"THE WORD WAS MADE FLESH." The perfection of the divine life was realised under the forms of human infirmity ; the abyss between the infinite and the finite was practically bridged over, and the *Logos* of philosophy, which had hitherto been dimly discerned only through clouds of speculation, is henceforth, to the eye of faith, a being who has been seen, known, apprehended. Such was the Jesus of history, such is the Jesus of John,—a Being as perfectly human as divine.

It has been often asserted that the Jesus of John is not a being perfectly human. Nothing can be more untrue. If there exists a true *son of man*, it is the Jesus of the fourth gospel. He sits *wearied with His journey* at Jacob's well ; He *groans in the spirit* at the sight of His friends in tears ; He *weeps* Himself at the grave of His friend ; His *soul is troubled* at the thought of His approaching trial.[1] The Jesus of John is *human* throughout.

Who is the *author* to whom we are to attribute such a picture as this?

He describes himself as one of the eye-witnesses of our Lord's life. "We beheld His glory," he says (i. 14) ; and if there could be any doubt of the literal meaning of this word *beheld*, the question would be set at rest by those other words (xix. 35) : "And he that saw it bare record, and his record is true ; " and by

---

[1] John iv. 6 ; xi. 33, 35 ; xii. 27.

the preamble to the first epistle of the same author :
" That which we have heard, which we have seen
with our eyes, which we have looked upon, and our
hands have handled, of the Word of life ; that which
we have seen and heard declare we unto you." [1]
Either he who thus speaks must be an audacious
forger, or he was himself an eye-witness of what
he relates.   Now it is no easy matter to make of
the holiest work that ever issued from a human
pen one continued act of fraud.   There are moral
inconsistencies which present difficulties quite as
insuperable as any logical contradictions.

That this character of eye-witness which the author
attributes to himself was really his, is also shown by
the position of sovereign authority which he takes up
with respect to the traditions received in the Church
and reported by the synoptists.   He does not scruple
to correct a misunderstanding to which their record
had given rise : " For," he says (iii. 24), " John was
not yet cast into prison,"—an evident allusion to those
words in Matt. iv. 12 : " Now when Jesus had heard
that John was cast into prison, He departed into
Galilee," and to the parallel passage in Mark.   He
takes the same independent line with respect to the
various sojourns at Jerusalem which the synoptists
had not mentioned ; also to the exact day of Christ's
death, which had not been indicated by them with
sufficient precision, etc., etc.   In all these instances,

---

[1] I John i. 1—3.

the author of the fourth gospel speaks as one who is better acquainted with the facts than the rest, and who knows that his personal testimony will be received without dispute by the whole Church, even if it does not agree in all points with the received tradition. This position, boldly taken up in face of the synoptists themselves, would have been impossible to any but an eye-witness and an apostle.

Let us take one step further. This apostle could have been none other than *the disciple whom Jesus loved*. This disciple is often mentioned in the narrative, but never by name. How is it that, while the author without scruple mentions all the other apostles by name, he never fails to conceal this one under a veil of anonymousness ? A strongly marked auto-biographic character is also impressed upon just those points in the narrative in which this unnamed disciple appears upon the scene,—as in the passage (i. 37—41) in which his calling is recorded, and especially in the narrative (xx. 1—9) where an account is given of the manner in which his belief in the resurrection of Jesus was formed. It was simply the sight of the grave-clothes, folded up and lying separately, which convinced him of the truth of this event. This incident belonging to the private life of the disciple whom Jesus loved is related by the author in the third person singular : "he saw and believed" (ver. 8); while in the preceding and following verses he speaks in the third person plural of that which relates both to his

companion Peter and to himself. Thus we see that
Peter did not so quickly reach to the same degree
of faith ; another means was needed for him—the
apparition of Jesus, of which mention is made elsewhere.

As the author was at the foot of the cross (xix. 35),
and as the beloved disciple seems to have been the
only one of the disciples present during the last
sufferings of Jesus (ver. 24), the identity of these
two persons seems also proved by this coincidence.
These are the indications which obliged even Baur to
acknowledge that the author *wished to pass himself
off* as the disciple whom Jesus loved.

Lastly, the author must have been one of the *sons
of Zebedee*. This follows first from the fact that neither
John, nor his brother James, nor their mother Salome,
who all play a part more or less important in the other
gospels, are mentioned by name in this gospel. The
same conclusion follows also from the passage in xxi. 2,
which, if not written by the author himself, is due, at
all events, to a tradition emanating from him. In
this list, the sons of Zebedee are placed last relatively
to the other *apostles* present (Simon Peter, Thomas,
Nathanael) ; their names have the precedence only
over two unnamed *disciples*, who were, no doubt, not
apostles. Now we know that, in the lists of apostles,
James and John are always placed at the head of the
Twelve with Peter and Andrew. Either, then, we have
here a deliberate degradation of them by the author,

or it must be from one of the two that this narrative
proceeds. As between James and John there can be
no doubt, since James died too early to allow us to
attribute this gospel to him. (Acts xii.)

This result of the study of the book itself is confirmed by the remarkable attestation which closes it.
It is certain that ver. 24 and 25 of chap. xxi. could
not have been written by the author himself. The
use of the plural "*we know*" proves that this is an
addition made by those to whom the author had
handed over his work to transmit to the Church at a
suitable time. Most likely these were the disciples
and pastors, mentioned in the Muratorian fragment
already quoted, who had urged the apostle to write
this gospel. The verb in the singular, "*I think*,"
(ver. 25) refers to the one among them who was
acting as secretary for the others, perhaps Papias. At
any rate, these persons affirm here that this gospel
is the work of the disciple whom Jesus loved, who
was still living at the time when they appended this
attestation to his work.[1]

Should we not then be justified, even if all tradition
relating to this document were wanting, in saying, in
the words of a German critic, who, nevertheless, does not
much favour evangelical orthodoxy:[2] "The character
of the language, the freshness and vividness of the

---

[1] Observe the contrast between the past tense, "*who wrote*,"
and the present, "*who testifies*," ver. 28.

[2] Credner.

narrative, the accuracy and precision of the data, the peculiar manner in which John the Baptist and the sons of Zebedee are mentioned, the love, the glowing tenderness which the author betrays towards the Person of Jesus, the irresistible charm thrown by his narrative over the gospel story,—all this leads us to the conviction that the author of such a gospel could have been no other than a native of Palestine, an eye-witness, an apostle, the disciple whom Jesus loved— that same John whose head had rested on His breast, and who had remained close to His Cross—that John whose subsequent abode in a town like Ephesus had fitted him for fulfilling this task among Greeks who were so eminent for their literary culture."

All other attempts to account for the origin of this document involve greater difficulties than they remove. Where are we to find a man in the second century, after the time of John, capable of writing such a narrative, of composing such discourses, of painting, in this style, scenes of such grandeur ? We know the eminent men of the second century ; their names are Ignatius, Polycarp, Papias, Justin, etc. How striking their mediocrity compared with the Johannean sub-limity ! And we must suppose that these men—holy, no doubt, but so inferior to our author—were stars of the first magnitude, while a man of genius, of an originality so great, remained completely unknown, and passed unnoticed in the midst of his contem-poraries ! This improbability far surpasses all those which it is usual to urge against the traditional opinion.

The conclusion, then, at which we arrive, by putting all these arguments together, is as follows :—

John, with some of the apostles and older followers of Jesus, alone remained, at the end of the first century, out of all that circle of eye-witnesses who had surrounded Him during His lifetime. Some of these were to be found at Ephesus. These were Andrew, — who had been the first, in company with John, to accost Jesus (John i.),—and Philip, who lived close by at Hierapolis. They felt that the portrait of their Master which had been bequeathed to the Church by the three evangelists, though it was substantially accurate, yet gave but an imperfect idea of the Person of Him whose glory had illumined their hearts. This was also the feeling of the heads of those churches in Asia to whom John had been for a long time preaching the Gospel, and who had heard things from his lips which they did not find in these books. On hearing the request which they addressed to him, the Holy Spirit moved him to take up his pen. Taking account of the writings already published, he composed his narrative straight off, as one who did not depend upon oral tradition ; with no intention of repeating that part of the history with which he knew his readers were already well acquainted, but with the object of throwing upon that life the stronger light with which it was illuminated in his own mind. Just as in a time of slow and irresistible upheaval of the earth, beds of rock come to the surface,—mighty strata which had been quietly depositing themselves during many ages at the bottom of the ocean : so now there came to light in this fourth gospel all the treasures of the recollections which for half a century had been accumulating and classifying themselves in the meditative mind of the beloved disciple. The plan of the work was not of his making ; that he found made ready to his hand—as, 1, the *glory of Jesus*, in its growing development, the Son of God realising under the forms of human existence the filial life in relation to God, and thus elevating our nature into a new position relatively to God ; 2, *faith*, developing itself amongst those who were attracted by this unique apparition, and represented in the persons of the disciples and of the author himself ; 3, *unbelief*, showing itself at the same time among those whom this same apparition repelled, personified in the Jewish authorities and the mass of the people, and, as it were, incarnated in Judas. Such were the three aspects under which his subject presented itself to his mind. They are distinctly set forth in the prologue (i. 1—18), and they reappear in the whole picture as the three essential aspects of the fact narrated. A plan such as this is not the work of man, but of the Spirit of truth. It is history apprehended from the point of view of its profoundest reality. We recognise here in John, to a degree peculiar to himself, the fulfilment of our Lord's promise, when, announcing the coming of the Spirit, He thus described the work He would do : " He shall glorify me in you."

Thus was produced this wonderful document which has already extorted from its adversaries so many retractations, and which will yet obtain from the present century, when once the delusions caused by the intoxications of a misleading critical philosophy shall have been cleared away, the homage which will for ever set it free from the opprobria under which it is still to this day suffering.

Four portraits of Himself—this is the whole of the legacy left by Jesus to His family on earth. But they are sufficient for its needs, because by the contemplation of these the Church receives into herself, through the communications of the Spirit, the life of Him whose characteristic features they set forth.

These four pictures originated spontaneously, and (the three first, at all events,) independently of each other. They arose, accidentally in a manner, from the four principal regions of the earth comprehended by the Church in the first century—Palestine, Asia Minor, Greece, Italy.

The characteristics of these four regions have not failed to exercise a certain influence upon the manner in which the Christ has been presented in the pictures intended for the use of each. In Palestine, Matthew

proclaimed Jesus as Him who put the finishing stroke
to the establishment of that holy kingdom of God which
had been fore-announced by the prophets, and of which
the foundations had been laid in Israel.   In Rome,
Mark presented Him as the irresistible conqueror
who founded His Divine right to the possession of
the world upon His miraculous power.   Amongst the
generous and affable Hellenic races, Luke described
Him as the Divine philanthropist, commissioned to
carry out the work of Divine grace and compassion
towards the worst of sinners.   In Asia Minor, that
ancient cradle of theosophy, John pictured Him as
the Word made flesh, the eternal life and light, who
had descended into the world of Time.   Thus it was
under the influence of a profound sympathy with those
about him that each evangelist brought into relief
that aspect of Christ which answered most nearly to
the ideal of his readers.

But, on the other hand, each of the evangelists has
also, by means of the picture which he has drawn,
pronounced a judgment upon whatever was impure in
the aspirations with which in some respects he sym-
pathised.   The spiritual and inspired Messianic idea
presented by Matthew condemned that political and
carnal view of the Church which is the very soul of
false Judaism.   The sanctified and divine Romanism
of Mark condemned the Cæsarism of mere brute
force.   The heavenly Atticism of Luke took the place
of the frivolous and corrupt Hellenism encountered

by Paul at Athens. Lastly, Humanitarianism—the Divine Humanitarianism of John—stands as an eternal witness against the humanitarianism, profane and anti-divine in its nature, of a world dazzled with its own greatness, and lost in evil.

Our gospels are at once magnets to draw to themselves whatever is left of divine in the depths of human nature, and, as it were, winnowing machines to sift out from it whatever is sinful. Hence the power both of attraction and repulsion which they exert upon the natural heart of man.

It has been sometimes asked why, instead of the four gospels, God did not cause a single one to be written, in which all the events should have been arranged in their chronological order, and the history of Jesus pourtrayed with the accuracy of a legal document. If the drawing up of the gospels had been the work of human skill, it would no doubt have taken this form; but it is just here that we seem able to lay a finger upon the altogether Divine nature of the impulse which originated the work.

Just as a gifted painter, who wished to immortalise for a family the complete likeness of the father who had been its glory, would avoid any attempt at combining in a single portrait the insignia of all the various offices he had filled—at representing him in the same picture as general and as magistrate, as man of science and as father of a family, but would prefer to paint four distinct portraits, each of which should represent him in one of these characters,—so has the Holy Spirit, in order to preserve for mankind the perfect likeness of Him who was its chosen representative, God in man, used means to impress upon the minds of the writers whom He has made His organs, four different images—the King of Israel, (Matthew); the Saviour of the world, (Luke); the Son, who, as man, mounts the steps of the Divine throne, (Mark); and the Son who descends into humanity to sanctify the world, (John).

The single object which is represented by these four aspects of the glory of Jesus Christ could not be presented to the minds of men in a single book; it could only be so in the form under which it was originally embodied—that of a life; first in the Church—that body of Christ which was destined to contain and to display all the fulness which had dwelt in its Head; and then again in the person of each individual believer, if that is true which Jesus said: " Ye in me, and I in you ;" and we are each of us called to make the personality of Jesus live again in ourselves in all the rich harmony of His perfection.

In the Church, then—in you, in me—we behold the living syntheses which were to be the result of that wondrous analysis of the Person of Jesus Christ which produced our several gospel narratives. The harmony of the four gospels is something better than the best written book; it is the *new man* to be formed in each believer.

From the earliest times, the canonical gospels have been compared to the four figures of the cherubim which support the throne of God. This comparison has given rise to many arbitrary and puerile exegetical fancies. We would rather compare them to the four wings, continually growing, with which the cherubim more and more cover the whole extent of the earth, and upon which rests the throne of the majesty of Jesus.

Let criticism beware : to destroy one of these wings is to mutilate the holiest thing on this earth.

2

JESUS CHRIST

" JESUS CHRIST has succeeded in making of every human soul an appendage of His own:"—so is the prisoner of St. Helena reported to have said in one of his private and intimate conversations. The assertion made by those august lips is true. By what means did Jesus reach this marvellous result?

Different men have different tasks and functions assigned to them ; and we each of us feel most powerfully attracted by that one leading mind which reigns supreme in our own sphere of life, and which, in it, offers us the support which is required by our weakness or want of intelligence.

But there is one task which does not belong to a few only, and which does not depend upon our special aptitudes or upon our particular tastes: it is that which is imposed upon us by *moral obligation*. The task of fulfilling this obligation is universal and absolute ; it belongs to us all, and to us all at every moment. It admits of no dispensation from its commands. The spirit who shall attain pre-eminence in this province in such sort as to become the point of support in work to all the rest, and shall thus make himself the fellow-worker with each man in the realisation of his supreme destiny, will have solved in practice the problem of the discovery of the universal centre of gravitation for all souls. He will be to them as a magnetic pole, towards which they will turn just so far as the law of right shall make itself felt within them ; he will be found to have grouped for ever around his person all who deserve the name of man.[1]

Of this problem Jesus first discovered the solution, and then actually realised it. He has been to humanity the genius of holiness. And was not this, in fact, what He meant when He so often described Himself by the title *the Son of Man?* Fifty-five times in our gospels does He choose, by preference, this title for Himself. His intention evidently is to define by it the relation in which He stands to humanity. A *son of man* in Holy Scripture means a *true* man.[2] *The* Son of Man means therefore the man *par excellence*, the *true* man, the perfect realisation of the type, man, the normal representative of the race as it was conceived in the mind of Him who gave it being.

But this title is not the only one by which Jesus designates Himself in His discourses. He also often

---

[1] See the fine development of this thought in the work of M. Wærner, *Kirchenfreund*, 1872, Nos. 18 and 19.

[2] Ezekiel xxvii. 3, and elsewhere.

calls Himself *the Son of God*, or *the Son* simply.[1] By this title Jesus defined the relation in which He stood to the Divine nature, or, it would be better to say, to the Person of God.

We see, then, how erroneous is the opinion, very common amongst the interpreters of Holy Scripture, which explains both of these titles as signifying the *Messiah*, and makes them consequently synonymous. They are, on the contrary, contrasted with and complementary to each other. In the one, Jesus wished to express all that He is to men ; in the other, all that He is to God.[2]

Notwithstanding the duality of relation, and even of nature, which belongs to Him, Jesus is nevertheless one single and unique Person. It is evident, then, that the contrast which we have pointed out is to be explained by a higher unity, by a *personality* which is the expression of the individual indissoluble consciousness of Him who thus speaks of Himself as *I*. And of this unity, which is perhaps the greatest mystery of theology, we are not forbidden to attempt to fathom the depths ; the Church has formulated it in the title, *the God-Man*.

But let man, as he enters upon this province of

---

[1] John iii. 16 ; v. 25, etc. ; Matt. xi · 27 ; xxviii. 19, etc. ; Mark xiii. 32.

[2] It is generally very easy to see the reason of the use of these two names by considering the different contexts in which they occur. Compare, for instance, John iii. 14 and 16.

thought, sacred above all others, never forget to take off his shoes from his feet,—that is, to renounce his own thoughts, and surrender himself to those of God revealed in the wondrous facts of redemption, and in the revelations which accompanied it.

This essay upon the *Person* of Jesus Christ will be divided into three parts : the Son of Man, the Son of God, and the God-Man.

We shall defer what we have to say more specially upon the *work* of Jesus Christ till the essay which follows.   It will only be after thoroughly investigating these two subjects that we shall be able to apprehend in all its profundity that remarkable expression which fell from a genius of another order, which we quoted at the beginning of this work.

1

THE SON OF MAN

We can study the facts of which the history of Jesus consists—the *material facts* of His life, to use the expression of Clement of Alexandria—while we are assuring ourselves of its reality by the stamp of truthfulness which marks the narratives which have preserved it for us.   This is the historico-critical point of view.   But we may arrive at the same result by following the opposite line.   We may start from the facts of the gospel story, accepting them provisionally, as known to us by the religious instruction we received in infancy, and observing the sense attaching to each of them, and the idea which binds them together into one whole; and if we find a real and deep harmony establishing itself without difficulty among all these facts disseminated as by chance through four distinct documents, we shall then be compelled to recognise in this interconnection between them, their historic and providential character. This is the synthetic method. The nature of the work would admit of no other.

We have then, first, to point out the idea which is, in our view, the key to all the salient events of our Lord's earthly life; then, taking these events one by one, to see if this idea can account satisfactorily for them.

The general idea which governs the earthly life of Jesus Christ is none other than that which He Himself enunciated when He gave Himself the title of Son of Man. His life is the realisation of the normal development to which, in principle, every human being is called.

Let us see if this simple idea will not throw light upon the whole career of Jesus from its beginning to its end.

The essential facts of the history of Jesus divide themselves into three series. The first includes His birth, the history of His development as a child and young man, His baptism at the age of thirty, and His temptation in the wilderness. This is the period of preparation. The second series comprehends (to express ourselves summarily, and grouping the facts together) His holy living, His teaching, and His miracles; and closes with the mysterious event of the Transfiguration. This constitutes the first part of His work as the Redeemer. The third series comprehends the supreme events of His history, His Passion and Resurrection, and finally, His Ascension, which is both the final term of the series, and the crowning point of His whole life. This constitutes the accomplishment of the second part of His work.

FIRST SERIES

I. *The Birth.*—According to our Gospel narratives, Jesus was not born in the ordinary course of nature. Have we not here, then, at the very outset of our undertaking, a rock upon which the thesis we have to maintain comes to shipwreck? If Jesus Christ is truly man, must He not have been born in the same manner as every other man? This objection, however, it is easy to see, proves too much; for it would oblige us to deny true humanity to the first man, upon the ground that he came into existence by a different process from that of ordinary human filiation.[1] Now,

---

[1] This would still remain true, even if we granted the Darwinian hypothesis, which, taken in its utmost strictness, still only applies to the body of man, not to his soul, unless indeed we are willing to give up, in the case of man, the distinctive feature of his being —his moral freedom.

would it not be a strange proceeding to deny real humanity to that being from whom all that bears the name of man has sprung? This instance proves that the quality of manhood does not depend upon the manner in which the individual being came into existence, but upon the possession of certain attributes which constitute humanity.

According to the account in Genesis, the body of the first man, that masterpiece of the creative wisdom, was formed out of the dust of the earth—that is to say, it came into existence as the crowning-point of that long development of animal life which the discoveries of geology have brought to light. But the spirit of man came from above. It was a direct inspiration from the Divine Spirit. The circumstances of the birth of Jesus Christ present a marked analogy with this mode of creation. His body was derived, through the medium of His mother, from humanity as it already existed. But it was the breath of God, the power of the Almighty Spirit, which called this embryo life into the orderly development and onward progress of human existence.

This analogy between the birth of Jesus and the creation of the first man reveals distinctly to us the divine idea which governed the earlier of these two events. Jesus was, by His miraculous birth, restored to the same condition of purity and innocence in which the first man existed before the Fall; and that was so ordered that He might be able successfully to enter once more upon that pathway of progress from innocence up to holiness which had been the course originally opened to man, but at the very outset of which Adam had fallen.

Man was not so created as to be able to reach his ideal by drawing the required strength from his own resources. He can only attain to that by the aid of continual communications from God. Now, as soon as he gives way to the sway of an evil power, these communications are interrupted; he does not any longer ask for, or receive them. Retrogression then takes the place of progress. Like a plant torn from its natural soil, man vegetates and perishes, instead of growing and bearing fruit.

In order, then, that the normal development of mankind, which had been interrupted by sin, might begin afresh, there was needed the appearance upon the scene of a personality raised above the influence of that downward tendency which had seized the whole race, free from that spirit of rebellion against God which had gained possession of us all, and completely open also to those communications from above which constitute for man the necessary condition of all true progress.

Jesus was that personality. His whole life proves it, as well as the new phase of history which has its origin in Him. Up to that time the course of human history might be summed up thus—" That which is born of the flesh is flesh." From His time the true

drift of that history might be formulated in the words
—"That which is born of the spirit is spirit." For the
distinctive characteristic of spirit, in the Bible sense of
that word, is holiness ; and where else shall we find
holiness, save in Jesus, and in that which emanates
from Him ?

But it may be said : If so, then Jesus was not really
a free agent, for it was not possible for Him to sin as
we do. We reply, that this special mode of birth did
not entail in His case the impossibility of sinning, any
more than did that of the first man, which was analogous to it; it simply restored to Jesus that power of
not sinning which man possessed before the Fall, and
which we have lost by the rupture of that link which
united us to God.

So far, then, from depriving Him of liberty of action,
this miraculous birth restored it to Him, by giving
Him back in its integrity that power of self-determi-
nation of which the tyranny of sin had in part robbed
us, and without which we could no longer fulfil the
holy and glorious calling opened to us by God.

The miraculous birth is, then, that divine act,
corresponding with the creation of the first man, by
which man has been placed in a fit condition for
carrying out that normal development to which he
was called, and answering in the end to the idea in
the mind of God.

II. *The Development.*—" And the Child grew and
waxed strong in spirit, filled with wisdom, and the

grace of God was upon Him " (Luke ii. 40). So does
the evangelist describe the development of Jesus as a
child. The expression *he grew* relates to His physical development. The words which follow, bringing
out the two ideas of *strength* and of *wisdom*, refer to
the development of the soul,—that is, to the ever-
growing energy of the will, and to its more and more
complete intuition of the true Good. Lastly, the
concluding expression, the *grace of God* resting upon
Him, indicates the religious principle which formed
the deep and sacred motive power of this twofold
development of soul and body. Thus did the Child
grow up to His twelfth year.

The development of the young man up to the age
of thirty years is also summed up in one sentence:
"And He increased in wisdom and stature, and in
favour with God and man " (Luke ii. 52). We find
here the three elements of the normal development of
man : a sound body, approaching day by day to the
stature of a full-grown man ; a soul drawing from God
an ever-increasing *wisdom*,—that is to say, the sense
of good, and good sense, in their deep-seated unity ;
lastly, the influence continuously exerted upon such a
being of divine *grace*. Here we have that true hier-
archy which constitutes the state of health in man's
life ;—the Spirit of God guiding the soul in the use of
its various powers, and the soul so sanctified governing
the body in its manifold functions.

What a wonderful phenomenon was this Child, this

young man carrying on this His normal development in the midst of a world in which every creature falls so far below His ideal! This was that progress *in absolute goodness* which humanity would have realised had sin not intervened. Mankind contemplated with wonder this new thing in the earth, and the eye of God Himself rested with an unmixed satisfaction upon the Being in whom at last He saw one who answered completely to His design. His presence in the midst of a fallen humanity was in itself a first step of the reconciliation between heaven and earth.

III. *The Baptism.*—The concluding act of this undeviating progress was the Baptism. Jesus was then thirty years of age; the period of human life when man reaches the culminating point of his powers, and when the faculties of his soul and the organs of his body lend themselves with the greatest readiness and flexibility to the execution of any work he has in hand. This, according to the evangelical record (Luke iii. 23), was precisely the age at which Jesus passed from His life of silent development in the retirement of Nazareth to that of His public and Messianic activity. The date at which His baptism took place constitutes, then, one feature of a profoundly human character in the record of this event.

There is another, not less remarkable from this point of view. Before descending into the river, the converts who came to John for baptism made confes-

sion of their sins to him.[1]   Jesus, presenting Himself
like any other Israelite, should have done the same.
In what did this confession consist ?   If there is a
human feeling which is alien to the heart of Jesus—
and there is one, and one only—it is that of penitence.
He made a confession like Isaiah, Daniel, Nehemiah,
laying before God the sins of the nation, and humbling
Himself for them in its name ; but with this difference
—that Jesus, in using the word *me*, did not use it
with any sense of personal participation in the general sinfulness, but only under the influence of the
profoundest sympathy.   What can be more human
than that feeling of solidarity in which the love of
Jesus rivets for ever, in that solemn moment, the
chain which binds Him to a guilty humanity !   This
was the spectacle which, a little later, moved John
the Baptist to utter these sublime words : " Behold
the Lamb of God which taketh away the sins of the
world."   He had recognised in Jesus, on the day of
His baptism, that sacred Victim who, while separating
between Himself and sin by a profound abyss as far
as His will was concerned, was at that same moment
making the sin of the whole race His own, in respect
of solidarity between Himself and them.

A third peculiarity of the baptism of Jesus, in which
the reality of His humanity reveals itself, is the act of
prayer with which He descends into the waters of the

---

[1] Matt. iii. 6.

Jordan.[1] In this prayer was expressed the first pure
utterance of the sigh of human nature in its sin for
pardon, and of the thirst of the same nature in its
purity for that which is the life of heaven,—the Holy
Spirit, without which the soul of man can but vegetate.
Prayer is the cry of human need; Jesus prayed with
the feeling of that need, which He must therefore
have shared with us.

The answer of God to that prayer was not long in
coming. The heaven was opened; that luminous sign
wherein was figured the communication of the Spirit
made its appearance; the voice of God sounded;—
three facts perceptible to the inner sense of John and
of Jesus, and which to them were signs of the highest
spiritual truths: the first, of the full revelation of the
divine decrees granted to Jesus; the second, of the gift
of divine power bestowed upon Him to enable Him to
accomplish the scheme of salvation; the third, of His
dignity as the well-beloved Son, without the assurance
of which He could not have executed that work. All
this is so human in character, that we find something
analogous to it in our own spiritual development.
How could we ourselves enter upon any sacred calling,
were we not enlightened from above respecting the
work which we have to accomplish? were we not
endued with the divine power which corresponds to its
requirements? were we not gifted with the assurance
of the adoption of our person and our work by God.

---

[1] Luke iii. 21 : "And, praying, the heaven was opened."

Himself? The difference between Jesus and ourselves in this respect is simply this, that He is charged with the general work of the salvation of mankind, while to each one of us is assigned only a slight part of that work to fulfil with Him ; and consequently He receives the Spirit in His fulness, while to each one of us is given only our own particular measure of His gifts.

There can be nothing, then, more human, from every point of view, than this scene of the Baptism of Jesus. We recognise in it a true man, but at the same time a man called to initiate the whole race into that higher form of life for which it is destined, —the life of the Spirit.

IV. *The Temptation.*—The scene of the Baptism is completed, in our three synoptic records, by that of the Temptation ; the two are inseparable even in respect of their significance, and it is in the latter of them that the truly human character of Jesus stands out with the greatest clearness. To be raised above temptation belongs to God only ; to tempt is the proper work of the devil ; but to be tempted belongs to the state of man.

Why, then, does God account it necessary to deliver up to the ordeal of temptation the Being upon whom He has just bestowed such rich gifts of grace ? Just on account of these very gifts. He has to learn in the school of temptation the habit of dedicating to God alone the gifts which He has received. Will not Jesus, in fact, be often tempted, in the course of His public ministry, to use His miraculous power for the amelioration of His personal and terrestrial condition, which would involve the abandonment of His true state as man ? Will He not, many a time, have an opportunity, offered Him by the enthusiasm of the people, of playing the part of a political Messiah and glorious earthly king, which would be nothing less than the abandonment of the office of a redeeming Messiah, such as God intended and the true needs of mankind demand ? Lastly, will He not often be exposed to the temptation of making use arbitrarily, and without moral necessity, of the almighty power entrusted to Him, which would be a supreme act of indiscretion towards God His Father, and an abandonment of His filial character ? In order to avoid these dangers in His future life, He must learn to know them beforehand; like the captain of a ship, who, before entering upon the ocean, must first have studied on the map the rocks which are scattered through the seas he will have to traverse.

Such were the uses to Jesus of the temptation in the wilderness. In His baptism He had learned what He had to do ; by His temptation He perceived what He was to avoid. Thus did the Father instruct—thus did He warn Him. Is not such an education exactly appropriate to the condition of man ? Is it not that which was needed by Him to whom had been committed the task of bruising, in the name of mankind as a whole, the serpent's head ?

SECOND SERIES

Up to this time the work of Jesus had been His own personal development. The hour has now arrived when this development is to bear its fruits for the good of the world. He has been receiving; now He is about to give. It is at this point that the second stage of His life's work opens,—that which relates to His public ministry. We will begin by His holy living, because that constitutes the basis of His whole redeeming work.

I. *His Holiness.*—Our sacred writings attribute to Jesus a holiness without spot; and one fact, unique in the life of humanity, confirms the truth of this assertion;—the absence in the discourses of Jesus of all expressions of repentance. We feel that in this one life remorse has no place. This fact is so much the more remarkable and decisive, in proportion as Jesus was more humble than other men, and His conscience more sensitive than theirs. The more advanced we are in the life of holiness, the more painfully do we feel the stains of sin. If the slightest defilement had existed in Him, He would have been more affected by it than we are by the gravest faults into which we fall.

But is not irreproachable holiness something in itself superhuman? Certainly not, if it be true that sin is no necessary element of human nature, and if we are not willing to throw the responsibility of it in some degree upon God Himself. The only question which we can and ought to ask here is this: Does the holiness of Jesus bear the marks of a human or of a divine holiness? This question is easily answered.

Two characteristics distinguish the holiness of God from that of man; the latter *progresses*, while the former is stationary and immutable; the latter is developed by *antagonism*, while the former is exempt from all conflict. Apply these two characteristics to the holiness of Jesus. Was there progress, was there conflict, in His moral life?

As to progress, this is what is said of Him in the epistle to the Hebrews: "He *learned obedience* by the things which He suffered." And this is the sentence which is put into His own mouth by that Gospel which is most accused of denying or of mini-mising His humanity,—that of John: "And for their sakes I sanctify myself, that they also might be sanctified through the truth."[1] To *sanctify* is not synonymous with to *purify*. To purify oneself implies that one is defiled; to sanctify oneself is simply to consecrate to God the natural powers of the soul and of the body, as soon as they come into exercise. *Pure* is the opposite of impure; *holy*, of what is profane, or merely natural. In themselves, the forces of our nature are neither good nor evil;

---

[1] Heb. v. 8 ; John xvii. 19.

they become the one or the other in proportion as, at the moment of their awaking into life, they receive the stamp of consecration to God, or remain in the service of that natural heart of man which is always egoistic. There may even arise cases in which holiness will require them to be entirely sacrificed,—that is, whenever they cannot be brought into the service of the special task which has been entrusted to their possessor. And it is in this that progress consists,—in the consecration of our natural gifts more and more to the work assigned to us by God, or even in renouncing them altogether,—plucking out the right eye, or cutting off the right hand, if the forces so expressed cannot be brought into the service of the mission entrusted to us.

Such was the holiness of Jesus. The dedication of His whole being to God progressed just in proportion as all the faculties which awoke within Him were either subjected to God, and dedicated entirely to His service, or else sacrificed because they were not applicable to His redeeming work. Jesus had in Him all those qualities of the heart which confer the power of enjoying the sweetnesses of family life, and all those intellectual powers which are the subjects of literary or scientific education. The parables prove that He could have been a poet or an eminent painter; many of His discourses exhibit the characteristics of an incomparable popular orator; the profoundest philosopher stands revealed in many of His sayings on morality. But if He had given Himself up exclusively to the practice of one or other of these functions, He must have renounced, or at all events have infringed in some degree upon, the fulfilment of that one task which His Father had appointed for Him; and progress in holiness consisted, in His case, in the exclusive dedication of all the powers comprehended in His personality to His work as Saviour of the world. It was precisely in virtue of this profoundly human character of His holiness that He could say: "*I sanctify myself, that they also might be sanctified through the truth.*" This sanctification of the life of man, which He was accomplishing in Himself, it was His purpose at a future time to reproduce in all those who should join themselves to Him by faith. Their holiness should be the same which He was at that time realising in His own person, and which the Spirit would communicate to them when the right moment arrived. What a decisive proof of the truly human character of His holiness!

It is equally proved such by the conflict which marks all its stages. Two tendencies, innocent in themselves, belong to our nature; the desire for enjoyment, and the fear of pain. But these tendencies, legitimate as they are in themselves, may come into antagonism with the mission which has been entrusted to us. Then is the moment for sacrificing them ; and hence arise the struggles to which the most innocent of beings may be exposed.

At the age of twelve years, Jesus found Himself for the first time in the temple. There He felt a happiness like that of a child in his father's house. It was to Him a paradise, and He would have wished to live there for ever. But the voice of His parents calls Him back ; He recognises in it the voice of God. " He is subject to them ;" and returns with them to Nazareth ; but assuredly not without a sacrifice and inward conflict. Here we see the purest of enjoyments sacrificed to the fulfilment of His appointed work.

In the wilderness He is tortured by hunger. What can be more legitimate than this call of nature ? But He unhesitatingly subordinates the fulfilment of its demands to the moral principle of trustful submission towards God. Again, He sees opening before Him those glorious visions of power, for the exercise of which He feels Himself fitted, and of which He would make so noble a use. But there is a condition. . . . The refusal is absolute, and the sacrifice is offered.

A few days before His passion He finds Himself once more in the temple. Some foreign pilgrims ask Him a question which awakens in Him the painful presentiment of the terrible death towards which He is advancing. The presentiment takes possession of Him, and even troubles Him. "Now is my soul troubled," He exclaims before all the people, "and what shall I say? Father, save me from this hour?" This would indeed be the cry of nature; but to this cry, which He might have uttered, another voice answers—the voice of the Spirit—overpowering the first, and finding expression in the prayer, so decisive and real, with which this conflict ends: "Father, glorify Thy name;" deal with me as Thou wilt, only do Thou, through me, reap Thine own glory! And it is in the fourth Gospel that we find the record of this inward conflict, so profoundly human in its character. Here the fear of suffering is offered up as a sacrifice upon the altar of His mission.

It is the same at Gethsemane. The first voice, the voice of nature, cries, "Let this cup pass from me." The higher voice, that of the Spirit—which is none other than that of the task divinely imposed upon Him—speaks in its turn: "Thy will, not mine, be done." And the first subordinates itself to the second; but not without a conflict which costs Jesus a bloody sweat.

For sin does not consist in having a nature that needs to be sacrificed—it is God who gave that nature to us, and if we had it not, we should have no victim to offer: sin consists only in the refusal to sacrifice it to God when He demands it of us. Jesus never opposed Himself to the Divine will by such a refusal, either when there was some pleasure to be foregone, or some suffering to be borne. He never allowed Himself the satisfaction of a desire, if it did not fit into the accomplishment of the task assigned to Him; nor refused to submit to any suffering which it demanded.

This characteristic of His holiness made of His life an uninterrupted series of conflicts; but this is the very point which gives to it its truly human character, and which enables us to recognise in Him the true *High Priest* of humanity, actually realising the motto inscribed on the forehead of the Jewish high priest: " Holiness to the Lord."

II. *The Teachings.*—What reader of Holy Scripture, after meditating upon one of our Lord's instructions, has not more than once been moved to exclaim, How divine! And yet what can be more truly human than these discourses, whether in respect of their contents or their form !

What is their origin? Within the Person of Jesus, when He was engaged in teaching, there was passing an event of the inner life, which it is important for us thoroughly to understand. Just as His holiness consisted in the care with which He kept His will free from every influence proceeding from Himself only, in order to keep it ever open to the impulses of the Divine will, so in His teaching, His whole art consisted in allowing no thought originating in self to rule His intelligence, and in keeping that faculty in a state of absolute dependence upon

the Divine mind. It was by this process, so simple
in itself, that He succeeded in making His human
speech the organ of Divine wisdom. "As I hear I
judge, and my judgment is just," He said Himself
(John v. 30); that is to say, before speaking, He
listened with the inward ear, and did not open His
lips to give expression to His thoughts till He
had received the answer of the Father to the silent
questioning which His heart had addressed to Him.
So did the judgment of God become His own, and
it was this which caused His own to be infallible.
"I speak not of myself," He says elsewhere; "as
my Father hath taught me, I speak these things."[1]
Here we have the explanation of the fact that His
precepts are at once so human and so divine.
They are divine, because in His teaching God is
allowed in each instance to speak first, before any
hearing is given to man. They are nevertheless
human, because equally in each case a human ear
receives the utterance of the Divine wisdom, and
a human heart and intelligence give it shape.

In view of this wonderful interdependence, shall
we not say that here we see human speech elevated
at last to its intended destiny—that of serving as
an organ through which the Truth of God may
utter itself? Here again, as always, we find in Jesus
a true man, doubtless; but in this true man, man
perfected. In His holiness He appeared as God's

---

[1] John vii. 16, 17; viii. 28; xii. 49, 50.

High Priest on earth, through the perfect submission of His own will to the Divine will. In His teaching He appeared as God's *prophet* here below, by the free submission of His intelligence to that of God. This was the second of the functions which constituted from the beginning man's destination— the image of God in him.

III. *The Miracles.*—The secret of the miraculous working of Jesus does not essentially differ from that of His doctrinal and moral infallibility. As in His teaching He did not err, because He took care in each instance to suppress every utterance of His own, which He might have invented, and to which He could have given expression as easily as we do, in order to give place to the word which came to Him from God, so in His miraculous working He took care to begin by renouncing every impulse of His own, in order to make His will the unresisting agent of the Divine will; and hence it was that the former derived from the latter the power to govern nature, and to set in action the new agency needed for bringing about the expected result. "I can of mine own self do nothing," says Jesus, in explanation of the healing of the impotent man (John v. 30); "The Son can do nothing of Himself, but what He seeth the Father do" (v. 19). The almighty power of Jesus rests upon His inability, on purely moral grounds, to do anything of Himself, in the same way that His infallibility rests upon His voluntary

ignorance, that is, upon His inability to say anything that was not derived from God.

His miraculous power is then human as well as
divine ; it is in each case a loan drawn by the
indigence, and at the same time by the trustfulness,
of man from the bounty of God.

Contemplate Him as He heals the deaf and dumb
man. He puts His fingers into his ears ; by this
clearly indicating that the miraculous power about
to be put in action will be an emanation from
His person. But on the other hand, He first raises
His eyes to heaven, while uttering a deep sigh ; thus
indicating no less clearly that the power which will
restore to this man the gifts of hearing and of speech,
comes from the region in which the Divine powers
have their dwelling. Listen to His words and His
prayers at the moment when He is calling forth the
dead man from his grave : "I am the resurrection
and the life," He says to the sister of the dead man,
—so making her understand in how close a relation
the great work He is about to accomplish stands to
His person ; but on the other hand : " Father, I
know that Thou hearest me always," is His exclamation before all the people. By this He bears
witness no less clearly to the Divine omnipotence
which is willing to lend Him its sceptre every
time He asks for it.

So it is with all the miracles of Jesus. They are at
once human and divine ; divine in respect of their

primary cause, human in respect of the agent to whom it pleases God to entrust His power. And this exercise of the will of God is not arbitrary in character. Our nature in its wantonness continually misuses the physical powers and faculties of intelligence with which we are endowed. Only reflect for a moment upon the use we make of the wonderful gift of speech! This is the reason why God cannot grant us a share in His power. To what use should we put it?—But if there appear upon earth a being whose will has placed itself under the dominion of the Divine holiness and charity, God will then rejoice in admitting him, as completely as possible, to fellowship in His power. And thus will at length be realised man's destiny as it had been already pictured by the psalmist: "Thou makest him to have dominion of the works of Thy hands; Thou hast put all things into subjection under his feet."[1] And the appearance of such a human being will not be a subject for joyful surprise, or a mere happy accident in the sight of God; it will be the fulfilment of His eternal purpose with regard to man. The function of *king*, as well as that of prophet and priest, attaches to the idea of man as God originally conceived it. It accords with the glorious destinies of man, that he should become the representative at once of the power, the wisdom, and the holiness of God, and should realise in his own person, by means

---

[1] Ps. viii. 6.

of this threefold mission, the visible image of God upon earth.

IV. *The Transfiguration.*—What will be the ultimate issue of a human life which has reached to this culminating point of perfection? Will it have to submit itself, as others do, to the law of decline, of decrepitude, and of death? No; death is, with man, *the wages of sin.* But if made one with God, man would overcome all the powers of decay which are inherent in the nature of his earthly body. A royal pathway had been originally opened to him; it led, through temptation and moral progress, from innocence to holiness—this was the first stage of the journey—then, through a glorious transformation, physical and spiritual, from holiness to glory.[1] In this idea we shall find the key to the story of the transfiguration.

The details of this event are known to all my readers. But a point which many of them will not have noticed is the place which it occupies in the development of the history of Jesus. On the one hand, this event marks the summit of His public ministry; on the other, it is the first step of the descent which ends in the cross. Read once more that very remarkable conversation which took place at Cæsarea Philippi, a week before the transfiguration,

---

[1] The transformation of the caterpillar into the butterfly, so often quoted as an emblem of the resurrection, is so, much rather, of that glorious transformation of which we are here speaking.

according to our three Synoptics. This is a decisive moment in the Lord's ministry. On the one hand, in the energetic profession of faith by Peter, and by His disciples, He reaps the fruit of the labours to which He had devoted Himself during the last two years ; on the other, He enters upon a new work in making known to them for the first time His approaching sufferings and His ignominious death.[1] This moment, then, marks the apogee of the public ministry of Jesus, and, if we may venture to say it, the point of transition from action to passion.

Jesus had thus reached that point of His existence when, according to the royal law of which we have been speaking, He was to raise Himself, by means of a transformation, out of the form of existence which belongs to earth, into the heavenly state. The transfiguration was the first step in this glorious ascent. That light which, from His inner being illumined from above, irradiates His body, and makes even His very raiment to glister, is the beginning of His glorification. Those two messengers from a higher world, who present themselves to Him, are ambassadors come to meet Him, and to introduce Him into the heavenly habitations. Lastly, that cloud—mysterious emblem of the Father's presence—is, as it were, the chariot in which the Holy One and the Just is to ascend into the world of glory.

---

[1] Matt. xvi. 13 *seq.* ; Mark viii. 27 *seq.* ; Luke ix. 18 *seq.*

But what happens now? The light disappears; the heavenly messengers vanish; the cloud is withdrawn. Jesus remains; He is seen amongst His disciples, the same as before; and soon, as if nothing had happened, He comes down the mountain with His disciples, who had been witnesses of this scene. How are we to explain this conclusion, so different from that which had seemed so nearly coming to pass?

One sentence of the narrative gives us the explanation we desire: "And, behold, there talked with Him Moses and Elias, who spake of the decease (literally, *the issue*) which He should accomplish at Jerusalem." So St. Luke expresses himself. Two opposite modes of departing this life offered themselves to Him at that moment. One, that to which He had a right by virtue of His holiness, and which, so considered, was in His case the normal issue,—the glorious transformation originally appointed for man, when not separated from God, and of which this transfiguration itself was the prelude. Jesus had it in His power to accept this triumphant departure; and it was right that God should offer it to Him, for it was the reward due to His holiness. But in thus re-entering heaven, Jesus must have entered it alone. The door must of necessity have closed behind Him. Humanity, unreconciled, would have remained on earth, struggling with the bonds of sin and death until its entire dissolution. Side by side with this mode of departure, Jesus contemplates another, to be accomplished at Jerusalem, that city which kills the prophets, and which would still less spare the Holy One of God, if He refuses to give way to its carnal will. This painful end to His Life is the subject of His conversation with the two great representatives of the Old Covenant, and is the one which, as He declares to them, He prefers and accepts. And they were fitted to understand this preference by the very contrast between the departure which Jesus chooses and their own. Had not one of them expired, as the Rabbis say, from the *embrace of the Eternal?* Had not the other ascended in a chariot of fire? Jesus initiates them into the victory of perfect charity. He turns His back upon the arch of triumph which rises before Him, and resolutely decides in favour of the pathway of shadows which leads to heaven through the grave. "Love," says the Song of Solomon, "is stronger than death." The transfiguration proves that it is stronger than something which is stronger than death itself; stronger than heaven and the attraction of heaven for the most heavenly mind. Jesus had the power to ascend; He exercises a free choice, and prefers to descend and take the road to Jerusalem.

After having fulfilled the task set before the innocent man,—that of becoming the holy man, perfect in all respects,—Jesus, on the point of laying His hand on the crown which was the reward due to His victorious course, turns away from it, because He sees before Him another task, a final work indispensable for Him if it was His purpose to ascend, not alone, but followed by a great company—the rehabilitation of fallen humanity.

The transfiguration constitutes therefore the transition to the last series of the essential events in the life of Jesus.

THIRD SERIES

I. *The Death.*—It is not our business in this place to paint over again those scenes of sorrow and of pain which are known to all the world; nor yet to enquire into the relation in which this sanguinary death stands to the salvation of the world; to set forth this relation will be one of the objects of the following essay. Our present task is solely to determine the relation of Jesus to His human family in that drama of blood which brought His terrestrial life to so sudden an end.

The Old Testament had spoken of a "*Servant of Jehovah,*" whose mission should be to expiate the sin of the world: "The Lord hath laid on Him the iniquity of us all. . . . He was wounded for our transgressions, He was bruised for our iniquities."[1] From ancient times the paschal lamb, whose blood had

---

[1] Isa. liii. 5, 6.

been for Israel in Egypt the means of his deliverance, had been the symbol of the office of this servant and victim in one. The brazen serpent, lifted in the midst of their camp, on the top of a pole, for the healing of the wounded Israelites, was likewise a significant emblem of the office which this redeeming Messiah was one day to fulfil.

Jesus applied to Himself these prophecies and types; He saw announced in them the fate which awaited Him. Accordingly, at the moment when He was about to go forth to His execution, He said to His disciples: "For I say unto you, that this *that is written* must yet be accomplished in me, And He was reckoned among the transgressors."[1] It was while facing this supreme task that He cried in agony at Gethsemane: "Father, if it be possible, let this cup pass from me." Two sentences which escaped from His lips shew us clearly the meaning which He attributed to the end which awaited Him: "The Son of man came to give His life *a ransom* for many;" and, a little later, when He gave the cup at the last supper to His disciples: "This is my blood which is shed for many, for the remission of sins."[2] Jesus then evidently felt that in His sufferings and death He was the representative of sinful humanity; His blood shed was in His eyes the expiation offered to God for the sins of mankind; the object of His death was to pay the ransom of His brethren.

---

[1] Luke xxii. 37 ; cf. Isa. liii. 12.   [2] Matt. xxvi. 28.

In His life He had acted out the task assigned to the ideal man. In His death He fulfilled that of fallen man.

Assuredly it was competent only to a man, a true man, to be in this way the representative before God of humanity in its guilt. An angel from heaven could not have fulfilled this mission. To bear the shame of a family, must one not be a member of it? In order that we may feel to the quick a great national crime, must we not ourselves belong to the guilty nation? Sympathy, carried to the extent of the miracle of actual solidarity and even self-substitution, presupposes complete community of life.

For a long time past, Jesus had been accustoming Himself to play the noble part of a bearer of the burdens of others. Had He not, many a time, as a child, interceded in tears with God for His younger brothers and sisters according to the flesh, and even for His parents, when He saw them yielding to some temptation? As a young man, at the age when the heart begins to open to the noble sentiments of patriotism, had He not comprehended all Israel in His sympathy, and many and many a time made the iniquities of this people, whom He loved so fervently, the subject of His sorrowing confessions? Arrived at man's estate, His pity extends to the whole world; all that bears the name of man, in the past, the present, and the future, finds unconsciously a home of refuge in the boundless charity of the Son of man.

He makes Himself, by the irresistible power of His
love, the living centre of humanity in its fallen estate.
He becomes, as it were, the sound and healthy heart
of this diseased body. John the Baptist salutes Him
as such when he calls Him the Lamb of God
taking away the sin of the world. Lastly, He offers
to God, in the name of His brethren, the compensation which is due to Him, and in fact renders
homage to that divine right which God Himself
cannot surrender till the conscience of man has at
last brought itself to acknowledge its claims without
reserve.

This substitution of Jesus for sinful humanity
implies not only the reality, but also the perfect
holiness, of His human nature. It was only in his
vesture of fine white linen that the high priest could
enter the holy of holies to intercede for the people.
He was not permitted to sprinkle the blood of any
but a victim without blemish upon the altar of propitiation. Accordingly, none but a perfectly holy
man could expiate sin, and intercede for the sinner.
In fact, only such an one could feel in his conscience
the hateful character of the sin that had to be washed
out, and estimate aright the greatness of the injury
offered to the Divine majesty by this act of rebellion.
Strange as it may seem, the moral compensation due
to God for the sin of mankind could only be offered
by a being who had not shared in it, and whose
conscience had therefore remained free from the

kind of pain which affects the man who has allowed
himself to be led astray and blinded by sin. In order
to be able to deplore and condemn sin in the way
in which God judges and condemns it, one must
be personally exempt from it. Man unfallen could
alone offer the compensation due to God from man
fallen.

Such was the work accomplished by Jesus on the
Cross, and which could only be accomplished by the
Son of man,—by Him who was at once true man and
perfect man.

II. *The Resurrection.* The agonised death of Christ
was the revelation in act of the judgment of God
upon the sin of mankind; His resurrection is the
revelation of the absolution pronounced by God upon
this same sin. Pardon is the taking away of sin
just in the same way as resurrection is the abolition
of death.

If then it is true that in Christ crucified we behold
mankind condemned, it is no less true that in Christ
risen we behold mankind justified. If it is we who
are dead in Him, in our guilt, must it not also be we
who in Him are risen again absolved ? So close is
the interweaving which His love has effected between
our lot and His, that after our death has become His
death on the Cross, His life becomes the principle
of our life in eternity. Jesus risen, then, personifies
humanity rehabilitated. In Him a man, a real man,
after having overcome sin by holiness, and disarmed

the law by expiation, has overturned the throne of death which had its foundation in the law of sin.[1]   A man had placed the sceptre in the hands of the king of terrors ; a man also took it from him.[2]

III. *The Ascension.*—Up to the time of the transfiguration, Jesus had been raising Himself step by step to the condition of human perfection.   After the transfiguration He devoted Himself altogether to the rehabilitation of fallen man. This twofold task having been fulfilled, what will be the crowning point of this life ? The transfiguration has already foreshadowed it in act. The heavenly transformation which began to take effect in Him upon the mountain, resumes its interrupted course, and consummates itself. Jesus had refused to enter into His glory before He had opened to His whole family access into heaven. That which He had generously denied Himself on the mount of transfiguration, God restores to Him on the mount of Olivet. Is it not the supreme law of the moral world that "he who loseth his life shall find it " ?

Two heavenly messengers—are they the same as at the transfiguration ?—once more descend to meet Him. The mysterious cloud reappears, and this time it opens to receive Him and carry Him out of sight

---

[1] 1 Cor. xv. 56, "The sting of death is sin ; and the strength of sin is the law."

[2] 1 Cor. xv. 21, "For since *by man* came death, *by man* came also the resurrection of the dead."

of His disciples. For the redemption of the world has been effected, and there is no fear that the door of heaven, about to open for the Redeemer, will close again after He has once passed through it. It remains thenceforth open to all who will accept His mediation.

He consents then now to be raised from holiness to glory, and that in order that He may be enabled from out of the midst of the latter to raise up His brethren into nearness to Himself.[1] This is the prize of that ascension, so laborious, so heroic, by which He raised Himself, first and alone, from innocence to holiness. The infallibility which He already possessed is changed into omniscience. [2] Instead of influence exerted at a distance, He is now endowed with omnipresence.[3] The omnipotence which He used to obtain as a loan, by means of prayer, is now transformed into omnipotence actually possessed by Himself. [4]

But in this glorious transformation of which He is the subject, He does not at all divest Himself of His

---

[1] John xvii. 1, 2, " Glorify Thy Son, that Thy Son also may glorify Thee : . . . that He should give eternal life to as many as Thou hast given Him."

[2] "Whatsoever ye shall *ask of the Father*, I will do it " (John xiv. 13).

[3] " I am with you alway, even unto the end of the world " (Matt. xxviii. 20). "Where two or three are gathered together in my name, there am I in the midst of them " (xviii. 20).

[4] " All power is given unto me in heaven and in earth " (Matt. xxviii. 18).

humanity. It is as man that He appears to the dying
Stephen : " I see the *Son of man* standing at the
right hand of God " (Acts vii. 56). Jesus Himself
had applied by anticipation the title of Son of man
to His personality when glorified : " I say unto you,
Hereafter shall ye see the Son of man sitting on
the right hand of power, and coming in the clouds of
heaven " (Matt. xxvi. 64).

Here then we see human nature elevated in the
person of its normal representative into the possession
of the Divine life, and become the organ of the
supreme thought and will. Here we see the chasm
between the finite and the infinite bridged over by a
member of our race. If God is love, must not this
have been the concluding step of the ascending
progress He had planned ? A higher aim was not
conceivable ; a conclusion less lofty would have left,
it would seem (and seem after trial) something still
wanting in the development of the Divine love.

We have then a right to conclude by saying : Jesus
was a real man, and this real man was man brought
to perfection. From the cradle to the cross, from the
cross up to the throne, the spectacle of His life extorts
from us the exclamation, of which Pilate himself,
while first uttering it, did not comprehend the full
meaning : " Behold the man ! "—man fulfilling his
normal development ; man sinking under the weight
of the judgment he had brought upon himself by the
fall ; man restored gloriously ; lastly, man exalted to

the full height of his destination, as perfidiously anticipated by the enemy when he whispered in the ear
of humanity, on its first entry upon its course, that
sentence which expressed the final goal of his history:
"Ye shall be as gods."

How is it possible, we would ask in conclusion,
to admit for a single moment that all these scenes
which we have been considering are mere human
inventions contrived in the service of the idea which
makes of them such a well-connected whole?
What! can we believe these pictures, so simple and
so pure, of the childhood and youth of Jesus, these
detailed narratives of the Baptism and Transfiguration, of the Passion and Resurrection, to be nothing
more than an artificially composed dramatisation of
that ideal of the perfect man, or of the Son of
man, which to our minds stands out from all these
narratives with such perfect clearness and with a
consistency so admirable, and which is nevertheless
so little the result of calculation! Oh! what honour
should we be doing to those apostles and first
Christians, who at other times are represented to
us as so narrow and so limited in their views, if
we supposed that they could have themselves conceived this idea in its singular elevation, grandeur,
and sublimity, and have illustrated it with so much
naturalness and ability in this series of pictures of
their own invention! No, the idea, as we conceive

servants, some devoted agents of His will.   Such were
Abraham, the friend of God ; Moses, who had spoken
with Him as a man speaks with his friend ; Elijah,
who stood before the Eternal, and was consumed with
zeal for His glory.   But what a distance was there
between the relation of these men to God, and that of
Jesus to His Father !   Even at twelve years old, when
He presents Himself for the first time in the temple of
God at Jerusalem, He feels Himself at once at home
as in His Father's house.   So much is it His home
upon earth, that it is inconceivable to Him that His
parents should even for a moment have sought for
Him elsewhere.   His reverence for Jehovah, while
quite as deep as that of the men we have mentioned,
or even more so, is not, like theirs, that of a servant or
of a worshipper only ; it is that of a son who both
loves and feels himself beloved.

His trust in God bears alike the character of filial
tenderness and of filial assurance.   Abraham has his
days of misgiving ; Moses his moments of bitterness
and even of murmuring ; Elijah his hours of self-will,
in which he withdraws himself from danger, and follows
the guidance of his own heart.   When this latter per-
forms the greatest of his miracles, the raising of the
widow's son, it is by means of a physical and moral
strain which reveals to us all the greatness of the
effort by which he succeeds in attaining the assurance
of the Divine concurrence in his act.   In the case of
Jesus, all is quiet, calm, and natural.   When perform-

it in our own minds, was not the mother of the facts, but their offspring. There exists assuredly a thought which gave birth to these events, but it is not ours. It is that of the God who makes history, of Him who, from all eternity, willed the salvation and the glory of man. [1]

2

THE SON OF GOD

BUT by the side of this wonderful collection of facts, which the idea of the Son of man binds together into one, we discern in our Gospels a series of features of quite a different nature, less numerous and less salient perhaps, when looked at from without, but in reality still more astonishing. We are speaking of all those indications in which there comes to light the *superhuman* character of Him who on earth so faithfully played the part of the Son of man.

And, in the first place, is it possible to contemplate thoughtfully the person of Jesus, as it is pictured for us by the pencil of the simple-minded and unambitious evangelists, without being struck by the absolutely unique relation in which this Man stood towards God; during the whole of His existence ? God had found in the world, before the advent of Christ, some faithful

---

[1] 1 Cor. ii. 7, "The wisdom which God ordained before the world unto our glory."

ing a much greater miracle than that of Elijah, the raising of Lazarus, He says, with a peaceful assurance, "Father, I know that Thou hearest me always." Later on, when He finds Himself reduced to extremity by the abandonment of His disciples, His confidence is not shaken. He feels all the more closely united to God, and says, " I am not alone, because the Father is with me."

We have in this a trait entirely unique, which distinguishes the piety of Jesus from that of every other man, and His worship from all other worship before or since. Accordingly, Jesus never combines under one expression the statement of the relation in which He Himself stands to the Father, and that of His disciples to God. He does not say, *our Father*, *our God*. In speaking of Him and of His disciples, He says, "My Father and your Father ; My God and your God."[1] If, in the Lord's Prayer, He uses the expression, *Our Father*, it is after having said : " When *ye pray*, say," thus putting the words into the mouth of the disciples, and not as speaking Himself in that manner.

From these facts of His life we pass to His positive declarations respecting His person.

Just as He designates God as *the Father*, in the strict sense of that word, so He calls Himself *the Son*, in a sense no less decided and exclusive. " No man

---

[1] John xx. 17.

knoweth the Son, but the Father; neither knoweth any man the Father, save the Son, and he to whomsoever the Son will reveal Him."[1]   "Of that day and that hour knoweth no man ; no, not the angels which are in heaven ; neither the Son, but the Father."[2]   By that expression He attributes to Himself a relation to God of a kind that is unique and quite unfathomable by any created intelligence ; a relation of which the Divine mystery can only be explained to us men by the help of a revelation of which He alone is the author.   As God Himself, He has *His* angels, who will constitute His escort on the day of His glorious reappearing.[3]   And during the whole of the present economy, the *name* by which God is to be worshipped and confessed by the Church, and which is distinctive of the New Covenant, is that of *Father, Son, and Holy Ghost*.   This is the formula of the new revelation which thenceforth complements that of *Jehovah*, which had been granted to Moses for Israel.[4]   To give in these passages to the word *Son* the sense of Messiah is impossible.   Let any one try to substitute the latter word for the former, and he will at once perceive the absurdity of the asserted synonymousness of the two expressions.   "No man knoweth the Messiah, but the Father ; neither knoweth any man the Father, save the Messiah." . . . . "Baptising them in the name of the Father, of the Messiah, and of the Holy Ghost."

---

[1] Matt. xi. 27 ; Luke x. 22.   [3] Matt. xiii. 41 ; xvi. 27.
[2] Mark xiii. 32.   [4] Matt. xxviii. 19.

Such words could have no meaning, unless it had been agreed upon beforehand to attach to the term " Messiah " the idea of a *Divine* being.

Let us add yet one more trait. The people had saluted Jesus by the title of *Son of David.* He takes occasion from this to ask the Pharisees how it comes to pass that in Ps. cx. David, impelled by the Spirit, calls that Messiah his Lord, whom the Israelitish teaching designates as *his son.* Then He leaves them under the pressure of this question, which admits but of one solution, and which invalidates by anticipation that accusation of blasphemy by which, in the course of a few days, they would endeavour to justify His condemnation to death.[1]

In presence of the Jewish monotheism, so jealous of the incommunicable rights of Jehovah, such a manner of speaking of Himself, from a Jew so eminent for piety as Jesus, would be absolutely incomprehensible, did not the fourth Gospel come to our aid, and give us the explanation of these extraordinary expressions, preserved for us by the Synoptists, by clearly revealing to us the background of the existence of this mysterious personage.

On one occasion, the Jews, scandalised by some expressions of this kind, were on the point of falling upon Him, when He suddenly casts at them this declaration, surpassing everything that He had previously said to them, and which, if it were not divinely

---

[1] Matt. xxii. 42, *seq.*

true, would be not merely false, but insane : " Before
Abraham was (literally, *became*), I AM."[1] Another time
a great number of His disciples, offended by one of
His sayings, forsake Him, and He, as if to carry
paradox to the extreme, even while explaining it,
questions them in these words : " What and if ye shall
see the Son of man ascend up where He was before ? "[2]
Finally, at the supreme moment, when He is preparing
to mount the Cross, notice the words in which He
prays for Himself and for His disciples : " Father,
glorify Thou me with Thine own self, with the glory
which I had with Thee before the world was. . . . .
I will that they also, whom Thou hast given me,
be with me where I am ; that they may behold my
glory, which Thou hast given me : for Thou lovedst
me before the foundation of the world." [3]

What means this " glory before the foundation of
the world," which Jesus claims to have restored to
Him ?   He tells us Himself : it is that of having been
the object, before all ages, of the Father's love. Before
He came to live here below as man, He had been
enjoying, as Son, in the heavenly life, the riches of
the Father's love, and of the condition of Deity.   And
now, arrived at the term of His terrestrial existence,
He claims once more the glory which He had before
possessed.   Here we see the mystery, hidden from
human reason, to which He was alluding, when, as is

---

[1] John viii. 58.   [2] John vi. 62.   [3] John xvii. 5, 24.

recorded in the Synoptists, He said : "No man knoweth the Son, but the Father."

Even in the Old Testament, mention had been made of an Angel of the Eternal, called also *the Angel of the Presence, the Angel of the Covenant, Adonaï whom ye seek*, and respecting whom God had said to Moses : "My name is in him,"[1] an expression which indicates not a mere angel or messenger, but the depositary of a knowledge, sufficient for our needs, of the Eternal.

Jesus had in Himself the certain consciousness that He was that Being. That which He felt to be behind Him, when He searched into the profoundest depths of His being, was not, as it is with us, the vacuum of non-existence, but the plenitude of Divine life. To Him, birth did not appear as the transition from nothingness into existence, but the passage from the fulness of Divine life into the state of dependence which belongs to man. "I came forth from the Father, and am come into the world," so He said when on the point of terminating His earthly career ; and He added, as if it were the natural consequence, "Again I leave the world, and go to the Father."[2]

God is love. Before He created the universe, He loved. And what was the object of this love, that never had a beginning ? It could not be anything external to Himself ; otherwise, God would have been dependent upon something not Himself. He possessed

---

[1] Exod. xxxiii. 14 ; Isa lxiii. 9 ; Mal. iii. 1 ; Exod. xxiii. 23.
[2] John xvi. 28.

then in Himself the object of His love, the Being in whom is realised everything that His thought conceives of as true, everything that His heart feels to be beautiful, everything of good that His will proposes to itself : His ideal—not such an ideal as is generally the ideal of man, the object of an ineffectual aspiration, a mere idea of the imagination—but an ideal such as that of God should be, the reflection of His own perfection, as real as Himself ; His image in the eternal mirror of the Spirit, a Person living eternally as He Himself does, the *Son* of His love, the expression, the *Lord* of His thought.

This is the Person with whom the Son of man felt Himself to be one and the same Being. We can understand how, in the consciousness of this identity, He was able to say, though He was born 750 A.U.C., " Before Abraham was, I am." The declarations of the Synoptists, implying the Divine nature of Jesus, can none of them be reconciled with the biblical monotheism, save by means of this supreme revelation respecting His Person, which is contained in the Gospel of John. And if this revelation were not authentic, if the Son of man depicted by the Synoptists were not really the Son of God in the sense declared by John, the New Testament would contradict the Old.

It may be asked by what means Jesus arrived at the apprehension of the mystery contained in His Person. M. Renan, starting from the idea that this

was nothing but an illusion on the part of Jesus,
supposes that He worked Himself up to this conception by degrees ; that He began by persuading
Himself that He was called to play the part of the
Messiah ; then little by little, drawn on, Himself, by
the enthusiasm of which He perceived Himself to be
the object in those about Him, He came to imagine
Himself to be a Divine apparition. . . . .

This explanation is not only contrary to all that
the moral purity of Jesus allows us to suppose—His
humility, His gentleness, His charity, perfect till
the end—but it conflicts also with a positive fact,
asserted, without the least appearance of intention
or collusion, by all our documents.   Jesus did not
arrive at the consciousness that He was the Son of
God through any intermediate stage of consciousness
of being the Israelitish Messiah.   On the contrary,
He recognised Himself as the Messiah, because He
had the feeling of Sonship towards God.   Now if He
was Son, He alone could be the King of Israel and
the Sovereign of the world.

At the age of twelve years, when He finds Himself
in the temple, it is not a conviction, more or less of
the intellect, of His Messianic dignity which expresses
itself in Him ; it is the purely religious consciousness
of the unique relation in which He stands to God
as a Son : " Wist ye not that I must be about my
Father's business ? "   This expression, *My Father*
does not imply the existence as yet in the mind of

the child of any definite dogma; it is a moral relationship to which He is referring. It is not in the region of theological science that His thoughts are moving, but in that of instinctive feeling; and that is just the reason why this declaration is of a nature to fill us with admiration, and to inspire us with absolute confidence in the child who thus speaks.

At the moment of His baptism, the revelation which He receives from the Father does not take the form of the assertion, "Thou art the promised Messiah," as would infallibly have been the case had the young enthusiast of Nazareth been the dupe of a generous patriotism. God reveals Himself to Him as His Father: "Thou art my beloved Son, in whom I am well pleased." Here again we discern a fact of the inner life, by which Jesus is made conscious of that relation of love which binds Him to Him who thus speaks to Him,—not by any means an intellectual conviction of the part which He is called to play with reference to His nation, upon the stage of the world. It is true that the conviction of His Messianic calling was the result of the experience He had just had of His special relationship to God. But this latter was the primary and fundamental fact in the development of His personal consciousness.

If we study the first Messianic act of Jesus, we are led to the same result. When, in John ii., Jesus drives the buyers and sellers out of the temple, the feeling which impels Him to this holy act is not the consciousness of the Messianic part He has to play,—it is His feeling of Sonship. His filial heart had been wounded by the sight of His Father's house thus profaned: "Make not *My Father's* house a house of merchandise," He exclaims. This is not the way in which He would have expressed Himself, had the Messianic sentiment been the one at that moment dominant in His mind.

Accordingly, those about Him, having begun, as it was inevitable they should, by believing in Him as the Messiah, rise at once to a higher intuition. Nathanael confesses his newly formed faith, in these words: "Rabbi, Thou art the Son of God, Thou art the King of Israel." The feeling of a mysterious relationship between God and this personage who has just seen through him, as by a flash of omniscience, at once gains the predominance in his mind over the conviction of His Messianic character; and this latter takes but a secondary place in his enthusiastic address.

This fact so well established is one of primary importance. It proves that the consciousness which Jesus had of His Divine nature was not a result to which He had worked Himself up gradually, by a factitious and merely human process. This consciousness existed in Him in an elementary state even from His infancy. Made more certain and absolutely clear to Him by the revelation which He received at His baptism, it formed from the first the basis of His public ministry. It was the feeling of this unique relationship which raised Him above all the narrownesses and all the ambitions of the false Jewish Messianism, and which impressed upon His work that exclusively religious and moral character, of which no alloy of any political element ever succeeded in impairing the purity. His consciousness of Sonship was not therefore, as M. Renan asserts, the last stage of a growing infatuation about Himself, of which that of His Messiahship had been the starting-point; on the contrary, His consciousness of His Messiahship was from the first involved in that of Sonship, as the corollary is implied in the principle; and as to the latter, it emanated directly from His personal contact with God. Thus it contains its guarantee in itself, as well as in the perfect holiness of Him who has testified to this fact of His inner life.

3

THE GOD-MAN

Up to this point we have been keeping within the province of faith, and have not crossed the borders of the domain of theology. We have ascertained and co-ordinated the facts contained in our Scriptures and the declarations of Jesus respecting His own person ; but whilst doing so we have discovered the existence of two classes of facts which seem to lead us to opposite conclusions.

If Jesus Christ is a being of Divine nature, how can He be at the same time the ideal man which implies that He is true man ? And if He is truly man, how can He be of Divine origin and essence ?

A clever woman once said : " God has given us the materials to form a certain arc, and we want to make a complete circle out of them." In other words : God has thought fit to put before us, in His revelation, certain facts which seem to be contradictory ; and we presume, unjustifiably, to attempt to harmonise them. But is this attempt blameworthy? I do not think so. Only it is important to understand that, in undertaking this task, we are passing out of the province of Faith into that of Theology. Faith realises the facts of revelation ; she feeds herself upon them, she draws her life from them, without seeking to discover in what way they are reconcilable with each other intellectually. Science endeavours to establish this harmony by the help of the hypotheses which are suggested to her by an earnest study of the facts. And, to use a figure more accurate perhaps than the one we have just quoted, she endeavours to construct the arch of the bridge upon the two pillars which Faith has provided for her.

In the particular case we are considering, the two facts which Faith receives from revelation, and hands over to be elaborated by Science, are the true humanity and the true divinity of Jesus Christ ; and the object of the labours of Science, of which the result neither confirms nor in any way invalidates the two facts which have been gained by Faith, will be to shew that there is no contradiction between these two fundamental data, but, on the contrary, that there exists between them a profound harmony. Only, it is important to bear in mind that these attempts at a solution of the difficulty do not any longer belong to the province of Faith, but to that of Theology. This is a point we beg the reader to consider well while reading the following pages.

Man ! God ! What an impassable gulf at first sight separates these two expressions ! But here it is proper we should call to mind two great principles of the monotheism of the Bible. The first is *the absolute freedom of God*. God is not, like a created being, dominated by a nature imposed upon Him from without, and in accordance with which He is compelled continually to make His caculations. " I am that I am," said Jehovah to Moses ; that is to say, in every instant I am that which it pleases me to be. The second principle is the *absolute perfectibility of man*. Man was made in the image of God. He is not therefore condemned, like the lower animals, to move incessantly in the same circle. His progressivity, if I may use the word, has no limit but that of the absolute good to which he aspires. The emblem of human life is a spiral, not a circle.

Once admit these two principles, and the problem which now faces us will appear no longer insoluble. It contains two questions: 1. How a Divine being —the Son—could, without ceasing to be God, make Himself man, and live as man? 2. How the son of man could, without ceasing to be man, be raised to the perfection of the state of Deity?

To the former question the first of the two principles we have laid down gives the answer. If God be absolutely free, He is not indissolubly tied to the condition of Deity. Where is the rich man who has not the right, if he think fit to do so, to make himself poor, and to live like a poor man? or where the king who, if he be really free, has not the power to lay down his crown, and make himself a simple citizen? This is the expression of St. Paul: "Ye know the grace of our Lord Jesus Christ, that though He was rich, yet for your sakes He became poor, that ye through His poverty might be rich." His riches consisted in the glory of the condition of Deity, His poverty in the state of dependence which is proper to humanity. He exchanged the former for the latter, because so alone could we be raised from out of the latter into the former. Would His divinity have been true riches to Him, if, when His love urged Him to strip Himself of it, in order that He might associate us with Himself in it, He had been indissolubly bound to that mode of existence, and had no power to adopt that which His love impelled Him to assume? Had that been so, the very freedom of the condition of Deity would have become in His case a chain, an intolerable slavery. He would not have been that which He wished to be, had He not been able to clothe Himself in our humanity.

The idea of this putting off of the condition of Deity, and entering upon that of humanity, is expressed by St. Paul still more clearly in another passage (Phil. ii. 6—8) : "Who, being in the form of God, thought it not robbery to be equal with God ; but made Himself of no reputation, and took upon Him the form of a servant, and was made in the likeness of men." St. John also expresses in his own way these two acts of un-clothing and re-clothing, when he says, "The Word was made flesh."

He had been in possession of the Divine omnipotence, and He enters upon a form of existence in which, instead of commanding and bestowing gifts, He has to receive, to ask, to obey ; and it is only at the last moment of this new stage of existence that He announces, as an event of recent occurrence, this fact: "All power is given unto me in heaven and in earth."

He had been a sharer in the Divine omniscience, and He accepts a condition in which He has ceaselessly to ask, constantly to learn, often to remain in ignorance, as when He says: "Of that day and hour knoweth no man, no, not the angels which are in heaven, neither the Son."

He had been filling all things, sharing in the omnipotence of God Himself, and He confines Himself within a human body, so localised that it could be said of Him : "*If Thou hadst been here*," such a thing would not have happened.

In Him there had been abiding the immutable holiness, and He accepted a state of being of which one of the fundamental laws is liberty of choice, the possibility of undergoing real temptation, and consequently the power to sin.

He had been loving with all the force of a perfect, infinite love, and this kind of love He exchanges for one which implies progress both in respect of intensity and of comprehension.

He knew Himself as the Son, with that knowledge with which the Father Himself knows Him eternally, and—this is that putting off upon which all those we have already mentioned depend—this consciousness of Sonship, which was the light of His life, He allowed to be extinguished within Him, to retain only His inalienable personality ; the individual life endued with freedom and intelligence as all human individuality is endued ; for our personality is made in the image of His. By means of this humiliation He was enabled to enter into a course of human development similar in all respects to our own.

Here we see the prodigy of love which is realised in the life of Christ, and revealed to us by His word. If this miracle is not possible, God is not free, and His love has limitations imposed upon it. By what mysterious principle? I know not. It is for those who deny the possibility of the incarnation to teach it us.

The second problem, that of the elevation of the Son of man to the condition of deity without any infringement upon His humanity, finds its solution, if we are not mistaken, in that other principle with which the theism of the Bible has supplied us; the perfectibility of man even up to the point of absolute goodness, in virtue of the *image of God* which is imprinted upon his nature.

The very moment of the humiliation, that is, the incarnation, was for Jesus the starting-point of the exaltation. In proportion as He develops as a child, there forms itself between God and Him a relation of a most intimate and tender nature, to which we sometimes see something faintly analogous in our children. This relation issues in the spontaneous creation of the expression, *My Father*, which Jesus utters for the first time at the age of twelve years, and which is a subject of surprise even to His mother. In proportion as He continues to grow in submission to His parents, in devotion to His brethren, in collectedness in prayer, and under the illumination of the Scriptures, He becomes more and more conscious, by the contrast between His own moral and religious state and the sin of which He realises, with sorrow, the existence in all, even the best of those around

Him, that His position in human life is an exceptional one. The peculiar character of His personality becomes to Him a great theoretical and practical problem. Who am I, and what is my work here below? As the only sound member of a sick family, must I not be called to be its physician?

The answer to this presentiment is given to Him at His baptism: "*Thou art my Son!* I have given Thee to the world, that Thou mightest save it." From this moment Jesus recognises Himself as the manifestation in human nature of the Being who is the eternal object of the Father's love, and as having the mission committed to Him of giving life to mankind. This revelation makes, however, no change in His real condition. It is to Him a fact of consciousness, and only that. He remains none the less confined within all the obligations and infirmities of earthly existence. In the wilderness, Satan's effort is precisely this, to induce Him to turn aside out of the right path by making Him feel painfully the contrast between His outward *condition* and the *consciousness* of His dignity as a Son which He had lately gained: "*If Thou be the Son of God*, make bread of these stones. . . . *If Thou be the Son,* cast Thyself down." He is to raise His position to the level of His nature, and thus to nullify the act of His incarnation at the very moment at which He has become conscious of it. The meaning of the refusal of Jesus to act upon this perfidious suggestion is: I may indeed know what I am *by right ;* none the less do I remain what I am *in fact*, till it pleases God Himself to lift the fact to the level of the right. The incarnation became therefore more than ever a permanent and free act on the part of the Son of man, from the moment at which He became conscious who He was.

Jesus even found, from that moment, in the recognition of His personal greatness, a motive for humbling Himself still more profoundly than He had hitherto done. Those words of John (xiii. 3—5)— " Jesus knowing that the Father had given all things into His hands, *and that He was come from God, and went to God;* He riseth from supper, and laid aside His garments, and took a towel, and girded Himself, and began to wash the disciples' feet "— express the feeling which dictated His actions through the whole of His ministry. The greater He knows Himself to be, the more does He understand that it is His proper work to set an example of the deepest self-humiliation, that so He may draw all that are His, without the possibility of any exception, into the practice of that self-sacrificing love which is the essence of the kingdom He is come to found.

Each one of His acts of obedience and of charity is a step towards a still deeper submission, towards a still more absolute self-sacrifice. He empties Himself now as man, as He had before done as God. And having reached the end of His course, instead of pleading His righteousness as a ground on which to claim the reward which is due to Him—the end of the just—He takes upon Himself the punishment of sinners. He had, by His incarnation, abandoned His life as God ; He surrenders to death His life as man. The second of these sacrifices is the complement of the first. Then did He reach the bottom of the pit which He had begun digging under His feet when He made Himself man.

Accordingly it is at this moment that there completes itself, with reference to His outward condition, an exaltation corresponding to that effected in His consciousness at His baptism. Taken into the arms of His Father, He had *felt* Himself a Son ; from this moment He *becomes* so once more as regards the conditions of His existence ; first, by His resurrection, which answers to His death, and which restores to Him in a glorified form the human life which He had freely sacrificed ; secondly, by the ascension, which answers to the incarnation, and by means of which He recovers the condition of Deity which He had no less voluntarily surrendered. But do not let us forget that He regains this condition without thereby renouncing His human existence. Thenceforth it is as Son of man that He possesses as His own the life of Son of God. How is this possible ? Can the Divine glory inhabit the forms of human existence without bursting them in every direction ? " All the fulness of the Godhead dwelleth in Him BODILY," is the answer of St. Paul, who had beheld the Lord in His glorified state first on the way to Damascus, and afterwards in the third heaven to which he was caught up, whether in the body or out of the body he himself could not tell.

Why should not that human nature, which was created in the image of God, have been destined from the first to become the free organ of the life of God, the agent of His omnipotence, the instrument of the sovereign activities of His love? The God-man would in that case be no other than the *true man*, such, that is, as God had conceived and willed Him to be from eternity. Is not that the meaning of that marvellous saying of St. Paul: "Those whom He foreknew [as His own through faith], He also did predestinate to be conformed to the image of His Son, that He might be the firstborn among many brethren."[1] Would not the mystery of the double nature, human and divine, of Jesus be in this way solved? What contradiction is there between the divinity and the humanity of Jesus Christ, when once it is an established fact that the man whom God had in view from the beginning—the ideal man—was the God-man?

Will it be asked still what is the share which the fact of the fall has had in the execution of this divine plan? Most certainly it did not determine its

---

[1] Rom. viii. 29.

purpose. It can never be allowable, from a truly Christian point of view, to glorify sin, exclaiming as St. Augustine does, when speaking of the disobedience of the first man : " Blessed fault !" God has assuredly not done *more* for man fallen than He would have done for man in the state of obedience. He has only dealt with him in a different way. Perhaps for unfallen man the dew of the Spirit shed upon him would have sufficed,—a Pentecost, to make him expand into that perfect holiness which is the necessary condition of the state of glory. Or, if the participation of the Son of God in our nature had been, even in that case, the means appointed by the will of God to bring about our exaltation into the Divine condition, this incarnation would certainly not have assumed the painful character of a redemption ; it would have been an incomparable festal celebration —the marriage between God and mankind.

Sin exercised an influence, not upon the *result*, but upon the *manner* of reaching that result. Fallen humanity lay helpless and paralysed, incapable of raising itself by its own power, or of finishing the course upon which it had entered towards its sublime destination. The Son of God beheld it in this its state of misery. He took into Himself that nature, divinely created, which sin had so profoundly vitiated. He restored it from its foundations ; He acted upon it in conformity with all the laws of its being ; He exhibited in His own person the development of which it was capable, and for which it was destined. He consummated in His own life the complete consecration of the life of man; and in His death the expiation of its rebellion. Then, taking possession of that state to which it had been destined, He works in those that are His, by means of a daily Pentecost poured upon them from the heights of heaven, that miracle of sanctification which He had first consummated in Himself, and thus prepares them for their exaltation into that position which He Himself occupies in glory.

God altogether in *One*, and through that One at last altogether in *all;* such are the means—such the end to be attained. This latter is eternal; the former had to be conformed to the conditions resulting from the fluctuations incident to man's freedom.

If once we admit the absolute perfectibility of man, and the sovereign freedom of God, I do not see any further obstacle in the way of this conception of the person of Christ, except the difficulty of comprehending a love which surpasses all that our poor hearts can imagine and lay hold of. But, as St. John says, "God is greater than our heart."

We hear, in our day, some who think themselves wise, crying, as from the housetop: "We are sons of God! Jesus, in telling us what He Himself is, has but told us what we all are." Sons of God . . .? We are not such yet; we have to become so. Or, if we are such now, it is only in respect of our destiny. We must become so in reality through Him alone, who, having first run the glorious race Himself, afterwards endues us with His might to run it after Him. That Son, who from all eternity had been acting out, with reference to the Father, a life perfectly filial, came to imprint this same filial character upon our human life, and thus to raise us from the rank of servants into that of children. It is for us to accept this new impress with which His Spirit would seal us. And will that be difficult for us, if we ponder well the fact that His intention is no less than to make of each of us a second *Himself*, a representative of that highest type of being, the God-man?

With such a destiny before us, it is worth while to live, to wrestle, to suffer, to die, as men. Let our life be even a *via dolorosa*, passing through a Gethsemane and a Golgotha, still what matters it if its end is a Mount Olivet and an Ascension!

3

THE WORK OF JESUS CHRIST

WE have followed Jesus through His life on earth. Accompanying Him thus step by step, we have recognised in Him a real man, but at the same time a man answering perfectly to the Divine intention ; and in this complete man we have recognised the apparition upon earth of a Divine Being, the Eternal Son, who came to exhibit the actual fulfilment by Himself, in our human nature, of the task which no other man had hitherto fulfilled, or would hereafter fulfil, and who has at last in His own Person brought our humanity up to the highest point of its sublime destination.

This study of the person of Christ comprehends in itself already in some measure that of His work ; for, like sin, salvation is a fact, not an idea. And this fact is the actual life of the Saviour. It would be impossible, therefore, to analyse the life of Jesus without in some degree studying His work.

Nevertheless, we may also consider by itself the influence which the very fact of the appearing of Jesus on the earth was destined to exercise, and, if I may so say, the fertile furrow which His passage through it was to trace upon the field of human life.

The work of Jesus in the world is twofold : 1. It is a work accomplished *for us*, destined to effect *reconciliation* between God and man. 2. It is a work accomplished *in us*, with the object of effecting our *sanctification*. By the one, a right relation is established between God and us ; the other is the *fruit* of this re-established order. By the former, the condemned sinner is received into the state of grace ; by the latter, the pardoned sinner is associated with the life of God.

The distinction which we draw between these two kinds of work done by Christ does not at all prevent the existence of the closest connection between them, in such a manner that the former may be truly called the treasury out of which the latter draws all its riches ; and the latter, the intended effect, without which the former fails of its purpose.

The combination of the two constitutes *salvation* in its plenitude, as the necessary condition of *glory*.

1

THE WORK OF CHRIST FOR US

To speak of reconciliation presupposes a previous hostility. Can there exist hostility between God and man ? Many will answer, Yes, but only on the side of man. As soon as man has sinned, he becomes afraid of God; he flees from Him; up to a certain point he hates Him. He would prefer that his Judge did not exist.

And, in fact, the history of all religions, ancient and modern, outside those which have had their origin upon the soil of revelation, proves that the sentiment which has contributed above all others to give them birth is that of fear. That was the case even among the Greeks, the race who attained to the purest intuition of God. The Greek word for the worship of the gods signifies, literally, *the fear of superior beings*.[1] Not only is it the fact that Paganism has never since those ancient ages raised itself above this sentiment of fear in relation to the Deity, but it has sunk continually deeper down into it, so that the multiplied forms of worship which we see before us in our day amongst the heathen are, for the most part, inspired only by terror. The aim which they propose to themselves is to propitiate a powerful but malevolent being, from whom they think they have nothing but evil to expect. And missionaries are certainly not wrong when they call the religion of the idolaters of our day a worship of the devil. The being who fills the imagination of the worshipper is a wicked being, an object of terror, of whom he endeavours to gain the favour, or to mitigate the anger, by the most extravagant and often cruel ceremonies.

---

[1] *Deisidaimonia.*

How infinitely he would prefer, had he the power, to be rid of him altogether !

And yet it would be to extenuate strangely the gravity of the state of things which sin has introduced into the relations between God and man, were we to ascribe the hostility, which is its characteristic, to one only of the two parties. Scripture does not regard the matter from this superficial point of view. As it knows the love of God better than man can do, so does it speak in express terms of His hatred and of His anger.

When Samuel, recalled from *Scheol*, appears before Saul, he says to him : "Wherefore then dost thou ask of me, seeing that the Lord is departed from thee, and is become thine enemy ? "[1] This expression, *thine enemy*, cannot mean here the object of thy hatred ; it can only signify the enmity of God to the rejected king.

In Romans xi., St. Paul, endeavouring to explain the temporary rejection of the Jewish people, says to the Gentile Christians (ver. 28) : "As concerning the gospel, they are enemies for your sake ; but as touching the election, they are beloved for the fathers' sakes." The word *enemy*, opposed as it is here to *beloved*, or well-beloved, can only be taken in the sense of *hatred*. In consequence of their rejection of the gospel, the Jews are themselves rejected, and become objects of the enmity of God. But in con-

---

[1] 1 Sam. xxviii. 16.

sequence of the election of the patriarchs, which extends to their descendants, they are none the less objects of His love ; and the hour of reconciliation will at last sound for them.

Lastly, when Paul, addressing himself directly to believers, writes to them, in chap. v. of the same epistle, verse 10, " For if, when we were enemies, we were reconciled to God by the death of His Son, much more, being reconciled, we shall be saved by His life," it is impossible to doubt that the word *enemies* means objects of the enmity of God, since, in the proposition which immediately precedes, mention is made of the *wrath* of God, from which we have been saved by the blood of Christ.

This idea of the wrath of God appears frequently in Holy Scripture.[1] We must, of course, separate from the idea of wrath, when we apply it to God, all the defilements which ordinarily attach to this sentiment in human beings. It is moral indignation in all its purity, the holy antipathy of the Good Being for that which is evil, without the slightest alloy of personal irritation, or of selfish resentment. It is the dissatisfaction which is excited in a pure being by the sight of impurity ; it signifies the outward manifestations which testify to this deep dissatisfaction, and the sufferings which result from it to him who has provoked it. The wrath of God, so understood, is a necessary consequence of the profound difference which separates

[1] Cf. Rom. i. 18, ii. 5 ; Eph. ii. 3, etc.

good from evil. To deny this would oblige us to consider evil not as the opposite, but simply an imperfect form, of good.

There are, I know, many who would not object to adopt as their own this idea of wrath existing in God, if we were content to apply it to sin in itself, but not to the person of the sinner. One often hears expressions such as these: God hates evil, but He ever loves the sinner. This latter remains still an object of mercy and pity to Him, even at the very time when his conduct falls under Divine reprobation. We cannot accept this distinction without reserve. In the passages quoted, it is the persons themselves, not their works only, that are designated as the objects of the enmity of God. Doubtless one of these passages (Rom. xi. 28) proves that the same man may be at once hated and beloved of God; hated in so far as he is a sinner, loved in so far as he is capable of salvation. But this simultaneousness of opposite sentiments in God can only be temporary. It is necessarily the state of transition into a fixed and definitive condition. Man is will—in that consists the essence of personality; and will cannot oscillate vaguely between good and evil. The end must be that it decides absolutely in favour of the one or the other. The relation between God and each man must also, therefore, at last reach a state of absolute simplicity. If the individual man frees himself from the power of evil, all enmity will cease.

If he gives himself up completely to the spirit of
rebellion, hostility will prevail more and more over
love, in God.   And let not God's immutability be
here objected to us; for it would be precisely an instance of mutability in God, if, while man changed,
God did not also change with regard to him.   This
progress of man in one direction or in the other is a
free act on his part; but it involves his doom.   In the
end the individual finds himself identified with the
principle to which he has surrendered himself, and
God can no longer separate them.   It is either the
state of changeless salvation, or of absolute damna-
tion—the two opposite poles of the moral world,
towards the one or the other of which, as all experience proves, all free beings are ceaselessly gravitating.

It follows from this that the relation of hostility
in which God stands towards the sinner, although
gradual in its development, is a reality, and may end
in a state of absolute fixity.   And it is this which
gives to the scriptural idea of reconciliation a character of such seriousness and solemnity.

Reconciliation is the fact which puts an end to this
double hostility, and which introduces a state of
things in which God can take pleasure in man as a
being who answers to His intention, and man can
rejoice in God as a master who no longer opposes
Himself to his happiness.   What is the nature of the
act which can serve for the foundation of so decisive a
change in man's future?   It seems at first sight that

it could only be the re-establishment of holiness in man's life. As it was sin which drew down upon us the Divine displeasure, would it not be naturally the opposite of sin—its destruction—which would restore to man the Divine favour?

The Bible does, in fact, recognise a reconciliation between God and man, effected by the re-establishment of holiness in the latter. Thus, in Rom. v. 9, 10, St. Paul speaks of a salvation which will be the consequence of the *life of Christ* realised in man. But, on the other hand, the Bible knows man too well, and his powerlessness by nature, to make a salvation of which holiness is the condition, the *first step* in his restoration. The reign of holiness within us can only be the fruit of internal communications from God. " There is none good but one," said Jesus : the creature can only be good through communion with Him, the Alone Good. Now it is precisely this bond of union with God which sin has broken. It must be re-knit by means of reconciliation, in order that holiness, the fruit of this union, may become once more possible to us. There is then, certainly, such a thing as a reconciliation which rests upon the fact of a reign of holiness established within us. But it is not with one of that kind that we are now concerned, but with that initial and preliminary reconciliation which precedes sanctification, and which can alone make it possible. The former is the transition from the state of grace to the state of glory, from the economy of faith to that of sight ; the latter, which comes first in point of time, constitutes the transition from the state of condemnation into the state of grace, from the life of sin into the life of faith.

What are the conditions of reconciliation, taking the word in the latter sense which is its usual acceptation in Scripture ? It is absolutely necessary, on the one hand, that God should be enabled to regard the *sinner* without feeling towards him that reprobation which is called forth in Him by the sight of *sin ;* and on the other hand, that sinful man should be enabled to see in God the judge of *sin*, without at the same time feeling himself the object of His displeasure and of His *condemnation*. By what means can this double result be reached—without which there can be no reconciliation ?

There is but one means—one only means—namely, that some man should make his appearance who shall accomplish these two tasks :—1. that of carrying through to its completion, without ever stepping aside from it, that course of normal development to which mankind was called, and to bring human life, in His own person, up to the state which had been appointed for it by God ; 2. that of repairing the evil brought in by our fall.

This is, in fact, what has been effected by Jesus Christ ; this is His work *for us*. On the one hand, He has consummated that development of humanity which had been left incomplete through the fault of the first man ; on the other, He has rehabilitated fallen humanity, and has replaced it on the road on which it has thenceforth the power to realise the destiny assigned to it. Upon these two bases reconciliation is possible between God and us.

1. Man, as created by God, was good, not in the sense that he was perfect, but that he had all that was needful for becoming so. It was goodness at its starting-point, not at its goal. Moral perfection can only be the fruit of freedom, the result of a series of decisions, perfectly voluntary, in the direction of that which is right. Man was therefore called to co-operate, himself, in the realisation of his moral destiny ; that was the reason why he was created innocent, but not holy.

Immediately after his appearance upon earth, that work began, by means of which he was to attain from his original state to that higher one for which he had been created. The task assigned to him was to transform the life of nature into the spiritual life, and that by means of the free sacrifice of the former, which was to be effected by constantly submitting to the successive manifestations of the Divine will. We know—and the condition of every man who comes into the world proves it—that man succumbed at the very beginning of the struggle, and that his moral life was vitiated by this fault even in its very germinating principle. We are all born as so many individual manifestations of this marred primordial human life, and the course of our development differs more or less in us all from the normal course of things.

What had He to do, to whom was assigned the task of restoring to us the favour of God? He must take up the thread of the normal development of humanity at the point where it had been broken through; recommence the moral labour which was to conduct man from innocence to holiness; go through that series of acts of obedience, of which each one was a sacrifice of the natural life; attain to that higher sphere of existence which Scripture calls the spiritual life, and thus sanctify the different spheres of human activity.

It is this that Jesus has done. We have perceived it while following, in the preceding essay, the course of His life as it is pictured for us in the gospel records. He realised in Himself the humanity which *was to be*, and accomplished, towards God and towards men, that pure and complete sacrifice of self which every one admires as that which is most perfect, and in which we see that absolute satisfaction has been given to the demands of morality.

It is just to such a life that the fine expression of St. Paul applies, borrowed from the imagery of the Levitical worship, "*a sacrifice for a sweet-smelling savour.*" [1] At the sight of this, God, if He is indeed a moral Being, that is to say, one capable of feeling love and joy, must have been *satisfied;* for satisfaction had at last been offered in this life to His eternal will.

---

[1] Eph. v. 2.

Henceforth the human race stands before Him embodied in a perfect example which is to become the originating spring of a humanity renewed after the image of this prototype.

To be united to this Second Adam, to be endued, if only in purpose, with His type of moral life, is itself, in the sight of God, to reproduce it; it is to have already accomplished the task ; it is to possess righteousness, and, as St. Paul expresses it, "to be accepted in the Beloved." [1]

II. Christ has not only *consummated* a humanity which had been arrested in its development—He has *rehabilitated* a humanity which had fallen. This is the second part of the task which He has accomplished for us, and by means of which He has effected our reconciliation. But it is the most painful part of His task, and the most difficult also for our intelligence to fathom ; the obscurity which envelopes sin and all its results wraps it in its shadow.

There exists in God one perfection which is not much in favour in our day in popular opinion,—that is, *justice.* According to the received definition of the word, this attribute consists in dealing with all men according to their works. How can we eliminate it from the Divine character? Would God still be God, if He were not just? He, the creator of freedom and of moral responsibility—would He be faithful to Himself, if, after having laid down these great principles of

---

[1] Eph. i. 4—6.

all morality in the nature and conscience of man, He did not do homage to them by judging man according to these rules which He had Himself established?

Right consists in the existence of such order among all beings as results from their very nature. Divine justice is the guardian of this order, and consequently the guarantee of the existence of right in the universe. It preserves order by means of punishment, when it has been disturbed by the wanton acts of wilfulness of free beings. Punishment may be defined as order preserved in the midst of disorder, without infringement upon freedom.

Suffering is the form which punishment takes. This it is which brings the creature to the consciousness of evil as evil. Evil *felt* is for him a revelation of evil *done*. In the physical sphere, what would become of man if he were able to burn one of his members without feeling pain in doing so? His life would be in danger every moment, without his being in the least conscious of it. It is the same in morals. Man must not have the power of sinning without receiving a warning through some internal or external suffering, that his soul has transgressed order, and is incurring danger.

But if the sinner dares directly to fly in the face of the Divine Majesty, and deliberately to deny the state of dependence in which he stands relatively to the Creator, mere suffering is no longer sufficient. It is man's very existence which is compromised. "The wages of sin is death." "I can live without Thee and in spite of Thee," man says to God when he thus acts. "Thy life was a gift, that gift is now withdrawn," such is the legitimate answer of Divine justice to this challenge. Immediate death—death by the shedding of the blood of the transgressor—for, as says Scripture, the blood is the life—such is the punishment of sin, as soon as it breaks out in the form of rebellion against the Author of life. It was the penalty with which God had threatened Adam: "In the day that thou eatest thereof thou shalt surely die." Nevertheless He did not think fit to execute the punishment in all its rigour. Adam sinned and lived on, and through a long course of centuries his descendants have continued sinning—and living. No doubt death has reigned, but apparently as the result of the natural decay of the organs and faculties. This death did not bear the stamp of a capital punishment; it was not by any means a manifest exhibition of the avenging justice of God. This attribute of justice therefore remained under a veil during this state of things, as did also the goodness and holiness, and all the other features, of the Divine character.

A day was to come when this abnormal state of things should give place to that full manifestation of justice, which had so long been delayed. And how was this manifestation made? Did God visibly put forth His hand, seize all the sinners that were living in the earth, and openly inflict upon each of them the punishment due to him ?   Did death, with one sweep of his scythe, cut down the whole of rebellious humanity ?

No; that which God desired was not the satisfaction of the demands of His justice by the effusion of torrents of blood; it was the revelation to the conscience of men of those demands which they had refused to recognise ; it was the willing acknowledgment of them by that conscience itself.   And why was this ?   Because herein lies the true restitution for wrong committed ; and herein, consequently, the true basis for the re-establishment of moral order when it has been disturbed.   When the will which has disturbed it has once convinced itself of having been in the wrong, and has passed sentence of death upon itself, then order has triumphed in the midst of the world of disorder.   God can the more easily relax the demands of His justice, when the righteousness of those demands has been recognised by the transgressor.

We must take this general view of the subject, if we are to understand the explanation which St. Paul has given, in a cardinal passage, of the sacrifice of Jesus Christ.   These are his words—"Being justified freely by His grace through the redemption that is in Christ Jesus : whom God hath set forth to be a propitiation through faith in His blood, to declare His righteousness for the remission of sins that are past, through the forbearance of God ; to declare, I say, at this time His righteousness : that He might be just, and

the justifier of him which believeth in Jesus" (Rom.
iii. 24—26).

According to this passage, some great act of restitution was indispensable. The justice of God had
been concealed from view during the whole course
of history. Sinners were not definitely conscious of
the punishment which they deserved. Some solemn
manifestation was needed, by which God should
exhibit the claims of His justice, and should teach
mankind this great principle, that whoever rebels
against God merits death. Had this measure been
dictated by personal resentment, or had it been the
act of vengeance of a superior, injured in his dignity
and authority, God, in executing it, would not have
failed to shew Himself prodigal of the blood of the
guilty persons. He would have destroyed them in as
large numbers as possible, and by this terrible catastrophe He would have proved that His toleration
towards the sinful world was the result of His long-
suffering to sinners, rather than of indifference to their
sin.

But what would have been the result of such a
punishment? It would have put an end to the history of mankind, and not even have left room for a
reconciliation. Now that at which God aimed was
a reconciliation; for He was not actuated by a sentiment of revenge, but by the generous inspiration of
His love, by the desire to pardon.

The very fact of redemption proves that that which

God desired was, not the *greatest*, but, on the contrary, the *least* possible amount of bloodshed consistent with the attainment of the required moral effect. *One* man sufficed for Him, in whose sanguinary death He manifested openly what had really been deserved by all ; *one* victim, at sight of whom all others might exclaim : There I see the retribution of which I had made myself worthy ! This death, of which I am but the witness, I had myself deserved to suffer.

That unique man who was commissioned to play this awful part in the history of humanity must be a *real* man. On this condition only could He identify Himself with those in whose place He was to stand ; for He was not to take their place only outwardly, but morally, by an act analogous to that by which we throw down the barrier which separates our own personality from that of our neighbour every time we intercede for him in any vivid and truly sympathising manner.

This real man must, finally, be *holy*, perfectly holy. For in order that that manifestation of His justice which God proposed to make to the world, in this central moment of its history, should become a complete demonstration of this Divine attribute, it was necessary that it should include two things : (1) the revelation of the claims of God upon a guilty humanity ; (2) the recognition of these claims by that humanity itself. Now these two things demanded perfect holiness in the Redeemer.

1. He in whose person should be displayed God's rights, must Himself be exempt from sin, in order that it might be made perfectly clear that it was not for His own personal faults, but for those of the whole guilty race, that He thus suffered. When Moses was commanded to lift a serpent upon a pole, in order to manifest the ultimate powerlessness of the plague which had been desolating the Israelites, God directed him so to lift up, not a real serpent, but an artificial image of one. Why was this ? Because in the former case the victory thus exhibited would have been only over the particular serpent thus nailed to the pole ; whereas, in the latter, the brazen serpent was evidently the type of the whole species. For the same reason the sin of humanity was to be nailed to the cross, not in the person of a sinner, but of a saint. The sin thus punished is seen not to be that of the particular victim, but of mankind in general. Isaiah had arrived at the understanding of this when he said : "We did esteem Him stricken, smitten of God, and afflicted. But He was wounded for our transgressions, He was bruised for our iniquities."

2. The end proposed to Himself by God—namely, homage rendered to His outraged Majesty—imperatively demanded that the personal will of Him in whom this revelation of the rights of God was made, should co-operate with holy zeal in this act of restitution. He must not suffer against His own will,—complaining against His destiny. It was necessary that He should

Himself ratify the justice of the punishment which He endured; that He should recognise it as deserved, not indeed by Himself, but by those in whose name He suffered. Thus only could such a punishment become really an *expiatory sacrifice*, an open declaration of rights of God hitherto unrecognised. Now such an expiation could not be offered by any one of the sinners who had made it necessary. And why not?

We have already given the answer: the conscience of the sinner is to a certain extent paralysed. It cannot raise itself to the level of the Divine justice whence issues the sentence which condemns sin. In order sincerely to ratify the penalty of which the sinner is the victim, sin must be hated as the Judge Himself hates it. In order to condemn sin as God condemns it, we must be holy as He is holy.

Now this is just what Jesus Christ was. It was because His conscience was a pure reflection of the holiness of God that He was able to accept and to undergo the penalty of sinners in the way that He did, acquiescing completely in the claims of God. Upon this narrow stage of the conscience of Christ, there met, face to face, two opposing powers, which, in us, can ordinarily contemplate each other only from a distance,—the holiness of God in its most delicate susceptibility, and the sin of man in all its forms, the coarsest as well as the most subtle. There, in this close contact between God and man, sin was judged as it ought to be, but as we had no longer the power to judge it. There were shed those perfectly holy tears which we are no longer able to shed. There was offered a full and complete satisfaction to God. The bitterest death was accepted as the just punishment of sin, and the Divine right to inflict such a punishment upon sinful man was recognised unreservedly. "*Holy Father*," was the exclamation of the dying Son in the last prayer which He uttered with His disciples.[1]

The manifestation of justice which God wished to make to the world attained therefore in this case the character of absolute perfection. To the adequacy of the punishment inflicted was added the complete concurrence of Him who consented to undergo it.

This reparative act had been foreseen and prepared for from all eternity.[2] This, according to St. Paul, was the ultimate result in which culminated all the sins committed up to that time, and of which God had not demanded punishment in a degree proportionate to their gravity. For centuries God had allowed to live in sin, even up to hoar old age, innumerable generations of transgressors, whose blood had not been shed for the expiation of their faults. Among the Jews alone had expiatory sacrifices recalled to the conscience of man the treatment merited by sinners. Those myriads of sins to which God had seemed to shut His eyes, had led up at

---

[1] John xvii. 25.   [2] Eph. i. 4—7; 1 Pet. i. 20.

length to this great judicial act ; and the sanguinary death of the Son, which had been decreed from all eternity, explained to the world why God had not smitten with His thunderbolts all those sinners who had braved Him to the utmost of their power, during the time in which He bore with them. As to the sins committed since, St. Paul does not mention them in the passage we are endeavouring to explain, because when once the manifestation of justice had been made by the sanguinary death of the Son, the state of things was thenceforth changed ; this Divine attribute is no longer concealed from view, whatever may be the toleration which God still extends to sinners.

And now what is the connection between that manifestation of the Divine justice in the cross of Christ, and the reconciliation of God with the sinful world ?

We should deceive ourselves if we thought that the sacrifice of Jesus Christ acted as a work of merit upon the relation between God and man, in such a manner as to make it needless for the latter to co-operate in any way in effecting the salvation which was to result from it. It is remarkable that in the passage from St. Paul which serves as a text to the whole theory thus set forth, the apostle, after having called Jesus a *propitiatory victim*, adds immediately, as a comment upon this statement, these words : " through faith in His blood." It is of the eternal decree of redemption that St. Paul here gives us the formula ;[1] and he does not fear to make the faith of man one of the effective elements of the amnesty which is based upon this decree. It had entered into it from the first as a foreseen and indispensable condition, to such a degree that, without it, St. Paul himself declares, the victim would no longer be *propitiatory*, and the amnesty would be annulled. What is the meaning of this ?

Between the living God and man as a free agent there is no place for a mere *opus operatum*. As Christ did not carry the complete development of humanity to its perfection in order to dispense us from fulfilling it ourselves, and thus leave us in the condition of unsanctified men, but His purpose is, by sanctifying Himself, to draw us after Him and to induce us to run ourselves that course of holiness of which He was Himself the first to reach the goal, so neither did He go through the act of expiation, in which is manifested the punishment due to the sinful world, in order to dispense us from offering to God the restitution which we owe Him ; His object was, on the contrary, to associate us with Himself in offering the collective satisfaction which He has consummated in the name of all, and to involve us, in a manner, in that solemn act of protest on behalf of the claims of God as against sin. Now it is *faith* that thus associates individuals with the act of restitution offered

---

[1] " Whom God hath set forth," or " foreordained."

by Christ. It is by faith that we apply to our own selves that which He did for the world, and to our own sin that which He suffered for the sin of the world. The sinful Israelite, before he slew the victim before the altar, laid his hands upon its head while confessing the sin on account of which he sacrificed it ; just so, it is through faith in Jesus Christ crucified that the sinner includes his own individual sin in that of mankind, which Christ has voluntarily taken upon Himself, and recognises in the death upon the cross that which he has himself deserved, but which God forbears to demand of him. By every act of faith he exclaims, as he looks to Jesus crucified, "There I see myself ! " or, as was once said by Betjuana, who understood the Cross better than many a theologian, "Jesus, come down from thence ; it is my place ! " Thus does he renew the atonement of blood offered to God by Christ, and make it valid for himself.

The forgiveness of God springs undoubtedly from His love—so the whole Bible declares. But His love meets with an obstacle in His justice. Sin is so grave a fact, that it has indeed originated this conflict between the attributes of God—justice requiring that the sinner should be dealt with according to his deeds, and love demanding his forgiveness. The obstacle opposed to love by justice had to be removed, in order that free course might be given to the gracious wish of God to exercise on our behalf His prerogative of pardon. This is precisely the result which has been reached by means of that great manifestation of justice, to which the conscience of mankind has given its adhesion in the first place in Christ Himself, and then again in each individual believer. Divine justice does not require, in order to leave the way open to mercy, to have its demands satisfied in act, but only to be recognised. Upon this recognition depends, in fact, the restoration of him who has put a slight upon these claims by sinning. Towards one who acknowledges them, justice lays aside her arms, and love is free to unfold her treasures.

We can understand, therefore, why we find the atonement made by Christ, and the faith by which we appropriate it to ourselves, to be the conditions of our reconciliation. There is nothing arbitrary in this. Faith in the atonement becomes itself an atonement. Its virtue in this respect is not derived from its *intensity*, nor even from its *nature* so essentially *moral*—characteristics always imperfect—but from its *object*, the perfect expiation made by Christ. That which satisfies justice is not a certain *quantum* of suffering equivalent to a certain *quantum* of sin; but it is, on the part of God, the complete revelation of this attribute of His Being; on the part of man, the unqualified adhesion which he gives to this revelation. Now this it is precisely which faith discerns in the sacrifice of Jesus, and which God, on His part, sees in faith.

It is with this feeling that St. Paul finishes the

passage quoted with these remarkable words : "that
He might be just, and the justifier of him which
believeth in Jesus." God would not be really just, if
He did not manifest Himself as such, and the world
would not have been compelled to believe in His
justice, if, once at least in the history of mankind, He
had not revealed this attribute in its plenitude. One
might even ask whether, without the Cross, the final
judgment would have been morally possible—whether
it would not have been for the impenitent sinner a
surprise, of which he might have had some reason to
complain. He might have said to God : " Thou hast
revealed Thy mercy to me by an act of free grace,
in such a manner that there was no room left in my
mind for believing in the possibility of final punishment. Thus Thou hast Thyself helped to mislead
my judgment, and to put my vigilance to sleep."
But by the manifestation of justice made upon the
cross, this language of the sinner is for ever excluded.
God has not forgiven without inflicting punishment,
and this act of punishment not only makes the forgiveness of others possible, but expressly holds in
reserve the future act of judgment with respect to
any who do not accept the forgiveness, or who abuse
it by taking it in a different sense from that in which
it was granted. God has therefore manifested His
justice in order that He might be just in fact—that is
to say, in order that He might not cease to be so, as
would have been the case had He acted otherwise ;

and in order that He might be enabled to act as such " in the day in which He will judge the world in righteousness by that man whom He hath ordained."[1]

To these words, " that He might be just," Paul adds, " and the justifier of him which believeth in Jesus." As, on the one hand, He would *not* have been just if He had forgiven without punishing, so, on the other, He would have been *only* just if He had punished without forgiving. In both cases the revelation of His moral character, which is one of the objects of the providential history of the world, would have remained incomplete. But, His claims having been once recognised by Jesus, and by all who believe in Him, God can refrain from enforcing them, and can legitimately declare to be *righteous* even the *sinner* himself. For this justification is not the final one. It is not that which opens to man the entrance into glory; it is that which introduces him into the state of grace, and which makes him breathe the life-giving air of reconciliation. Final justification presupposes the faithful use of this boundless grace. If God proclaims the sinner righteous who recognises His rights, it is because this recognition contains in principle the moral restoration of man to the full height of the Divine holiness. It is impossible to lay hold of the object of faith, the atonement made by Christ, without breaking altogether with sin, which has been the cause of such a death, or without laying within ourselves the founda-

---

[1] Acts xvii. 31.

tion of sanctificatiou. This consequence of faith is the result, as we have seen, of the nature of its object.

We cannot, therefore, completely agree either with a view which is very prevalent in our day, and which has been unfolded in a very brilliant manner by M. de Pressensé in his *Vie de Jésus,* according to which the atonement consisted only in the perfect obedience offered to God by Christ in the active consecration of Himself which He made to Him by closely uniting His will with His ; nor with the old orthodox formula, according to which Jesus on the Cross became, as the representative of the sinful world, the object of the displeasure and reprobation of God.

The first of these two conceptions does not admit of our accounting sufficiently for the preponderating part assigned through the whole of the New Testament to the blood of Christ in the work of redemption. This blood is not in Scripture the symbol only of obedience carried to its utmost limits, but certainly also of expiation by suffering and death. Accordingly, St. Paul not only says that Christ was an *offering* unto God for a sweet-smelling savour ; but, uniting the two aspects of Christ's work on our behalf which we have just explained separately, he says, "*an offering and a sacrifice* for a sweet-smelling savour." [1] There is to be seen, assuredly, in Christ crucified, the Divine judgment upon sin, and not only the renunciation of sin. It is this which is so keenly

---

[1] Eph. v. 2.

felt by the conscience of a Christian who accepts unreservedly the teaching of the New Testament The first method of reconciliation, which we have expounded—the sanctification of the life of man by Christ—ought not to make us forget or deny the second.

On the other hand, the old orthodox view offends in some respects against Christian feeling trained in the school of Holy Scripture. Does not St. Paul call Jesus a sacrifice *for a sweet-smelling savour ?* Does he not apply this expression to Him at the very moment when He is sacrificing Himself for us, and when He is being made, as the same apostle says, a *sin* and a *curse* for us ?[1] Never certainly was any act done upon the earth more pleasing to God than this sacrifice, which was inspired by the purest love for mankind, and the deepest reverence for the Divine holiness ; and never was the person of Jesus so much the object of the favour and blessing of His Father as in that moment in which He identified Himself with the *sin* of the world, in order to bear, in His own Person, the whole *curse* which was attached to it, and which included even a temporary abandonment of Him by God Himself. For Jesus, as we have seen, met the first claims of God, not by satisfying, but by revealing and recognising them. The sufferings He underwent upheld the *principle* of justice and of judgment : they were an equivalent in quality, not quantity. They

---

[1] 2 Cor. v. 21 ; Gal. iii. 13.

represented our own in such a way that we may be spared from undergoing them ourselves, if we profit by His. From this point of view the doctrine of substitution, against which so many objections have been raised, no longer presents anything to offend the moral sense. Assuredly *one* could, without injustice, suffer for *all*, if His suffering was not a *compensation* for the lack of theirs, but a revelation made to all of what all would have deserved to suffer, and what those will really suffer who are not brought back to God, in penitence and faith, by the spectacle of this expiation.

Jesus *sanctified Himself for us ;* by so doing He realised in His own person the ideal of human nature ; Jesus *was crucified for us ;* so did He atone for the outrage that had been offered to God by sinful mankind : these are the two aspects of the work which He accomplished *for us ;* these are the two means by which He has rendered possible the reconciliation between God and us. The believer who accepts this twofold work is regarded by God as having fulfilled it himself, since this acceptance is the means and the pledge of its accomplishment by the believer himself.

The wonderful greatness of the atoning work of Christ will appear so much the more clearly, when we remember that He accomplished the two tasks included in it, simultaneously, and, if we may venture so to express it, at one stroke. Picture to yourself a train which has run off the rails, and has fallen down a precipice. A deliverer appears, who succeeds in, at the same moment, lifting it on to the rails again, and conducting it to the end of the journey. Thus did Jesus, in His passage through the world, at the same time lift fallen humanity out of its state of condemnation, and consummate the moral development, which had been scarcely begun, of unfallen humanity.

To the execution of these two tasks belong all the salient facts of His history ; to the latter, His miraculous birth, by which He begins anew, from the very first step, the course of life laid down for man ; His baptism, by which He effects the lifting of natural and psychical into spiritual life ; His transfiguration, the seal of His individual perfection ; and His ascension, the absolute realisation of the glorious destiny of humanity. To the former task belong His death and resurrection—that is to say, the atonement offered by man, and the absolution given by God.

Rationalism has a special predilection for the former aspect of this sublime work, that which relates to the perfecting of the moral nature of man ; orthodoxy has only understood the latter—that which relates to expiation. We believe that a perfect intuition of the method of the reconciliation of the world, of the justification of sinners, and generally of the relation of Christianity to human nature, can only be formed in the mind of him who combines in one, as we have been endeavouring to do—the two aspects of the work of redemption. Jesus, the *consummator* of creation, and the *repairer* of the fall ; Jesus, the second Adam, in whom man accomplishes the task which had been originally set him, and comes forth from the grave absolved from the sin of the humanity of the past—this is the complete Jesus, considered from the point of view of His work on our behalf. Every man who accepts Him by faith in this twofold character, becomes immediately, in the sight of God, all that He is Himself. For that which Jesus has been *for* him, He will infallibly become *in* him : "That the love wherewith Thou hast loved me may be in them, and *I* in them."[1] In other words : "Thou wilt be enabled to love them as Thou lovest Me, because it will be Myself whom Thou wilt love in them." This is the mystery contained in that favourite expression of Paul : Christ *our righteousness.*

2

CHRIST IN US

We have, in accordance with the New Testament, distinguished between two *justifications*, the one preliminary, founded solely upon faith ; the other definitive, resting upon holiness firmly established in the soul of the believer.[2] Sanctification, or the work of

---

[1] John xvii . 26.

[2] " Much more then, being now justified by His blood, we shall be saved from wrath through Him. For if, when we were enemies, we were *reconciled* to God by the *death* of His Son, much more, being reconciled, we shall be *saved* by His *life*." (Rom. v. 9, 10).

Christ *within us,* has its place between the two, as the consequence of the former, and the condition of the latter.

Many Christians are perplexed by an apparent contradiction which strikes them in the Scriptures. On the one hand, salvation is granted to faith—to faith only. St. Paul continually affirms it ; and this thought makes its appearance in all the other apostolic writers. On the other hand, they all equally speak of a judgment which is to take effect, *according to the works* of each.[1] St. Paul is not less explicit upon this point than all his colleagues.[2] How are we to reconcile these two doctrines ?

The solution is to be found precisely in the distinction which we have just drawn. It is, as it seems to us, this : Every favour received from God ought to have for its effect a step of moral progress, but this effect can only be produced by the co-operation of the person favoured. Every grace granted by God issues in a trial of man's fidelity. Now that which is true of the details of the Christian life is true also of the whole. The fundamental grace, that of the forgiveness of sins, presupposes no other moral condition than faith only. But this immense act of grace is no sooner granted by God, and accepted by man, than there results from it a new task, with the responsibility which attaches to it. This is the work of sanctifica-

[1] Matt. xvi. 27, and parallels ; John v. 29 ; Rev. xx. 12, 13.
[2] Rom. xiv. 10, 12 ; 1 Cor. iv. 5 ; 2 Cor. v. 10 ; Gal. vi. 7.

tion ; the renewal of the life in the likeness of Christ.
And this is the *work*, according to which the believer
will one day be judged. This is the fruit which will
be demanded of him in return for the grace given.
We cannot fail to be reminded here of the unmerciful
servant, in whom the mercy of his master did not
produce that effect of mercy towards his fellow-servant,
which should have resulted from it. The sentence of
absolution which had been already pronounced upon
him was annulled ;[1] and the sinner, who had been
justified freely, but in whom that act of mercy had
not borne its proper fruit, was placed once more under
the jurisdiction of the law. St. Paul threatens with a
precisely similar fate Christians of evil lives in Corinth,
Galatia, etc.[2]

The reason is that justification by faith is only the
door of entrance by which we are admitted into the
state of salvation; whilst final justification, which is but
the simple acceptance by God of holiness actually
realised, is the door of exit through which we reach
from the state of salvation into that of glory.

Thus are the two scriptural principles of justification by faith, and of judgment according to works,
brought into harmony. Though apparently opposed
to each other, they are both equally true ; only they
apply to two different periods of the Christian life.

Few, even among Christians, seem to understand

---

[1] Matt. xviii. 23—35.

[2] 1 Cor. vi. 9, 10 ; Gal. v. 19—21 ; vi. 7, 8.

this great and important truth : that the attainment
of holiness in the soul of the believer is the *object* of
the Divine work, and that the forgiveness of sins is but
the *means*.   How many express themselves as if when
forgiveness, with the peace which it procures, has been
once obtained, all is finished, and the work of salvation complete !   They seem to have no suspicion that
salvation consists in the health of the soul, and that
the health of the soul consists in holiness.   Forgiveness is not the re-establishment of health, it is but the
crisis of convalescence.   If God thinks fit to declare
the sinner righteous, it is in order that He may by
that means restore him to holiness.   The righteousness
which He *imputes* to him for the moment is to become his actual and personal property ; otherwise it
will not fail to be withdrawn from him.

There is, therefore, an indissoluble connection between justification and holiness ; and it is with regard
to this connection that we must now endeavour to
come to an understanding.   This will be the best way
to reach at the same time a comprehension of the true
nature of Christian sanctification.

Two different powers of sanctification are contained
in justifying faith.   One is included in the object
itself of this faith ; the other proceeds from the new
relation which faith establishes between the soul and
God.   The former belongs to the *human* side in the
work of sanctification ; it is the inward law which
impels the Christian to undertake this great task.

The latter belongs to the *divine* side of this work; it is the new force which makes it possible to him.

St. Paul, in Rom. vi. and viii., has unfolded in succession these two aspects of Christian sanctification.

I. The *object* of justifying faith is not an idea, it is a fact; it is the work of reconciliation which Jesus Christ accomplished in His life and in His death. Now this fact is essentially moral in its nature. That which constitutes the propitiatory power of the life of Jesus is the perfectly normal character of its holiness. That which gives to His death its power of expiation and reparation is not a certain amount of suffering undergone, no matter in what manner; it is the perfect submission with which these sufferings were accepted, as the legitimate consequence of sin.

If the object of faith be in its nature essentially moral, how can faith be limited to the mere acquiescence of the reason? Must not the act of faith share the nature of its object? The assent which we give to a work of art is æsthetic in nature, like that creative operation which, in the author's mind, produced the masterpiece that we admire. Just so the adhesion which we give to the purely moral work of reconciliation accomplished by Jesus Christ will have its spring necessarily in the moral sense, and will, like the work itself—that masterpiece of the human conscience—take the character of an act of the conscience.

Is it possible to acquiesce in the holy life of Jesus Christ, in His incessant victory over even the most

legitimate natural instincts, in His perfect self-
dedication to the will of the Father, in His unbroken communion with Him, as picturing to us
the normal human life which ought to have been
that of us all, without appropriating to ourselves
ipso facto the moral principle of that life, and making
it henceforth the soul of our own? To give our
adhesion to a life so offered to God is equivalent
to offering ourselves.

Would it be possible to accept the moral redemption
offered by Him as an act which ought properly to have
been offered by ourselves,—to ratify in our own conscience the sentence which the normal conscience of
the Redeemer pronounced upon the sin of the world,
when He underwent the punishment due to it, without
making of that sentence *ipso facto* a sentence of death,
passed in our own heart and will, upon our own sin?
This assimilation of the conscience of Christ crucified,
which is involved in the act of faith, is that which
St. Paul, in his strong language, at once literal and
figurative, characterises by these expressions: *to be
crucified with Christ; to be baptized* (immersed) *into the
death of Christ.*[1] To join ourselves by an act of the
will to the death of Christ for sin, is to die to sin,
that is, to break altogether with it. It is the response
called out in the heart of the believer himself by the
object of faith, which had been so profoundly felt
by that other member of the Betjuana people, who

---

[1] Gal. ii. 20; Rom. vi. 3.

exclaimed : " The Cross of Christ condemns me to become a saint." That word "*condemns*" expresses in a very natural manner the effect which the sight of the cross produces at first upon the old nature in us, when it feels itself drawn by faith to gaze upon that instrument of a terrible death upon which the sin of mankind has been once for all condemned in the person of the Son of God.

It is then of the essence of justifying faith to create in the soul of the believer, by the very nature of its object, an insuperable antipathy to the sin so painfully expiated by Christ, and an inexhaustible sympathy with the goodness so wonderfully realised in His person.

We may compare the life of Christ on earth to what would be, in the life of any one of us, a moment of miraculous insight and holiness in which it should be given to us to discern perfectly the real nature of sin, and to pass judgment upon it, as God Himself does. This ray of heavenly light would radically renew the conscience, the heart, and so the whole life, of him whom it reached. Such has been the effect produced upon mankind by the appearance upon earth, and by the work of Jesus Christ ; and in order to feel its effects in ourselves, it suffices to allow this supreme object of faith to unfold within our inmost being the power which is inherent in it.

II. At the same time, in order to become victoriously efficacious, this connection which establishes itself between the object of faith and the soul of the believer, must be sealed by a direct act of God.   Here we have the divine side of the relation which connects sanctification with justification.

As long as the state of hostility between man and God lasts, no intimate communication is possible between the one and the other.   God especially could not, during this state of things, quicken man by His inspiration, by His Spirit.   This communication of His own individual life presupposes a reconciliation already effected, and peace restored between Him and man.   But as soon as a right relation is restored between the two, the gift of the Holy Spirit becomes as natural as before it was impossible.   The state of condemnation was the barrier which prevented the Spirit from giving Himself.   No sooner is this obstacle removed by the act of justification, no sooner does man find himself placed once more in his normal position with reference to God, than the Divine blessing again takes the course which had been forcibly interrupted ; grace is again poured forth, and like a torrent whose banks have been broken down, the Holy Spirit flows freely into the reconciled heart.

Jesus had pointed out this relation in which His atoning death stood to all future Pentecosts, whether collective or individual : " If I go not away," He had said, " the Comforter will not come unto you ; but if I depart, I will send Him unto you."[1]

---

[1] John xvi. 7.

These remarkable words prove at the same time, that, in order to understand this new aspect of Christ's work, we must call to our aid the third period of His existence,—that of His heavenly glory and ministry.

Not only is it true that Jesus participates, since His ascension, in the omnipresence, the omnipotence, and the omniscience of God, in such a manner that He can at any moment help and deliver those that are His, in the difficulties of their earthly existence; but above all, that after having, during His sojourn here below, completely appropriated to Himself the Divine Spirit, and made of it His own personal life, as God Himself does, He is become the sovereign dispenser of it to His brethren.   And this is the divine source of Christian sanctification.

If chap. vi. of the Epistle to the Romans makes us understand the imperative *obligation* of holiness which is for the Christian conscience the result of the fact of justification, in chap. viii. the apostle reveals to us the divine *power* which renders the justified man able to fulfil this obligation : " For the law of the Spirit of life in Christ Jesus hath made me free from the law of sin and death.   For what the law could not do, in that it was weak through the flesh, God sending His own Son in the likeness of sinful flesh, and for sin, condemned sin in the flesh : that the righteousness of the law might be fulfilled in us, who walk not after the flesh, but after the Spirit."[1]

---

[1] Rom. viii. 2—4.

This passage, no less cardinal than that in chap. iii., from which we have drawn our light upon the subject of redemption, opens to us a view into the scene of the Divine operations in which the work of Christian sanctification is being carried on.

God began His work by sending His Son, clothed in a body like ours, to realise in that body itself perfect holiness, so passing sentence upon sin by signalising it as that which ought not to be, and excluding it from that part of our being in which He had chosen to take up His abode, and from which He extends His dominion over all our faculties. This work once accomplished in Jesus Himself, there emanates from His glorified person, as a life-giving power, His Spirit, who wins the same victory in us that Jesus has won in His own person, and who realises in our life, as Jesus did in His, the righteousness demanded by the law, on this sole condition, that we take for the governing law of our conduct, not the flesh as it is in us, but this Spirit.

Our holiness is not therefore a mere imitation of that of Jesus, which we realise in ourselves by our own resolutions; it is actually His own—that which He realised here below through conflicts and sacrifices, and now communicates to us from out of His life in glory. It is human life such as He has made it in His own person, freed from sin, and pleasing to God, which He reproduces in us through His Spirit. Himself the Prototype of this new life, He is at the same time its source and author in the soul of the believer. He makes to shine forth in the heart of him who looks to Him in faith, His own image ; He makes it to shine there with such power that it begins to live in the man ; it becomes the new man in him, and the believer is thus "changed from glory to glory, even as by the Spirit of the Lord."[1]

Jesus had Himself indicated this relation which should one day exist between His holiness and our own, in that expression, often thought difficult, but which, after all that has been said, seems to me very clear : "I sanctify myself, that they also might be sanctified through the truth."[2] In other words, the holiness which I realise in my own life shall become theirs by my communicating it to them ; and then they shall be indeed holy as I am holy. Jesus has included the same thought in those mysterious images, *drinking His blood, eating His flesh*, which evidently have reference, according to the explanation which He Himself gives of them (v. 63), to the operation by which His Spirit appropriates to the believer His flesh,—that is to say, His life dedicated to God, and His blood,—that is to say, His death *for* sin, together with the death *to* sin which is involved in it.

From the point of view of ordinary orthodoxy, which makes the whole work of Christ to consist in the atonement, and the whole of salvation in the

---

[1] 2 Cor. iii. 18.   [2] John xvii. 19.

forgiveness of sins, one might ask why Jesus Christ
did not come down from heaven to ascend the cross
immediately, why He *lived* before He died. It may
no doubt be replied that the holiness of the victim
was a necessary condition of the atonement; but
this answer would evidently be incomplete. The
true solution is to be found in the view of Christian
holiness which we have just propounded. Jesus
Christ lived because His holiness was at last, after
His death and ascension, to become ours.

Perhaps it will be asked what is the connection
between the passages in which our sanctification is
attributed to the Holy Spirit, and those in which
it is attributed to Christ Himself living in us?[1] The
answer is easy. In reality these two classes of expressions refer to one and the same fact. What is
the work of the Holy Spirit? It is to impart Christ
to us, with everything that is His, and to make Him
live again in us, as the grain of wheat which lies
dead in the earth is made by the power of nature to
live again in each of the grains in the ear. And, on
the other hand, by what means does Christ live in
us? By the operation of the Holy Spirit. There
takes place in the believer, by the power of that
Divine agent, an effect similar to that which produced
the miraculous birth of Jesus Christ. "My little
children," said St. Paul, "of whom I travail in birth
again till Christ be formed in you."[2] Our holiness

---

[1] Gal. ii. 20.   [2] Gal. iv. 19.

does not, properly speaking, consist in our changing and becoming better *ourselves ;* for after fifty years of faithful labour it may happen that all at once we find ourselves, when our own nature gains the upper hand, as bad as we were half a century before ; it is rather *He,* He Himself, born and growing in us, in such a way as to fill our heart and gradually to drive out our natural self, our "old man," which cannot itself improve, and whose destiny is only to perish.

How is this kind of incarnation practically effected, by which Christ Himself becomes our new self ? By a process of a free and moral nature, described by Jesus in words which surprise us, because they place His sanctification upon nearly the same footing as our own : "As the living Father hath sent me, and I live by the Father ; so he that eateth me, even he shall live by me."[1] Jesus derived the nourishment of His life from the Father who had sent Him, and lived by Him. The meaning of that is, doubtless, that every time He had to act or speak, He first effaced Himself; then left it to the Father to will, to think, to act, to be everything in Him. Similarly, when we are called upon to do any act, or to speak any word, we must first efface ourselves in presence of Jesus ; and after having suppressed in ourselves, by an act of will, every wish, every thought, every act of our own self, we are to leave it

---

[1] John vi. 57.

to Jesus to manifest in us His will, His wisdom, His power. Thus it is that we live by Him, as He lived by the Father; that we "*eat Him*" (this is the image He employs), as He was nourished by the Father. The process is identical in Jesus and in ourselves. Only in Jesus it was carried on with God directly, because He was in immediate communion with Him, whilst in our case the transaction is with Jesus, because it is with Him that the believer holds direct communication, and through Him alone that we find and can possess *the living Father*. In that lies the secret, generally so little understood, of Christian sanctification.

But no one would be able to practise this sublime art without from the first taking up the glorious position opened to us in Jesus Christ through justification, such as St. Paul teaches. When that apostle wishes to teach us how we can attain to die unto sin, and to live unto God, this is the way he expresses himself: "Likewise reckon ye also yourselves to *be dead* indeed unto sin, but *alive* unto God, through Jesus Christ our Lord."[1] This language is scarcely conformable to that of reason. Human wisdom says, "Disengage yourself by degrees from the bonds of sin; learn gradually to love God and to live for Him." But in this way we never break radically with sin, and give ourselves wholly to God. We remain in the dull troubled atmosphere of our own

---

[1] Rom. vi. 11.

nature, and never attain to the contemplation of the full light of the Divine holiness. Faith, on the contrary, raises us, as it were, at one bound, into the regal position which Jesus Christ now holds, and which in Him is really ours. From thence we behold sin cast under our feet; we taste of the life of God as our true essential being in Jesus Christ. Reason says, *Become* holy in order to *be* holy. Faith says, You *are* holy: therefore become so. You are holy in Christ; become so in your own person. Or, as St. Paul says to the Colossians (iii. 3, 5), "Ye are dead . . . . *mortify* therefore your members which are upon the earth."

This is, perhaps, the most paradoxical feature of pure evangelical doctrine. He who disowns it, or puts it from him, will never cross the threshold of Christian sanctification. We do not get rid of sin by little and little; we have to break with it, with that total breaking which was consummated by Christ upon the cross. We do not ascend one by one the steps of the throne; we spring upon it, and seat ourselves there in Christ, by the act of faith which incorporates us in Him. Then from the height of that position, holy in its essential nature, we reign victoriously over self, the world, Satan,—all the powers of evil; it is in that atmosphere of absolute holiness that we put on the image, both divine and human, of the Son of God.

The relation between justification and sanctification

is perhaps one of the points upon which the difference of view which distinguishes the two great forms of Western Christianity is the most keenly felt; though it is nevertheless true that a completely scriptural conception of this important subject cannot be said to be in perfect agreement with either the one or the other way of viewing it.

Protestantism, we must confess, has always shewn itself weak and embarrassed, when called upon to point out precisely the organic connection between these two elements of salvation — forgiveness and holiness. Theologians of this way of thinking have generally looked for this connection in the feeling of gratitude;[1] or else they have contented themselves with simply adding on the exposition of the law to that of grace, without seeking to discover the internal relation which connects the latter with faith and the former with obedience.[2] But a simple juxtaposition is not sufficient; and as to the feeling of gratitude, it could never furnish any solid foundation for the duty of Christian sanctification. How could the emotion of gratitude provide the motive and justification of an act demanded by the author of the benefit received, if that act were not in itself morally good? Gratitude is an *incentive* well fitted to make the practice of duty easier for us; but it could never supply the *principle* of the duty itself.

---

[1] See, for instance, the *Heidelberg Catechism.*

[2] As in the *Catechism of Osterwald.*

On the other hand, Catholicism rightly lays great stress, in the question of sanctification, upon real, vital, even substantial, communications from Christ to the believer. It understands, better than Protestantism, the sacred mystical truth of the incarnation of Christ in each of His members. But why does it connect it in so childish a manner with outward rites, material usages, which, first instituted as symbols, have since been transformed into meritorious acts and necessary conditions, and have had the effect of excluding the one only true means,—justifying faith, and the free access to the throne of grace which that opens to every believer?

In their almost total ignorance of justification by faith, as it is set forth by Paul, and their desire nevertheless to do justice to his teaching, the most enlightened among the Catholics—and indeed some pious Protestants with them—make, as St. Paul does, justification to depend indeed upon faith, but on condition that the latter shall possess certain indispensable qualities. Thus, men imagine they find in the *fervour* of faith, or in the charity which is its necessary *fruit*, the secret of its justifying power. And the idea of *merit*, which had seemed to be excluded by the substitution of faith for works, returns again in full force through this tacit addition of works to faith. But what is the result? As the most exemplary fervour is but lukewarmness when compared with its ideal, and the riches of the fruits of faith but scarcity, in proportion to that abundance which faith in the Divine work ought legitimately to have produced, it thence follows that these sincere souls never feel themselves certainly justified, or completely freed from condemnation. Never, consequently, do they arrive at that high position which is our birthright in Christ, and which faith assures to us, not by the degree of its intensity, or the abundance of its practical effects, but solely by the nature of its object.[1] Or, if they are for an instant transported to these heights, as, for instance, at the time of the celebration of the Sacrament, the blessed moment is no sooner passed, than, human frailty making itself felt once more, they fall again, and are obliged to wait for a fresh sacerdotal absolution, before they can regain the height of the state of justification, and then hold it in a manner just as unstable and insecure. A joyless system! which, no doubt, answers the purpose of the priest by making his intervention constantly necessary, but does not answer that of the Christian, who is held down by it in a state of perpetual nonage.

Is not the time arrived for these two sections of the Western Church, who have, as it were, divided the truth upon this cardinal doctrine, at last to reunite and set it forth in its fulness: when justification, as Protestantism has understood the doctrine, more especially Lutheran Protestantism, or, to express ourselves better, justification according to the

---

[1] Meditate upon that wonderful passage, Eph. ii. 1—10.

meaning of Isaiah, of Jesus, and of Paul, shall be placed, without reserve or subterfuge, at the base of the work of salvation, but with the earnest and decided intention to erect upon it the edifice of sanctification, the work of Christ within us, as understood by Catholicism ; that is, the infusion of the holy life of Christ into the faithful soul by the Holy Spirit.

Christ, substituted for us before God, as our *righteousness;* Christ, substituted for us in ourselves, as our *sanctification:* " Christ, made unto us," as St. Paul says, "wisdom, and *righteousness*, and *sanctification*, and redemption " (1 Cor. i. 30) ; such is the plenitude of Christian salvation.   Let us learn, both of us, so to regard Christ, and the true form of union will have been discovered.   It is that which Paul has before indicated in the words (Col. ii. 20), " And ye are complete in Him."

We have studied the work of Christ, both in the part which has been accomplished once for all, and in that which is still in process of being accomplished.   Let us now endeavour to comprehend it in its totality, by taking into our view its future stages and its crowning glories.   From this more general point of view it presents itself to the eye of faith as a twofold victory, gained over the two great enemies of humanity.

One has seen devoted men dedicating their lives to the restoration of their impoverished or dishonoured families.

One has seen others who have made the deliverance
or the glory of their country the whole object of their
ambition.

But one Man set before Himself a still more lofty
object. At a time when the idea of the *human race*
was only beginning to dawn upon the most advanced
minds, that mass which we call *humanity*, divided
into nations hostile one to another, almost wholly
disintegrated by the egoism of individuals, presented
itself to His mind in its essential unity; He took
this humanity in its entirety to His heart as His
own people,—His family whom He should save. He
looked the two tyrants who were oppressing it, and
whose rule over it seemed to form an integral part
of the very existence of that race—Sin and Death
—in the face. And He dared to say, This being,
sinful and mortal, is not man such as God intended
him to be, or now wills him to be. God reigns
over all! Let sin flee before Him, and let death
perish! And let holiness and immortality, those
two characteristic features of the work of God, shine
forth upon this earth which He has created for the
manifestation of His glory!

And this grand idea He has adopted and elaborated.
This task He took upon Himself as that of His life;
He did not shrink back in presence of the apparent
impossibility of its accomplishment. In order to
execute the work of which He alone dared to conceive the idea, He did not begin with any great plan

of social reform. His first work was upon Himself : He realised the essential, true, Good in the humble sphere of His personal existence—in that which was apprehended immediately by His moral consciousness. In that field did He fight with the first enemy, sin, and overcame it. He refused it any foothold in His heart and life, and made the holy will of God to be the absolute master of His existence.

This first victory gained, He found Himself face to face with the second enemy, death. This adversary appeared even more invincible ; for death is not, like sin, the result of a free determination of the human will ; it is a law which seems to pass upon humanity with the power of fate, and to envelope Nature herself. Nevertheless, in presence of this terrifying sight, the courage of the Divine hero did not flinch. He looked the gloomy tyrant in the face, and by the light of God He perceived that it was but a phantom, which at the single word *grace*, when it descended from heaven, would vanish away. He recognised in death, inflicted upon man, the result of a sentence of condemnation ; and He boldly believed that if once the condemnation were removed, the throne of death would be overturned. He discerned two causes of that condemnation—*sin* which calls for it, and the *law* which pronounces it. As for sin, He had already overcome it in His own person ; and He was reserving to Himself the task of overcoming it in humanity also. Already had He kindled here below, in His own person, a central fire of perfect holiness, and He beheld, grouping themselves around it, all those who seek for light, and who *do the truth*.[1]

But the law? It is a Divine manifestation. It cannot be treated in the way sin is; it cannot be destroyed; all that can be done is to disarm it, and this can only be effected by meeting all its just demands.

Here is the way in which this Man resolved to vanquish the law: He had in His life offered to it that perfect obedience which it demanded; He had by His death offered the atonement which was required by the transgressions of its violators. By this means He had gained over to His side the justice of God, which hitherto had been against us. And as God had pronounced upon the guilty a sentence of condemnation which was their death-warrant, Jesus staked His righteousness to pronounce upon those who believed in Him an absolution which is their life.

Sin being vanquished, the law satisfied, the two foundations of the kingdom of death were undermined, and its power fell.

In the resurrection of Jesus Christ the victory which had just been obtained over death was for the first time displayed. And this first prey torn from the tyrant's grasp is the guarantee of the deliverance and future resurrection of the whole of justified humanity. The Church glorified will be the magnificent harvest

[1] Cf. Luke xii. 49, and John iii. 21.

of which Jesus risen was the firstfruits. Complete incorruption, moral and physical, will crown the work which the heroic love of Jesus dared to conceive and succeeded in accomplishing. What were the works of Thrasybulus, of Tell, of Washington, compared with that of such a deliverer ?

" Since by man came death, by man came also the resurrection of the dead. . . . . O death, where is thy sting ? O grave, where is thy victory ? The sting of death is sin ; and the strength of sin is the law. But thanks be to God, which giveth us the victory through our Lord Jesus Christ."[1]

How can we think it any longer wonderful that He Who conceived and has accomplished such a work as this, ceases not to gather around Himself all the slaves of sin and death that are to be found here below, who feel the weight of their chains—all who exclaim with St. Paul, " Wretched man that I am ! Who shall deliver me ? " Is it surprising that this Being should have succeeded in reaching that result which astonished the genius whom nothing, it might have seemed, could any longer astonish, that of " making of every human soul an appendage of His own."

Jesus is necessary to the human soul, because He has made Himself its indispensable fellow-worker in the accomplishment of its moral destiny.

---

[1] I Cor. xv. 21, 55—57.

4

THE FOUR PRINCIPAL APOSTLES

THE person of the Lord has been presented to us in four pictures, of which each, as we have seen, brings into relief some one particular aspect of His relations with God and with the world.

The work of Christ for the salvation of humanity is also set forth in the New Testament under four different points of view.

Ancient orthodoxy ignored all such contrasts. Modern criticism exaggerates them, and makes them out to be contradictions. Perhaps the time has now arrived at which a just appreciation of this diversity will make its way in the Church, and when the thoughtful Christian, far from ignoring the unity which is at the bottom of this variety, will admire the abundance of various forms in which, under the influence of different factors, one and the same life can clothe itself.

Will any one ask how such contrasts could arise among writers equally inspired? The question itself shews how ill the idea of inspiration has been understood in the Church, and what a transformation it will have to undergo. Just as the water with which we water the seed sown in the ground does not create the plant which grows out of it, but stimulates the development of the organs which had previously been formed in the germ, and sets their power in action, so in the same way the Holy Spirit does not substitute Himself for the individuality of the sacred author; He awakens his faculties, He groups his experiences, He places him in immediate contact with salvation, and by that means confers upon him a special gift— the distinct intuition of that aspect of gospel truth which answers most specially to his own character and needs. For, as M. Reuss most admirably says, speaking of the difference between the sacred writers, "The pole which attracted the magnetic needle of their sentiment, or of their intelligence, was not situated for all at the same point on the sphere of revelation."

This is just what St. Paul himself wished to express when he made use of the expression, "*my* gospel." [1]

The four different conceptions of the nature of Christian salvation which we are about to study are those of Peter, of James and Paul, and lastly of John.

We place Peter at the head, not only in conformity with history, which assigns to him the first place chronologically, but chiefly because his conception of the gospel seems to us the most instinctive, that which reproduces most simply and directly the first impres-

---

[1] Rom. ii. 16 ; xvi. 25 ; 2 Tim. ii. 8.

sion. We are aware that the epistle in which this conception is set forth is later in date than the epistle of James, and than the larger number of those of Paul. But the preaching of Peter, as a missionary, furnished, nevertheless, the body of doctrine which served as a foundation for others which were brought out later.

The elements contained in the preaching of that apostle divide themselves into the two types of doctrine, apparently opposed to one another, of James and Paul. A contrast does exist ; and this contrast seems even to bear the traces of deliberate intention. How far does this difference extend ? This is the point we have to determine accurately.

If we speak here of James, it is not that we regard him as one of the apostles properly so called. But his qualification as *the Lord's brother*, his moral character, which very soon gained for him the veneration of the first Christians, and the high position which he occupied in the Church at Jerusalem, confer upon the epistle which he has left us, and upon the conception of the gospel of which that epistle is the depositary, a dignity in some degree apostolic.

The higher unity into which the contrast between James and Paul resolves itself manifest itself in John. The type of gospel which characterises the writings of this apostle is in many respects a reproduction of that which we meet with in Peter. But these two types differ as the maturity of the old man differs from the artless freshness of the child, or as the rich colours

shed by the setting sun differ from the fresh tints
poured forth by it at its rising.

1

THE APOSTLE PETER

We will first collect all we can ascertain concerning the personality and the religious development
of this apostle. We will then compare with these
facts the intuitions which characterise his teaching,
whether in the Acts or in his epistle.[1] And thus we
shall endeavour to determine what was the special
benefit offered by the gospel salvation which won
his heart and satisfied his deepest aspirations.

The surname of *Peter*, which Jesus gave to Simon,
son of Jona, at his first interview with Him, indicates
the impression he made upon Him. He recognised
in him a young man of courageous impulses, and an
energy always ready to take the initiative—the man
given Him by God, to serve, if we may use the expression, as a kind of pivot for the work He was about to
undertake. We can see nothing in this honourable
designation to make us suppose that Peter was
endowed with a profound contemplative genius, or
with a mind gifted with great dialectic sagacity.

[1] We speak here deliberately of only *one* epistle of Peter.
The ecclesiastical tradition of the first centuries concerning the
second epistle, as well as the study of that document itself,
compel us to exclude it, if not from the Canon, at least from the
number of the genuine apostolic books.

Jesus was thinking only of aptitude in the sphere of *practical* life. All that is implied by a superiority of this kind is, either a calm and sound judgment, if the task to be taken in hand is to edify and to preserve, or else warmth of heart, freshness of imagination, and the faculty of giving oneself up enthusiastically, if the work is rather to found and create.

Now it is evidently to this last type of men that St. Peter belonged. This apostle had always more of free impulse than of reflection. This characteristic makes us understand at once the contagious energy of his faith, and its surprising moments of weakness.

It was doubtless in consideration of these ruling qualities of his mind that Jesus set Peter at the head of the college of the twelve, and entrusted him with the direction of the work they were about to do;[1] which, however, in no way implied any permanent or universal supremacy over Christendom in general. Even at Jerusalem the words of James seem to have had more weight than his; and as to the Gentile churches, the absolute independence of St. Paul's apostolate was recognised by the representatives of the apostles, and by Peter himself, in a decisive conference. The primacy as a leader which was assigned to Peter, was by common consent limited to the mission of the twelve with regard to Israel; and the province of the evangelisation of the heathen world, which was recognised as a wholly distinct sphere, was

---

[1] Matt. xvi. 18 ; Luke xxii. 32 ; John xxi. 15—17.

entrusted by the Lord to Paul. "When they saw," says St. Paul, "that the gospel of the uncircumcision was committed unto me, as the gospel of the circumcision was unto Peter; (for He that wrought effectually in Peter to the apostleship of the circumcision, the same was mighty in me toward the Gentiles)."[1] How, with such words before us, can we, without charging Paul with heresy, continue to maintain that the Western Churches, all of which belong to the domain of the Gentiles, are under the patronage of the Apostle Peter? The province of Paul was placed not *within* that of Peter, but *alongside* and *outside* of it. There existed between these two agents of the Lord a relationship of association, but not at all of subordination.[2]

We know nothing of the moral development of Peter up to the time of his first meeting with Jesus.

That ardent spirit, that fervent heart, that lively imagination, had, certainly, up to that time, found their religious sustenance in the intuitions revealed to Israel by the word of prophecy, and typically figured in the Levitical worship. At every Passover at which he was present, the young worshipper beheld the chosen people assembled in their metropolis and in their temple. He took part in the sacrifice of the paschal lamb and in the sacred feast which followed, and he saw in those rites the pledge of the future deliverance and glory of that people.

---

[1] Gal. ii. 7, 8.   [2] Gal. ii. 9, "The right hand of fellowship."

The land of Canaan appeared to him as the centre of that kingdom of God which was to extend the dominion of the law of Israel to the ends of the earth ; and the caravans which he saw returning after the feast into all the different countries of the heathen world, appeared to him as so many bodies of troops destined to prepare the way for the conquest of the world.

These views, though not erroneous, had to undergo a transformation before they could correspond perfectly with the truth of things. This process began when Peter became a disciple of John the Baptist and heard that bold preacher laying down, without reserve, holiness as the foundation of the Messianic work. It was completed when, from the school of John the Baptist, the young patriot passed to that of Jesus. Then it was that all those theocratic ideas upon which his spirit had fed began to take in his mind a direction more and more spiritual.

But this transformation was not effected without a crisis. We know that none among the apostles had more difficulty than St. Peter in accepting the idea of the sufferings of Christ and of His rejection by the people. We call to mind his protest, as bold, to say the least, as the noble confession which had preceded it : " That be far from Thee, Lord. This shall not be unto thee." The vision of Messianic glory which filled his heart left no room in it for expectations so gloomy. The Cross was therefore, to him especially,

a terrible surprise; the death-blow to the false
Messianic idea which he, like the rest of the apostles,
had inherited from the prevalent doctrine of his time.

But as no one was more confounded than Peter by
that catastrophe, so no one was more overjoyed and
transported by the resurrection of Jesus. The Messianic ideal, which had suffered temporary eclipse in
his heart, shone out afresh, transformed and transfigured, like Jesus Himself. The kingdom which he was
expecting took then, to his eyes, a heavenly character.
The brightness of that glorious state of things would
doubtless extend its rays even to the earth; but the
kingdom of the risen Messiah meant thenceforth, to
Peter's mind, something different from, and better
than, a Mosaism universally victorious, and a perfected
earth.

Among all the apostles, then, Peter is the one who
must have felt most keenly in his heart the reaction caused by his Master's resurrection. This event
occupied, in his life, the place which the apparition of
Jesus in glory did in that of Paul; it divided his
life into two halves, as distinct from each other as the
shadow and the light of noonday.

These results, gathered from the Gospels, will interpret to us the peculiar aspect in which the Christian
salvation is presented to us in the sermons attributed
to him in the Acts and in his epistle.

We notice naturally, above all, in these records of
Peter's faith, the traces of the vivid impression made

upon him by the time which he spent here below in the company of Jesus. He feels profoundly the greatness of the privilege which attaches to the position of an eye-witness which had been granted to him. It is with this feeling that he says in the Acts : "We who did eat and drink with Him ;" and that, in his epistle, he addresses to the Christians in Asia Minor, who had not enjoyed the same privilege as himself, those touching words : "Whom having not seen, ye love."[1] We may notice also the freshness of personal recollection in that picture of the meekness of Jesus : "Who, when He was reviled, reviled not again ; when He suffered, He threatened not ; but committed Himself to Him that judgeth righteously."[2] The author of these words need scarcely have designated himself, as he does, "a witness of the sufferings of Christ."[3]

But the event which formed the principal object of his faith is evidently the Resurrection, with its complement, the Ascension. " God has raised up Jesus,"—this is the theme of his discourse. " Blessed be the God and Father of our Lord Jesus Christ, which according to His abundant mercy hath begotten us again unto a lively hope by the resurrection of Jesus Christ from the dead, to an inheritance incorruptible and undefiled, and that fadeth not away, reserved in heaven for you:"[4] this is the introduction to his epistle. Might we not imagine ourselves listening to

---

[1] Acts x. 41 ; I Pet. i. 8.
[2] I Pet. ii. 23.
[3] I Pet. v. I.
[4] I Pet. i. 3, 4.

an account of the moral resurrection of the apostle
himself on that Easter morning ?   His mind delights
in recurring to the fact of the Resurrection.   Baptism
itself appears to him as the act by which the conscience
of the believer joins itself consciously to Jesus Christ
risen (iii. 21).   We see clearly that it is by this
decisive event that Jesus became to him the rock of
his faith.

Peter was a man of heart and imagination.   This
is the impression left upon us by his whole epistle.
We see in it no trace of systematic doctrinal exposition ; it is entirely of a practical character ; and if,
from time to time, the author takes a spring into the
sphere of dogmatic teaching, he cannot sustain himself
long in those regions which are evidently unfamiliar
to him, and he descends again immediately into the
domain of moral application.   But these practical
instructions are clothed in the freshest and most
poetical imagery, which Peter borrows for the most
part from the symbols of the theocracy.   All his
theology is summed up in one word : the New
Covenant is the Old, realised under the form given by
the Spirit.

For the land of Canaan, that heritage which Israel
profaned, Christ substitutes henceforth the heritage
which man can neither corrupt nor defile, and which is
already reserved in heaven for us.[1]   The lamb which
every Israelite set apart five days before the Passover,

---

[1] 1 Pet. i. 3—5.

and which represented that to which the nation owed
its deliverance in Egypt, was but the symbol of the
Lamb without blemish and without spot, whom God
had fore-ordained before the foundation of the world,
and who has now redeemed us by His blood from
that subjection to vanity which we have inherited
from our fathers.[1]

The Church is the reality symbolised by the ancient
people of God. To her belong all the titles of honour
which Moses had given by anticipation to Israel,
and which were applicable to it only in virtue of a
typical consecration : " Ye are the chosen generation,
the royal priesthood, the holy nation, the peculiar
people." [2]

Just as the ancient Israel lived in great measure
dispersed in the heathen countries, so does Christendom
live on earth, disseminated in a great number of
churches, which, like colonies that have been founded
in a foreign soil, keep up an aspiration after return
to their native country. That is, if I am not mistaken,
the true meaning of the expressions made use of by
Peter in the introduction to his epistle (i. 1, 2): " To
the *expatriated elect* of the dispersion, in Pontus,
Galatia, etc."[3] The Jews used to designate by the
expression *the dispersion* (*diaspora*) all that portion of
the nation which lived in the heathen countries, far

---

[1] 1 Pet. i. 18—20.
[2] 1 Pet. ii. 9, 10 ; cf. Exod. xix. 5, 6.
[3] We adopt this translation of M. Renan as the most exact
and the most *French*.

from the Holy Land and from the Israelite metropolis.
We cannot think that St. Peter at all intends to say,
as has been supposed, that he is addressing only
ancient Jews; too many passages evidently presuppose the pagan origin of some at least of his
readers. Neither does he intend to say, as M. Renan
thinks, that those Christians among the Gentiles are,
as it were, a part of the people of Israel, and that for
them also " Jerusalem is the only point in the world
in which they are not in a state of exile." How could
Peter, in any sense whatever, make of the earthly
Jerusalem the true home of the heathen populations,
now Christian, of Asia Minor? Far from the Church
being confounded in his eyes with the Synagogue, the
moment at which he was writing was the critical one
when the name of *Christians*, by which believers were
beginning to be designated, expressly distinguished
them from the Jews, with whom the heathen had until
then confounded them; when those edicts of toleration which covered the Jewish religion ceased, for that
reason, any longer to shelter them; and when they
found themselves exposed to persecution, that dread
contingency for which St. Peter specially labours to
prepare them in this epistle.

The true sense of this expression, "*to the expatriated
elect,*" comes out clearly, in the first place, in the very
fact of the association with each other of these two
words, which forbids our assigning to the second of
them a coarse material sense; but above all, from the

passage, ii. 11, where this same word[1] is used certainly in the spiritual sense: " I beseech you as strangers and pilgrims, abstain from fleshly lusts, which war against the soul." Christians, as strangers and pilgrims here below, must not allow themselves to be caught by the allurements of this land of exile, nor to be hindered in their march towards the heavenly country which has been won for them by Jesus Christ. The Canaan, then, from which they are separated, is not the earthly one, but that heavenly Canaan of which Palestine was but the image. And the churches dispersed through the empire are, in relation to the Church triumphant in heaven, a *diaspora*, like that composed of the Jewish communities dispersed through the pagan countries, in its relation to that part of the nation which is fortunate enough to inhabit Jerusalem and the Holy Land.

With this allegorical sense of the words, *expatriated* and *dispersion*, in the introduction to the epistle, agrees the figurative use of the name *Babylon* in the last lines of this document. This term is borrowed from the same symbolical language which reigns in the whole epistle. The Fathers were not mistaken there. M. Renan fully admits and confirms their interpretation.[2] Babylon indicates the capital of the

---

[1] *Parepidemoi.*

[2] *Antichrist*, p. 122. We should have other reasons to add to those adduced by M. Renan, but it seems to us superfluous to do so.

vast empire in which the Christians are now dispersed, as the Jewish tribes had formerly been in Chaldea. It is in Rome that St. Peter is writing, and it is from thence that he sees with his mind's eye those edicts of persecution issuing, which are soon to reach to all the provinces of the monarchy.   It is in this way that the first and last words of the epistle answer to each other: *the exiles, Babylon*.

We could cite in addition many other instances ; they would lead us to the same result.   The state of salvation presented itself to the eyes of Peter as a supra-terrestrial theocracy, a transfigured Canaan. Beauty incorruptible, holiness raised above all possibility of profanation, such are the features of that higher order of things of which the foundation was laid by the resurrection of Jesus Christ, and which awaits us in that upper world.   It is *glory*, in the scriptural and perfect sense of that word.

This is the divine magnet, of which the attraction had mastered the warm heart of the apostle.   The Resurrection was the fact in which he had seen this ideal approaching him, and had been able to grasp the pledge of its realisation.   The dominant characteristic of his faith became, consequently, the glorious expectation of that state—*hope*.

That would naturally have happened in the case of a devout Jew, who had become a Christian and an apostle, and in whose character the ruling forces were the impulses of the heart and the fire of the imagination.   In such an one the old Israelite ambition must disappear in presence of the Cross, and revive at the sight of the Risen One, but transformed then into the hope of the true glory,—of that which has holiness for its principle, and heaven for its stage.

There remains one important point to be cleared up.   It is asserted that Peter was an advocate for the maintenance of the Mosaic law within the Church ; that not only did he continue to observe it himself, with all the Christians of Jewish origin, but that he wished even to impose it upon converts from among the Gentiles, as a condition of salvation.[1]

But if Peter had attributed such importance to the observance of the law, whether for the Gentiles or for himself, how could he have freed himself and them from it, *even for a time*, at Antioch ?   How should his party at Corinth be expressly distinguished by St. Paul from the party designated as that "*of Christ*," which, according to 2 Corinthians,[2] was certainly that of the judaizing Christians ?   There is yet another consideration.   If we attributed that opinion to Peter, we

---

[1] M. Nicolas, *Etudes sur le Nouveau Testament*, pp. 224, 235, 243—245.   M. Sabatier associates himself completely with this way of thinking, in his article on Paul of Tarsus, the Apostle of the Gentiles, *Revue Chrétienne*, July, 1873.   (" Mark, Barnabas, Silvanus forsake Paul, and attach themselves to the twelve.")   MM. Reuss and Renan are more cautious in their judgment, though they also come under the unhealthy influence of Baur, an influence from which the Church recovers only by slow degrees.

[2] 1 Cor. i. 12 compared with 2 Cor. x. 7, xi. 21, 22.

should be absolutely compelled to charge the whole narrative of the Acts with falsehood, since in it Peter himself combats this Pharisaic tendency; we should have to do violence to the plain meaning of Gal. ii., in which St. Paul contrasts the apostles with the *false brethren* who wished to compel the Gentile Christians to practise circumcision;[1] we should have, lastly, to make up our minds to brand as unauthentic St. Peter's first epistle, one of the documents of the New Testament to the authority and use of which in the Church we have the earliest testimonies. For there is not a single mention of the law in that epistle, which could not have been the case had its author still regarded the Mosaic observances as necessary for Christians; so much the more as, from the beginning to the end, his thoughts are moving in the sphere of precepts of morality.

All the documents, impartially consulted, agree in shewing that St. Peter, as well as most of the Christians of Jewish origin, continued to observe the law as a form originally of divine institution, and not yet abolished by God Himself; but without imposing it upon the Gentiles, and consequently also without making its observance a condition of salvation; since if such observance had been in their view a second

---

[1] v. 6. " But (δὲ) those who seemed to be somewhat (James, Peter, and John, v. 9) *added nothing* to me" (that is to say, imposed nothing new; in connection with v. 2, "I *communicated* unto them that gospel which I preach among the Gentiles.")

condition of salvation equivalent to faith, they evidently could not have absolved the Gentiles from it. From this point of view we can understand the vacillations of Paul and Barnabas in their practical conduct. A pious observance does not stand on the same ground as an absolute moral obligation ; it is a conventional matter from which it may be allowable temporarily to dispense oneself.

In the first epistle, Peter insists more exclusively than Paul upon moral duties, but without ever resting them upon any other foundation than that of faith ; he leans, at the same time, more strongly than James, upon the gospel verities ; for instance, upon redemption by the blood of Christ, the descent of Jesus into *Scheol*, His resurrection, etc., but never in any other aspect than that of their practical application.[1]

We have, then, a right to say that in him we find

---

[1] The essay of M. Nicolas on St. Peter's first epistle presents a strange specimen of scientific levity. This writer wishes to prove that the object of this epistle is to labour at the *reconciliation* of Paulinism and Judæo-Christianism. To this end M. Nicolas says : " If we consider, lastly, that *this epistle concludes* by an apology for St. Paul, whose epistles, sometimes hard to be understood, are wrested from their true sense by ignorant persons . . . (1 Pet. iii. 15, 16)." (p. 266.) Now these words, quoted as evidence of the tendency of the first epistle of Peter, do not belong to that treatise ; they are found, as everybody knows, in the second epistle !—It is, then, a fact that it is possible to write a criticism on a book of the Bible, by consulting for the purpose volumes of learned Germans, . . . while at the same time omitting to read the book itself. What a criticism of criticism—of this specimen of it at least !

the simple synthesis, not formulated systematically, of the elements, whose antithesis in relation to each other is about to be presented to us in the conceptions of Peter and of Paul.

2

THE APOSTLE JAMES

As Peter personifies in himself the normal transition from the Jewish economy into the free grace of Christianity, James represents—I beg to be allowed the expression—the transition into that transition.

The person best known under this name in the gospel story is the son of Zebedee, the brother of the apostle John, and himself an apostle. He suffered martyrdom about fifteen years after Pentecost, in 44, by order of King Herod Agrippa.[1]

The New Testament mentions another apostle of the name of James the son of Alpheus; this latter was not, like the former, of the rank of the chief apostles; he belonged to the lower group of the college of the twelve.

Lastly, mention is sometimes made of a James surnamed *the brother of the Lord*.[2] This title leaves no room to doubt the identity of this person with the James who is placed at the head of all the lists of the brothers of Jesus given in the Gospels and in the Acts.[3] It remains to enquire whether or no, as many learned

---

[1] Acts xii. 2.   [3] Matt. xiii. 55, for instance.

[2] Gal. i. 19, for instance.

men in all ages have thought, this James was the same
as the one last mentioned, the apostle James, the son
of Alpheus. According to a very ancient tradition,
Joseph, the reputed father of Jesus, had a brother
named *Cleophas*. Now this name may be considered
as the Aramaic equivalent of the Greek *Alpheus*, so
that James the son of Alpheus may well have been
the nephew of Joseph, and the first cousin of Jesus.
We must, according to this supposition, give to the
word *brother*, in the expression " the brother of Jesus,"
the sense of *cousin ;* and it is permissible to suppose
either that, after the death of Cleophas, his wife and
son came to live in the house of Joseph and Mary, or
that, after the death of Joseph, Mary and Jesus, her
only son, took up their abode with Cleophas. Brought
up together, the children of the two families would
have been, in the language of ordinary life, designated
as brothers, not cousins.

But this combination is inconsistent with the many
passages in the Gospels which prove that the *brothers
of Jesus* were not, during His lifetime, believers, nor,
consequently, apostles.[1] There is no exception made
to this statement. The incompatibility of these two
characters is true, therefore, also in the case of James.
Besides, in the Acts and in 1 Corinthians, the brothers
of Jesus are distinguished from the apostles.[2]

---

[1] Mark iii. 21, 31 ; John vii. 5: " Neither did His brethren
believe in Him."

[2] Acts i. 13, 14 ; 1 Cor. ix. 5.

It is impossible, therefore, to identify James the apostle, the son of Alpheus, with James the Lord's brother; and it is consequently natural to suppose the latter to have been either a son of Joseph by a former marriage, or a son of Joseph and Mary, a younger brother of Jesus.

It is to this James, called the *Lord's brother*, that ecclesiastical tradition is generally agreed in ascribing the first of our catholic epistles which sets forth the view of Christian doctrine we have now to analyse.

James and Peter both of them came out of a world of the most marked Jewish character; but there were well-defined differences in the disposition and in the development of the two men. Both of them were of simple, upright, practical natures; but Peter's temperament was vivacious and impressionable, whilst in James the conscience and the judgment seem to have predominated.

According to the accounts given by the Fathers, James must have always led a severely ascetic life, after the manner of those Israelites who took the life-long vows of a Nazarite, such as were Samson and John the Baptist. The following is the way in which a Father of the second century, Hegesippus, describes, in language a little emphatic, his manner of life: " He was a saint from before his birth. He never drank wine or strong drink; he abstained altogether from animal food. He never cut his hair. He never allowed himself the use either of anointing or the bath."

Did James choose this kind of life, which was regarded amongst the Jews as especially holy, from a secret feeling of rivalry or jealousy with regard to his Brother, whose high destiny was not entirely unknown to him? One could understand on this hypothesis the sort of hostility of which we seem to detect indications in his conduct during the ministry of Jesus.[1] His resistance was at last overcome by a manifestation of the Risen One, of which—and this is a strange circumstance for those who make Paul the fierce enemy of James—the first epistle to the Corinthians alone has preserved the memory.[2] James recognised in the vanquisher of death the Messiah whom he had failed to discern in the person of his Brother during the days of His flesh—*the Lord of glory.*[3]

As soon as he entered the Church, he took a prominent position in it. The extraordinary consideration accorded to him, although he did not bear the title of apostle, was due doubtless to two causes,—to his relationship to Jesus, which carried weight with the Jewish Christians in whom the purely spiritual appreciation of things was as yet not highly developed,—and to his

---

[1] Mark iii. 21, 31 ; John vii. 5.

[2] 1 Cor. xv. 7: "After that, He was seen of James." It is well known how eagerly this slight hint has been laid hold of, and how largely it has been amplified by the Judæo-Christian apocryphal Gospels.

[3] James ii. 1.

rigorous legalism, which he did not at all renounce after he had reached the life of faith, and which gained him the favour of the whole Jewish people. This circumstance rendered him more fit than any other person to act as a link—a sort of bridge of connection —between the Synagogue and the Church. Thus he was quite naturally the person to carry on the work of the forerunner, taking his place apparently as a member of the Jewish nation, of which he strictly observed the law, and at the same time loudly proclaiming Jesus as the national Messiah, the King of Israel.

Accordingly, none of the apostles seem to have had so much prestige with the mass of the people as he had. Not having taken part with Jesus in the public conflicts into which His ministry brought Him, his popularity suffered less than theirs from his profession of the Christian faith. Moreover, the twelve were occupied with their mission, which often called them away from Jerusalem, while James, settled in the metropolis, became by degrees the centre of the most highly revered of the churches of Christendom. Whether the office of bishop—that is to say, in the primitive language of the Church, head of the college of presbyters—was officially conferred upon him, or whether this pre-eminence grew naturally out of his circumstances, makes little difference. It is a fact that he governed the mother-Church. Paul, in the account he gives of the conference which he held with the three representatives of that Church, places him *before* Peter and John.[1] It is in his house that, at the time of Paul's last visit to Jerusalem, the council of presbyters meets to receive the apostle of the Gentiles.[2] It is in his hands that Paul deposits the collection he has been making in all the churches of Asia and Greece on behalf of the Christians in the capital. As late as the fourth century, the episcopal chair of James was still shewn in Jerusalem.[3]

Faith in Christ would, we can easily understand, naturally take, in such a man, a peculiar form, especially as compared with the faith of Peter. To the causes of difference which we have already indicated, we will, with Neander, add the following :—Peter, in common with the other apostles, had only known Jesus from the commencement of His public ministry, whilst James had lived with Him on familiar terms from his childhood. The person of Jesus had therefore, in his mind, a reality independent of His office as the Messiah. And when this latter character was at length revealed to him in his Brother, it was only a new feature which had to be added to the conception which he had already formed of Him ; it was not the foundation of the knowledge he had of His person. His new faith was only the crown of the relation in which He had stood to him before.[4] There is perhaps

---

[1] Gal. ii. 9.   [2] Acts xxi. 18.
[3] Eusebius, vii. 19 (Læmmer's edition).
[4] Is there any allusion to this fact in 2 Cor. v. 16?

some connection between this fact and the difference that marks the Christian intuition of Peter and of James, a difference which we might define by saying that, in the mind of the former, Christianity appeared as a Judaism *transformed*, whilst the latter seems rather to have regarded it as a Judaism *completed*.

This result, to which we are led by the historical data which we gather from the New Testament and from the Fathers, is in accordance with the contents of the epistle which Christian antiquity attributes to the first bishop of Jerusalem. As we read this letter, we seem to ourselves to discern all the time, as through a transparent veil, the well-known form of this personage, unique in its kind.

The author designates himself, not as an *apostle*, as he would doubtless have done had he been invested with that office, but as a *servant* of the Lord Jesus Christ. The title of the Lord's *brother*, given to him by the Church, would have been in him pretentious and unsuitable.

He addresses his epistle "to the *twelve tribes* which are scattered abroad." It might seem from this address that those for whom it was intended were still Jews. But this conclusion is inadmissible; for faith in Jesus Christ is expressly presupposed in the readers of this epistle, in many passages.[1] Looking at it from another side there is no indication that we

---

[1] i, 1. "Servant of the Lord Jesus Christ (the Messiah);" ii. 1, "Jesus Christ the Lord of glory." (Cf. also v. 6 and 8.)

are to attribute to these words, as we have done to
some similar expressions in 1 Peter, a spiritual sense,
and to see in them a figurative description of the
Christian Church generally.   What meaning then are
we to give to this address?   Neander seems to us to
have solved the difficulty: " The author," he says,
" regards the recognition of Jesus as the Messiah as
an essential feature of true Judaism.   Believers are
in his eyes the only true Israelites.   For Christianity
is in his view Judaism come to its perfection."   Such
in truth must the relation between the two economies
have appeared to the mind of a man in whom the
faith in Christ had been but the matured flower of the
Israelitish life.

The epistle contains some minor features still
more characteristic.

It insists repeatedly and urgently upon the duty of
prayer.   Now we know that the Lord's brother was
peculiarly a man of prayer.   Hegesippus asserts
that he was so continually kneeling upon the
temple steps, interceding on behalf of the people,
that " his knees had become hard like those of a
camel."

In the whole of this epistle there breathes a spirit
of vigorous moral energy, and even of high austerity.
Religious belief has no value, according to James,
save so far as it is accompanied by the practice of
what is right.   Pious words without good works are
but so much wind.   We must learn to hate the world,

the enemy of God, if we would possess in its reality the love of God. We discern clearly in these indications the character of the man who, in the mouth of the whole Jewish nation, bore the title which the Athenians of old had given to the best of the Greeks, *the just one*, and who, in virtue of his holy life, so universally admired, and of his constant intercession for Israel, was also called *Obliam*, that is to say, the *wall* (or bulwark) *of the nation*. We learn from the Jewish historian, Josephus,[1] that many in Israel regarded the murder of this just man as the sweeping away of the last of the embankments which still protected Jerusalem from the in-pouring of the Divine judgments.

It is remarkable that James speaks of Jesus in his epistle by the title, *the just one*, by which he was himself known : " ye have condemned and killed the just."[2] It is as if he had desired to cast his crown beforehand at the feet of his Divine Brother.

Lastly, let us not forget that to write such an epistle, so weighty, so firm, so severe even, "to the twelve tribes which are scattered abroad"—that is to say, to all the Judæo-Christian communities, and even to the whole Jewish nation, so far as it was destined to become Christian—a man was needed who should feel himself possessed of exceptional consideration, and of the authority, in some sort, of a prophet. Now James, the Lord's brother, is pro-

---

[1] *Complete Works of Josephus.* Kregel Publications. 1962.   [2] **v. 6.**

bably the only Christian personage who ever occupied such a position.

It is therefore with more reason than good taste that M. Renan says of the epistle of James and of 1 Peter: " The circumstantial details which we meet with in these epistles, anticipate facts known to us from external evidence, and may be included in them." And this remark applies, as we are about to see, to the moral situation of those for whom the epistle was intended, no less than to the character of its author.

When St. Paul summons Jewish morality to the bar of judgment, at the beginning of the epistle to the Romans (ii.), the principal fault with which he charges it is that it substitutes the profession of the lips for practical obedience to the law. Every one knows that this is precisely the danger against which, above all others, James warns his readers. Here then, already, we have come upon a point in which the epistle perfectly fits the needs of Judæo-Christian communities.

Religious fluency, the lust of teaching, the rage for casuistical discussion, have in all ages been the characteristic features of pharisaic piety. The third chapter of the epistle is entirely devoted to attacking these faults.

One of the distinctive features of the Church in Jerusalem, and of the Judæo-Christian communities, seems to have been the general poverty of their

members.   Rationalism wishes to see in this poverty
the natural result of the community of goods which,
as it is pretended, had established itself after Pentecost.   But did not Jesus Himself, during His sojourn
here below, already see a clear line of demarcation
beginning to be drawn between the indigent portion
of the people who received Him favourably, and the
richer classes who, with few exceptions, openly took
part against Him ?[1]   The occasional acts of liberality
mentioned by Luke in the picture he gives us of the
primitive Church, could not have produced effects so
general, and above all, so lasting.   Recruited for the
most part from among the poorer classes of the popu-
lation, the churches of Judea depended for their work
and for their subsistence upon the rich who detested
them.   These are the very simple causes of that indigence which the rest of Christendom was so often
called upon to aid.   This state of general poverty is
just what we perceive in the communities which James
addresses.   The appearance of a rich man is an event
to be noticed : every one is tempted servilely to do
him homage.   " Let the brother of low degree rejoice
in that he is exalted, and the rich in that he is made
low."   As for the opulent grandees, Pharisees, and
Sadducees, living in Jerusalem amidst the pleasures of
a life of the most unbridled luxury, James addresses

---

[1] Luke vi. 20—26.   " Woe unto you that are rich ! woe unto
you that are full ! . . . Blessed be ye poor : blessed are ye that
hunger."

them bluntly in these words: "Go to now, ye rich men, weep and howl! your riches are corrupted, and your garments are moth-eaten. Your gold and silver is cankered; the rust of them shall eat your flesh as it were fire!"[1]

M. Renan reads in these words a condemnation of riches *as such*. We see fermenting here, according to his view, the spirit of social revolutions. We are to recognise in the words the programme of the Ebionites,[2] of which James has made himself the organ. M. Renan is mistaken here, as he is also in his explanation of the analogous passages in the Gospels. It is not rich men in the abstract, but rich men such as those James saw actually before him, that he is here characterising and condemning; just as Jesus had done before him. "Do not rich men *oppress you,* and *draw you before the judgment seats?* Do not they *blaspheme* that worthy name *by which ye are called?*" They "keep back the *hire of the labourers,* whose cries reach to heaven." They "*live in pleasure;*" they "*nourish their hearts* as in a day of slaughter." Is it not indeed they, "who have *condemned* and *killed the just* who did not resist them?"[3] It is not therefore against riches in themselves, but against that misuse of riches which he was witnessing every day in Jerusalem, that James rises up to protest.

---

[1] ii. 1—6 ; i. 10 ; v. 1—5.
[2] A sect which makes a principle of poverty.
[3] ii. 6, 7 ; v. 5, 6.

Scarcely eight years intervened between this prophetic warning and the catastrophe which, in the year 70, fulfilled it. It must have been in fact a little before the year 62 that this epistle was composed. For that was the year in which Ananias the high priest caused James to be cast down from the top of the temple. The latter was at that time at the highest point of his favour with the people. That was, doubtless, the time at which he composed his epistle. It was intended for circulation amongst the Judæo-Christian churches of Palestine and Syria, the only countries in which were to be found communities of wholly Jewish origin, such as are presupposed in this letter. Perhaps the epistle was distributed at Jerusalem during one of those great national feasts which still drew to that city the representatives of all those churches, of those " *thousands of Jews which believe,*" according to the expression of James when speaking to Paul.[1] If such is the origin of our epistle, we can easily understand how it came to pass that this document appeared first in the canon of the churches of those countries, in the Syriac version of the New Testament called *Peschito*, and did not gain currency in the West till a somewhat later date.

We are now in a position to estimate aright the spirit of this document, and to define more accurately

---

[1] Acts xxi. 20.

the conception which its author had formed of the Christian salvation.

Salvation depended, in his eyes, upon the moral conduct of man—upon the faithfulness with which he fulfilled the will of God : " Was not Abraham our father justified by works, when he had offered Isaac his son upon the altar ? Ye see then how that by works a man is justified, and not by faith only." [1] This doctrine, at first sight, seems contradictory to that of Paul. It looks even as if James had deliberately intended to controvert Paul, and to oppose formula to formula.[2] Does not Paul say (Rom. iii. 28), " Therefore we conclude that a man is justified by faith without the deeds of the law " ?

But there are grave difficulties in the way of this hypothesis of a deliberate intention on the part of James to controvert Paul's teaching.[3]

The principal one is that the faith of which James affirms that it does not justify, is quite of a different kind from that of which Paul affirms that it suffices for justification. They differ with respect to their object and their nature. When Paul teaches justification by faith, he means faith in the redemption

---

[1] James ii. 21, 24.

[2] M. Nicolas thinks such was really the case. Such is the opinion also of M. Renan : " James is the adversary of Paul. . . . A whole paragraph of his epistle is intended to warn the faithful against Paul's doctrine of the uselessness of works, and of salvation by faith only." M. Renan goes so far as to insinuate that James's words, *O vain man !* are addressed to Paul.

[3] They are well pointed out by M. Reuss.

accomplished by Jesus Christ, or at least—when he is dealing with Old Testament personages—faith in the gracious promises of Jehovah, of which this redemption was the fulfilment ; whereas the faith which James declares to be insufficient for salvation, means simply— he says so himself—that belief in the one only God which distinguished the Jews from the heathen ; consequently it consists in adhesion to an article of the Jewish faith : " Thou believest that there is one God ; thou doest well : the devils also believe, and tremble." [1] But where has St. Paul ever taught that man could be justified by faith in a dogma not specially Christian ?

The theory of salvation by faith in *the unity of God*, which James attacks, belonged to a cycle of ideas totally different from Paul's ; rather let us say, it belonged to the system of his most declared adversaries—to pharisaic orthodoxy. We have many indications of this fact. Does not Justin Martyr, in his dialogue with Tryphon the Jew, say to him : " As for you Jews, you affirm that even when you are sinners, yet if you know God, He will not impute to you your sins ? " And do we not, in a document of the second century, belonging to a school of the most marked judaistic tendency,[2] find these words : " A monotheistic soul has this privilege above that of an idolator, that even when it has lived in sin it cannot perish " ?

---

[1] ii. 19.   [2] The *Clementine Homilies.*

This Jewish prejudice, which makes of the mere acceptance by the intellect of the dogma of the unity of God the sole and sure condition of salvation, is attacked by Paul with as much indignation as by James himself: "Behold, thou art called a Jew, and restest in the law, and makest thy boast of God . . . . and thou dishonourest God through breaking the law!"[1] Had then the blows of James fallen upon Paul, he would have been unintentionally striking at one of his own allies!

Compelled then to give up the idea that James deliberately attacked the apostle Paul, many writers have put forward the supposition that his purpose was to warn his readers against the abuses which might be made of his doctrine *if misunderstood*.

But why, in that case, are we to give to this doctrine, as we have just stated it, an entirely different interpretation from that of Paul? Or why, at any rate, does he not begin by stating to the reader whatever in the doctrine was well founded and in conformity with Scripture, and then go on to refute the misunderstandings to which it might give rise? Lastly—and this is perhaps the most cogent argument—is there the least likelihood that there should ever have prevailed among the Judæo-Christian communities, for whom James was writing, any inclination to exaggerate the doctrine of grace, as taught by Paul, and to push

_____

[1] Rom. ii. 17, 23.

it to the length of antinomianism ?[1]   Was not Paul himself, with all his teaching and all his actions, a constant object of suspicion to Christians of Jewish origin ?[2]

Neither does the selection, common to both these sacred writers, of Abraham's example, prove that the one intended to allude to the writings of the other. For this patriarch was, in the eyes of the Jews, the very personification of salvation. To discuss his case was to discuss the principle itself of salvation.

There remains a third hypothesis—that James contradicted Paul without knowing it.

In order to maintain this, we should have first to efface from the epistle of the former of these two writers some maxims which lead logically and directly to the doctrine of the latter, and consequently to the precise opposite of that which is attributed to James himself. "Whosoever," he says, "shall keep the whole law, and yet offend in one point, he is guilty of all." Compare this maxim with the confession, "In many things we offend all,"[3] and we shall agree that Paul could not have laid down better premises upon which to build his gospel of justification by faith, and that James could not have taught anything which would more radically undermine the doctrine of salvation by works.

---

[1] That is, systematic and practical opposition to the law.
[2] Acts xxi. 20—22.
[3] ii. 10, and iii. 2.

Let us examine more closely the idea of salvation which James endeavours to inculcate into his readers in the well-known passage which gives rise to this dispute.[1]

We must, it appears to me, if we are to state with perfect definiteness the relation in which this passage stands to the teaching of Paul, draw three distinctions, which arise out of the passages themselves, and which bear upon the meaning of the three words common to both the formulæ which are usually considered contradictory to each other.

Paul says : Faith justifies without works.   James says : Faith does not justify without works.

Three words occur in both of these formulæ— *justify*, *works*, and *faith*.   And no contradiction, it is evident, exists between the two authors, except so far as they both attributed the same meaning to these three words.   But we shall find that they did not do so—the fact is quite otherwise.

First, as to the word *justify*, we have already remarked, in the essay on the work of Christ, that Holy Scripture recognises two kinds of justification : one, that by which man passes from his natural state of condemnation into the state of grace,—this is, if we may venture so to speak, *initial* justification : the other, that by which the believer, already a participator in the Divine reconciliation, *abides* in it, even to the end, and is finally received into glory ; this is con-

---

[1] ii. 17—26.

tinuous, daily justification, of which the issue is *definitive* absolution.

Now the justification of which Paul habitually speaks is the former of these two—that by which we *enter* into the state of salvation. His mission being to open the door of the new covenant to the heathen, it was this that must of necessity chiefly occupy his attention. And he makes this justification depend entirely upon faith. The passage in James, on the contrary, is written with reference to the latter; which is quite natural, since it is intended for Jews, who, having been born in the state of covenant with God, did not need to be *admitted* into it, but only to *persevere* in it. Now for this, holiness is the indispensable condition. Every gift of grace received, whether it belong to the initial or decisive stage of the spiritual life, is a talent entrusted to us. God expects a substantial moral result from it. Otherwise the talent is soon withdrawn. It is upon this side of the truth that James insists, in perfect agreement with Jesus, who has said to each of His disciples, " By thy words thou shalt be justified (in the day of judgment), and by thy words thou shalt be condemned;" and who, applying to the relation in which He Himself stands to God this same condition of faithfulness in practice, expresses Himself thus : " If ye keep my commandments, ye shall abide in my love (the love that I have for you); even as I have kept my Father's commandments, and abide in His love (the love that He has for me)."[1] Now could Paul have meant to attack this assertion? On the contrary, is it not he who addresses these words to men who came under the same category as James's readers? " Not the hearers of the law are just before God, but the *doers* of the law shall be *justified* . . . in the day when God shall judge the secrets of men."[2] Is not that the very formula of James, complete? And, speaking of himself, does he not say, " For I know nothing by myself; yet am I not hereby justified : but He that judgeth me is the Lord."[3]

James does not then, by any means, teach an *initial*[4] justification for which good works would be *required*, which would be really contradictory to Paul; and Paul does not teach a *final* justification for which good works are *not required*, which would be really contradictory to James.

In the Bible idea of justification, as soon as it is clearly understood, there is room at the same time for both these formulæ ; man is justified by faith without works ; man is not justified by faith without works. For they relate to two different moments in the Christian life : one, to that in which the sinner first reaches faith ; the other, to that in which the believer is judged according to the fruits of his faith.

---

[1] Matt. xii. 36, 37 ; John xv. 10.

[2] Rom. ii. 13, 16.

[3] 1 Cor. iv. 4, referring to the final judgment alluded to in ver. 3 and 5.

[4] That by which the state of grace is begun.

Or, to say the same thing in another way : James would be in contradiction to Paul, if he affirmed that, in order to *obtain* grace, the sinner's faith must be accompanied by a certain *quantum* of meritorious works ; and Paul would be in contradiction to James, if he taught that the believer could be *finally* saved whilst still living in sin. But that is just what neither of them does say.[1]

The distinction which we have just drawn is confirmed by the different manner in which the two writers quote the example of Abraham. Paul brings forward the moment at which he was for the first time *declared righteous* by Jehovah.[2] James recalls a much later moment in the life of the patriarch, that at which, already believing and justified, he accomplishes his greatest work of obedience, the offering up of Isaac, and receives a solemn confirmation of this justification which he had already obtained.[3]

The example of Rahab, quoted by James, is not contradictory to this explanation, as might be supposed. At the time when this woman saved the spies, she had been already for some time a believer. She herself relates to them how the fame of the exploits of the God of Israel on behalf of His people

---

[1] See upon the necessity of sanctification for final salvation, according to Paul : 1 Cor. vi. 10 ; vii. 19 ; xvi. 22 ; Gal. v. 6, 21 ; vi. 7, 8 ; Eph. ii. 10, etc.

[2] Gen. xv. ; cf. Rom. iv. 3 ; Gal. iii. 6.

[3] Gen. xxii. ; cf. James ii. 21.

had reached her, and how she had believed in Him, as the Lord of the whole universe.[1] The work which she did on behalf of the spies was therefore subsequent to her entrance into the life of faith. It was the act in which the reality of her faith came into light. And God responded to it by granting to her a new gift of grace, that of her temporal preservation.

To this distinction between the two applications of the word *justify*, may be added another, with regard to the use of the word *works*. The works which Paul declares to be unavailing for justification are works which *precede* faith,—those which he himself calls *the works of the law*,[2] forced from the sinner by the constraint of the law, and destitute of that which alone could give them any moral value in God's sight—the spirit of love. The works which James set forth as necessary for justification are those which are wrought *in* faith, and which St. Paul designates by the name of *good works*, in opposition to the works of the law.[3]

Neither, lastly, is the third word, *faith*, taken in the same sense by the two writers. We know what Paul understands by faith—an act of the moral consciousness [4] which takes possession of the whole man—feeling, intellect, and will. On the other hand, we have

---

[1] Josh. ii. 9—11.

[2] Rom. iii. 20, 28.

[3] Eph. ii. 10. "Created in Christ Jesus unto good works." In antithesis to the works of the law, ver. 8, 9 : "By grace are ye saved . . . not *by* works."

[4] pp. 182, 183.

already seen what is meant by faith in the language of James. It is true that this language is not his own ; it is borrowed from that of his readers. According to this terminology, more Jewish than Christian, faith consists in the adhesion of the intellect to a truth of the reason—that of the unity of God.[1]

It is easy to understand in this way the difference of the relation in which faith and works are made to stand to one another by the two authors. According to Paul's view, the active element of the soul, the will, is included in the idea of faith ; works then emanate spontaneously *from* faith, in which they are virtually contained, as the consequence is contained in its premise. In the language of James, the adhesion of the will is to be added, subsequently, to faith (belief), so as to bring forth works—and that, as a new fact, *perfects* faith.

But in reality James, when he himself calls a faith *dead* which is not accompanied by works as its complement, makes us perceive that true faith—that which alone merits the name, and which is in his eyes *living* —is inseparable from the will which brings forth works ; and this leads directly to St. Paul's view.

When, in answer to the vain boasting of a dead orthodoxy, which has knowledge only without works, St. James says, " Shew me (if thou canst) thy faith *without* thy works, and I will shew thee my faith *by* my works," are not works put forward in these words,

---

[1] pp. 231, 232.

as they are in Paul, as the embodiment of faith—as the security that it is living?

To recapitulate,—The justification intended by Paul is, that by which man *enters* into the state of salvation; but James is speaking of that by which he *abides* in it.

Works are, in Paul's view, those which are anterior to faith; in James's view, they are those done in the state of faith.

Faith, as conceived by Paul, is that of the consciousness, which is the act of the whole man, and operates through the will; faith is, according to James, the belief of the intellect, which is dead in itself, unless the will import into it life and efficacy.

When once these distinctions have been grasped, we perceive the simultaneous truth of the two formulæ in which the two points of view are summed up.

And now we are in a position to attempt a definition of the form under which the Christian salvation presented itself to the mind of James.

That which, above all other things, occupied the mind of the brother of Jesus evidently was *good works*. In Peter the dominant idea was the brilliant picture of the perfect state which the coming of Christ was ultimately to bring about. James dwelt more upon the severe aspect of salvation—upon that holiness which alone leads to glory.

The ruling principle of this holiness he discovered in the *law*, the revealed expression of the Divine will.

But he did not separate the Jewish law from that commentary and complement to it which is given to us in Christ—from the *word planted in us* by the preaching of the gospel. Explained by Jesus, changed by His Spirit into a principle of the inner life, the law had become for him the *royal law*, a *law of liberty*, the *wisdom which is from above.* [1]

James, then, did not take the view of the law of an ancient Pharisee, who would have seen in it only a means of establishing his own righteousness, and of laying up before God by his obedience a store of merits ; but who, separating the observance of the law from those succours of Divine grace which attached to it even under the old covenant, would at last have found in it only a principle of condemnation. James assigns to the law the same position as do the authors of the Psalms and Proverbs, who endeavoured to fulfil it in a spirit, not of pride, but of obedience. Far from undertaking this work in any confidence in their own strength, they accomplished it only in communion with the God of that covenant which had already been opened to the faithful Israelite by many ordinances of mercy. Thus the law was to them a daily object of joy and admiration, a treasure more precious than gold, food sweeter than honey.

Such was James's feeling. The gospel therefore naturally presented itself to him as the crown and consummation of this institution intended for the

---

[1] i. 18, 23—25 ; ii. 8—11 ; iii 17.

moral education of the people of God—as the *perfect* law, perfect in respect of the spirituality of its commandments; perfect in respect of the living model of its fulfilment presented in Jesus; perfect in respect of the Divine strength, abundantly sufficient for its purpose, which is granted to man to fulfil it in his turn.

The part played by Jesus, according to this idea, is pre-eminently that of the supreme *legislator;* of the *judge*, who alone can save or destroy; of the *Lord of glory*, whose hand places the crown upon the head of him who has overcome.[1]

It is not easy to see what, from this point of view, was the method of appeasing the conscience after a fault had been committed. Was it the sacrifice of Christ alone, or was it necessary to add to that the observance of the rites of the law? Perhaps this question did not even occur to the minds of James and the Judæo-Christians whom he was addressing. The Levitical rites, being symbolical of the sacrifice of Christ, were associated in their minds with the contemplation and the celebration of the latter. What is certain is, that in Peter's view the question was settled. His epistle does not allow us to doubt it; the whole redemptive power had definitely passed over from the typical sacrifices into that of the Cross. But the epistle of James does not contain one word

---

[1] Legislator, iv. 12; judge, iv. 12, v. 9; Lord of glory, ii. 1; giving the crown, i. 12.

which betrays the opinion entertained by its author on this subject.

In all times there have been and there will be upright natures, instinct with force and power, severe to themselves, who seek in the gospel an instrument of sanctification rather than of pardon, who see in Christ a pattern and a force rather than an atoning victim. Pardon, they think, should of necessity accompany serious labour undertaken with a view to moral amelioration. Such natures have, it seems to us, a right to see themselves reflected more or less in that of James. The conception of the nature of salvation which is suggested by this habit of mind needs to be complemented rather than corrected. It contains no error, but the truth does not as yet shine forth in it distinctly. If this should surprise any of my readers, let them remember, with regard to James, as well as to Jude, that neither of them had been invested by Jesus with the dignity of apostles.

The teaching of Paul had had the effect of affixing an eternal stigma in the Church of Christ upon *dead works*—external observances without the inner life; that of James, to brand with lasting condemnation a *dead faith*—intellectual belief separated from moral activity. These two errors—like two reefs which rise to the surface at different points of the ocean, but which beneath the surface are blended in one and the same rock—both belong to the same religious principle, that ever-recurring Pharisaism which at one time *knows* without *acting*, at another *acts* without *feeling*.

The writings of Paul are especially indispensable in ages of formalism ; they lift the banner of that spirituality which is characteristic of all true obedience, such as is worthy of the God who is a Spirit.   James's epistle is especially appropriate in times of intellectual dogmatism and of dead orthodoxy ; it contains the protest of the moral principle upon which Divine salvation rests.

The epistle of James forms a part therefore, as do also the writings of Paul, of that sacred viaticum which the Lord bequeathed to His Church for its use during the whole period of its development and of its earthly activity—of the authentic canon of the New Testament.   And here it is fitting to do homage to the breadth of view, to the freedom of mind, to the boldness of faith, with which the churches of the fourth century, at the very time when they were proclaiming loudly the divinity of the Scriptures, dared, without grudging, to assign a place in their infallible canon to writings which included formulæ which, taken in the letter, were mutually contradictory upon the subject of salvation.   How far does Luther, with his unguarded assertions, dictated by the too exclusive pre-occupation of his mind with the controversies of his own time, stand below these courageous synodal decrees which governed the closing acts of the formation of the Christian canon !

In view of this fact, have we not a right to speak of a *providential canon*, and to recognise in this collection of writings as it has been issued from the hands of the Church, the fruit of guidance from above?

3

THE APOSTLE PAUL

We have said of James that he was a *unique* man; he was so indeed, among all the eminent persons of the primitive Church, on account of the special point of view which he represents. But there is another servant of Christ who has still more right to this epithet, from the novelty of the path opened by him, and the grandeur of the work he has accomplished.

St. Paul was, like James, a man of strong moral sense and of firm and upright judgment. He possessed also, like Peter, wealth of imagination joined to depth of feeling, as well as a spirit of bold enterprise in the sphere of practical work. But he was distinguished from both of them by the possession of dialectic skill of the most flexible as well as penetrating kind, and, at the same time, of that faculty for rapid and large intuitions which is so rarely combined with closeness of reasoning. From this combination of gifts, which are seldom developed to so eminent a degree even separately, and still more seldom when two or three of them are combined in one man, has resulted one of the most powerful and fertile natures in the domain of action as well as of thought, which humanity has ever produced.

It was not in Palestine that this rich intelligence was developed, but under the skies of Asia Minor, in the midst of the life of Greek literature and art, at Tarsus, —one of the most brilliant centres of civilisation in that age. It is hard to believe that a spirit so wakeful as that of this child should have been insensible to the influence of the atmosphere in which it came into being. The traces of the study of Greek poetry and the numerous comparisons taken from the social life of the Greeks, which we meet with in his epistles, and which distinguish them in so marked a way from the Gospels and from the writings of the Twelve, in which we never find anything of the kind, betray, not, it is true, a highly developed Greek culture, but at all events a very real sympathy with that people, and with its life and works of genius. Now such a sentiment could only have been formed in him before the time when he became imprisoned in the strait-waistcoat of a Pharisaic education.

It is therefore probable that he passed the whole of his childhood at Tarsus, and that it was not till he was about twelve years old,—the time when the child became, according to the saying of the Jews, *a son of the law*, because he was from that time subjected to all the customs of the law,—that he was sent to Jerusalem.[1] There he had a married sister ; and he

[1] Acts xxiii. 16. In his article upon Paul of Tarsus, M.

very soon received instruction from the most celebrated Rabbi of the time, Gamaliel. Here began for
the youthful Saul a severe discipline, which must have
had the effect of at the same time curbing the impulses of his ardent nature, and narrowing the sphere
of activity of his lively intelligence. In the lessons of
Pharisaic rabbinism everything turned upon the explanation of the precepts of Moses, and their different
applications. It was a kind of casuistry in which
masters and pupils often found occasions for displaying a rare sagacity. To these intellectual exercises—
a real gymnastic training, for which the law was, if we
may so say, the machinery—were added, at least
amongst the more earnest youths like Saul, serious
practical efforts at realising that ideal of the true
Good which was shadowed forth by the law. We
know from the later declarations of the apostle, that
he devoted himself to the fulfilment of the duties of
the law with no less zeal than to the study of their
theory.

The consideration in which the doctors were held
at that time is almost incredible. Their person was
regarded as sacred; and of their words it was said
that they were equivalent to those of the Most High.
A young man could become a *rabbi* at the age of
sixteen. From that time he had the right to expound
the decisions of the school to the people, and upon

Sabatier says : " *While he was still of tender age*, he was sent to
Jerusalem." This does not follow necessarily from Acts xxii. **3**.

his person was shed a reflection of the glory which shone around the heads of the great masters. Thus there opened before Paul a vista of the highest honours, and he seems to have climbed the first steps of the ladder which was to lead him up to them with a firm and decided step. "I profited in the Jews' religion," he says himself, when later in his life he recalls this time, "above many my equals."[1] But it is easy to see how self-love and ambition would have gathered strength in him in such a course of life, especially in the case of a nature so highly gifted as his. And the eyes of the noble and pious youth were by no means blind to the wrong feelings which were developing themselves within him. Under cover of the holiness of which he bore the appearance, he detected in his heart the plague-spot of impurity of which he could not cleanse himself. He has himself described this grievous conflict in the admirable seventh chapter of the epistle to the Romans. It was covetousness, he says, (v. 7 and 8,) which had revealed to him his condition of moral corruption. With regard to the first nine commandments he might have deceived himself, and have sincerely declared himself free from blame. But the tenth, "Thou shalt not covet," condemned him without mercy, and reduced him to despair,—a touching confession, implying as much of purity in his external conduct as of candour and severity in his examination of his conscience.

[1] Gal. i. 14.

By the illumination shed by the law, the depths of his evil nature, hidden from the eyes of the world, were brought into the broad daylight of his conscience.

The secret sin with which Saul had to struggle broke forth at last in a definite act. It was the great blot upon his youth, and became the bitter memory of all his after-life ; but the Divine mercy was able to make of this sin an occasion for miracles of grace. He declared himself, with a fanatical zeal, to be the enemy of Jesus and of His followers. Probably the pride which had been fostered in him by his talents and success was the primary source of this violent animosity. That persecution of the Christians to which the young disciple of the Pharisaic doctors gave himself up with a kind of frenzy, was a revenge for the little consideration in which Jesus and the apostles had seemed to hold his teachers and the Pharisaic philosophy of which he was himself so proud. At the same time, it was probably something more than this. It was the endeavour to make up by some great meritorious act for those shortcomings of his own righteousness, which he was compelled more and more to acknowledge. Never were the words more applicable which Jesus had spoken to His disciples : "They shall put you out of the synagogues : yea, the time cometh that whosoever killeth you will think that he doeth God service." But this act, which was intended to establish his own righteousness, did but serve to complete its ruin. The blood of Stephen, shed by Paul and his fellow-disciples, envenomed the wound of his conscience instead of healing it. And then it was that Christ, taking advantage of the moment in which his conscience was most athirst for righteousness, came suddenly from the throne of His glory to reveal Himself to him, and to give him in his own person that for which he was so ardently seeking —the *righteousness of God*, that is to say, the sentence of absolution which God the righteous Judge, alone can pronounce without appeal upon the sinner.

This righteousness which Jesus brought him was something quite different from the ideal which he had formed to himself of this grace—the first of all graces in his eyes. He had pictured to himself as the object of life the power of settling accounts, as it were, satisfactorily with God, upon the footing of a strict application of the terms of the law, and of offering to Him a faultless obedience as the work of his own moral strength. And now righteousness was, on the contrary, to be granted to him as the work of another, and to be imputed to him gratuitously. It descended upon him from heaven, instead of springing from the ground of his own heart as the fruit of his own labour. He has himself described this contrast better than we could do it : "If any other man thinketh that he hath whereof he might trust in the flesh, I more : circumcised the eighth day, of the stock of Israel, of the tribe of Benjamin, an Hebrew of the Hebrews ; as touching the law, a Pharisee ; concerning zeal, persecuting the church ; touching the righteousness which is in the law, blameless. But what things were gain to me, those I counted loss for Christ . . . . that I may be found in Him, not having mine own right-eousness, which is of the law, but that which is through the faith of Christ, the righteousness which is of God by faith."[1]

We observe here—and not less distinctly in other passages—a difference, which appears at first sight strange, between the sentiments of James and those of Paul with regard to the law. James seems to look upon the law as a basis upon which to rest his moral activity,—a beneficent and friendly principle. Paul represents it rather as a ground of condemnation. In James's view, the law does but transform itself into the gospel ; in that of Paul, they are two opposite principles. Whence arises this difference of view ? James took the law in that fulness of meaning in which it includes all the numerous institutions of *grace* with which God had already furnished the old covenant. He had no thought of fulfilling it without having first strengthened himself in God by the use of all these means, just as now the sincere Christian never separates the practice of evangelical duties from communion with Jesus, and the use of the Divine means of grace which He has bestowed upon His church. Paul, on the contrary, treats of the law in the sense in which it was understood by the Pharisees among the Jews, and

[1] Phil. iii. 4—9.

by his Pharisaic adversaries in the Church itself. It is the law solely as a moral commandment and as a meritorious observance—the Divine command isolated from communion with Jehovah Himself, and regarded, consequently, as the opposite of grace. For it was the object of the Pharisee to do some work by which he might prevail with God, as being the act of his own personal righteousness.[1] In the eyes of James, this opposition between the law and grace, between the work of man and the work of God, has no existence. For the idea of merit does not falsify in him, as it does in Pharisaism, the relations between God and man. Human obedience is the work of God Himself in man by the instrumentality of the law.[2] To the Pharisee, on the contrary,—and it is at this point of view that Paul places himself in discussing this question with his Pharisaic adversaries,—obedience, being purely the work of man, gives him a *right*, if it is complete, to the promised recompense, and becomes the foundation of his glory in the present age, and in that which is to come.

If we do not distinguish between these two points of view from which the law may be regarded, we shall not be able to understand the very different manner in which this divine institution is spoken of, as well as

---

[1] " What good thing shall ⅄ do, that I may have eternal life ?" (Matt. xix. 16.)

[2] James i. 17, " Every good gift and every perfect gift is from above ;" ver. 18, " Of His own will begat He us with the word of truth," etc.

its relation to the economy of salvation in James's epistle and in those of Paul.[1]

Paul was now, then, in possession of that grace for which he had laboured and wrestled so earnestly. He had found in Christ crucified and risen, the righteousness which he had vainly sought to obtain by his own works. Faith—not belief in the dogma of the unity of God, but absolute trust in this Jesus, Who was delivered for his offences, and raised again for his justification—was henceforth, in his eyes, the sole condition of his receiving this grace from the hands of God. The divine mystery with respect to the salvation of the world was revealed to him. That which was needed to rehabilitate the fallen world was not, as he had up to that time thought, to extend the supremacy of the law to all the heathen nations—to *judaise* or even *pharisaise* them. What advantage, then,—he must have said to himself, after his late experience,—would it be to them to possess a law which makes demands, but does not provide the means of fulfilling them; which passes sentence of condemnation, but offers no effective means for removing the burthen which it imposes? He understood that Christ had put an end to this *régime;* that it was no longer a question of saying to a man: "Do this, and your works shall make you righteous

---

[1] We may observe also, that the fact that Paul's point of view is not foreign to James, nor that of James foreign to Paul, follows clearly from Jas. iii. 2 : "For in many things we offend all;" and Rom. vii. 10 : "The commandment which was ordained *to life.*"

before God ;" that henceforth it was true that all
that had to be done had already been done by
Christ ; that we become righteous by accepting His
perfect work ; and that the proclamation of this
good news was for him to take the place of the
work of proselytising on behalf of the law.[1] To
preach Christ as the righteousness of sinful man,
appeared to him thenceforth to be the work of his
life. It was not only the actual calling which had
been addressed to him from the Lord through
Ananias, that made him feel this need; it was
principally the result of the work that had been
accomplished in himself. It was the shining forth of
the light which had arisen within his own soul.[2]

We know how from this time he fulfilled this
mission of a preacher of justification by faith. It was
the primary part of his work. We cannot give a
sketch even in outline of this heroic work. In three
great bounds, if we may venture so to call his three
great missionary journeys, he traverses the heathen
world, and conquers it for the gospel. Just as the
full revelation which had been granted to him upon
the cardinal point of justification by faith is the primordial illumination which is reproduced in all subsequent illumination in the Church, so was it his

---

[1] Rom. x. 4, 18.

[2] " For God, who commanded the light to shine out of darkness, hath shined in our hearts, to give the light of the knowledge of the glory of God in the face of Jesus Christ " (2 Cor.
iv. 6).

model apostolate which opened the way for that of all missionaries who have followed.

But his work as a missionary was but half of Paul's task. At the same time that he was extending Christianity over the heathen world, he was obliged to labour at setting it free from those swathing bands of Judaism in which the new religion had at first been confined. The bird could not spread its wings until it had freed itself from its native prison.

Paul, more thoroughly than any other apostle, had recognised—and that through his very Pharisaism—the radical unfitness of all commandments and rites to justify and convert mankind. That was the reason why, more distinctly than any one else, he had cleared the idea of Christian salvation of all admixture of legal alloy. But—and here only are we in a position to conclude the treatment of this subject—it is untrue to say that Paul, in teaching such doctrines, had the Twelve for adversaries. We have seen that they observed the law, though not as a condition of salvation. The law was to them a divine and national institution, which, so long as God did not abolish it, continued to be the normal form of Jewish life. This common observance was therefore for them a remaining link, connecting them with this unconverted people which was their proper mission field. James himself did not go farther than the Twelve. If there was any difference between him and them, and especially Peter, it was solely upon this point, that he insisted upon the observance of the law for the Judæo-Christians *absolutely*, in whatever country they might live ; whilst Peter, Barnabas, and their colleagues, seem to have allowed of a certain *relative* liberty for believers of Jewish origin, when they lived amongst the Gentile churches. This is evident from the passage in Galatians with regard to the contention between Peter and Paul, chap. ii., particularly ver. 12 : "Before that certain came from James, he did eat with the Gentiles ; but when they were come, he withdrew and separated himself." The concordat agreed upon at Jerusalem (Acts xv.) had not stated explicitly what was to be done in this particular case. And this it was which gave rise to the contention at Antioch. Both ways of acting, upon this secondary point, were in reality compatible with the decision that had been arrived at. The only words spoken on that occasion which could be applied to this question—"Moses of old time hath in every city them that preach him, being read in the synagogues every Sabbath day"—belong to the speech of James, not to the apostolic decree. Accordingly, the reproach which Paul addresses to Peter bears only upon his *inconsistency*,—upon the flagrant fact that he built up again by his subsequent conduct what he had before pulled down—the obligation to keep the law. With James himself Paul would not have so contended. He would have accepted James as he was.

In fact, St. Paul granted to the Judæo-Christians

the full right to continue observing the law, whether under James's more rigorous form of it, or in the milder manner practised at first by Peter at Antioch. He saw nothing to condemn in that course, provided such observance was not made essential to salvation. Upon this point, therefore, he was in full agreement with the Twelve.[1] The Pharisaic judaisers alone made any division. But the difference was, that Paul felt himself *from that time* completely freed from the law *by the death of Christ*, Who had by fulfilling, abolished it; whilst the Twelve, in order to put into practice with complete freedom of conscience this abolition, waited for *the return of Christ*, Who, by changing the whole existing state of things, would inaugurate the concluding age. This liberation from the law, for which, according to them, an external event was to give the signal, Paul found for himself in the moral fact of belief in the work of Christ,[2] so completely, that he felt himself at liberty not only to renounce the observance of the law, but even to subject himself again to it whenever such submission could further the cause of Christ. Such observance was to him so much a matter of indifference from a moral point of view, that he was free to choose between the two usages in every case as it arose. It is this voluntary subjection, so different from the judaising bondage, which he describes when he speaks of putting himself *under the law to them that*

---

[1] Gal. ii. 1—10.

[2] See the admirable but difficult passage, Rom. vii. 1—6.

are under the law, and of *becoming weak to the weak.*[1]
It is also because of this conviction and this principle
of action, that at Jerusalem he was able to accede in
perfect good faith to the request of James, that he
would join himself to some Nazarites who were fulfilling a vow in the temple ; with the express purpose of convincing the Judæo-Christians, who came
in crowds to the feast, that they were mistaken in
taking him for a fanatical adversary, an enemy on
principle of the observance of Jewish rites by Jews
who had become Christians. Had he indeed ever
deterred a single Judæo-Christian living in a heathen
country, from circumcising his sons, or from bringing
them up according to the national customs ? No ; the
observance in itself did not seem to him to deserve to
be so far honoured as to be made a subject of contention. It would fall of itself like a dead tree.[2]

Never did anybody, we venture to say, infuse
into the treatment of practical difficulties more of
condescension, of conciliatoriness, and of gentleness,
than did Paul in settling this anxious question with
the apostles. Just as inflexible as he shewed himself towards the *false brethren,* the judaisers, with
whom the very principle of justification by faith

---

[1] I Cor. ix. 20—22.

[2] The above exposition seems to us fitted to correct many false
ideas which have been disseminated of late upon this subject by
the school of Baur. We are sorry to see even M. Sabatier
associating himself in some measure with such erroneous views.
Revue Chrétienne, pp. 394, 395.

was at stake, so was he conciliatory with regard to all concessions, in the practical application of the principle, demanded by the other apostles, and by the Judæo-Christians generally, who had not yet reached such complete liberty as he had.[1]

It was this flexibility in conduct, running parallel with that which he practised in his reasoning, which brought upon him those accusations from his adversaries of double-facedness and of astuteness, of which we find indications in his letters. It was this condescension, carried almost to an extreme in the case of James, which caused his arrest and his long imprisonment. With respect to this again, St. Paul has been strangly misrepresented in some portraits recently made of him. He has been painted as a stiff, severe, peremptory man. Possibly these defects did exist in his natural character. But the strong man had been broken like an oak tree by a thunder-bolt. When, on the road into which his human nature had allowed itself to be led by its own wisdom or self-will, he suddenly discovers that he is at open war with the God whom he thought he was serving, his heart melts in a moment, as in a furnace. This is the annihilation of his pride, of his old self,—it is death. And the lion comes forth transformed into a lamb, out of this terrible crisis.

---

[1] Cf. the two cases of Titus (Gal. ii. 1,3), and of Timothy (Acts xvi. 3).

It was the radical transformation which he had gone through at Damascus which fitted St. Paul for accomplishing the most difficult of tasks—that of establishing the kingdom of God among the Gentiles without breaking with the Judæo-Christian Church, the cradle of the gospel. To effect this, what tact was required in the methods to be adopted ! what sustained perseverance in delicacy of treatment of them ! After each of his missionary journeys, Paul hastened to return to Jerusalem, to grasp the hand of those among the apostles who might still be there, especially of James, the leader of the flock. And he did not arrive with empty hands. He came to lay at the feet of the saints of the capital the tribute of gratitude offered by the whole of pagan Christendom.[1] Never was the *base metal* put to a nobler use. Thus did the whole world acquit itself of the sacred debt which it owed to Israel.

St. Paul understood perfectly that the successive layers of the building which he was erecting among the heathen nations could only rest firmly upon the historic foundation laid in Israel by the Lord Himself ; that otherwise they would remain suspended in the air, and would soon fall to pieces. It was on this account that he said : " I went up to Jerusalem . . . . lest by any means I should run, or had run, in vain."[2] It was, then, no empty form, as some have asserted, when Paul and Barnabas on the one hand,

---

[1] Gal. ii. 10.   [2] Gal. ii. 2.

and James, John, and Peter, on the other, gave each
other the right hand of fellowship as the result
of a critical conference. It was the symbol, deliberately adopted, of a real fellowship between them.[1]
Distinct as to their manner of service, and as to
the fields of work they occupied, these workers were
one with respect to the Master whom they served,
and to the work which they were doing for Him.

It might be said that James, established at Jerusalem, was like the fixed point of the compass,
while Paul, embracing the whole world in the immense circuits of his mission, represented its move-
able needle. This formed an instrument at once
twofold and single, moved by one and the same
hand.

We have brought into prominence that one among
the elements of salvation which was the central
point of the life, the thought, and the activity of
St. Paul; that is, the state of justification before
God. Let us now turn our attention to the vast
perspectives which opened before his view as soon
he had attained this blessing, which had been the
object of his most intense aspirations. One may
compare these fruitful intuitions to a series of
luminous rings developing themselves around a
brilliant focus which formed their centre.

But we must first clear out of our way two opinions

---

[1] Gal. ii. 9.

which have been often proposed, but which seem to us rather unproved hypotheses than results of ascertained facts.

It has been asserted that St. Paul's ideas underwent a transformation with regard to many points in the course of his apostolate, and that his epistles bore the traces of these modifications. We have in the first place a psychological objection to make to this view. Was not that crisis in his soul's history, which transformed St. Paul, so radical a renewal of his whole being, that his nature must have issued from this recasting all of one piece, if I may so say, and such as it was to remain to the end? With respect to his epistles, we recognise indeed in them a progress in the *exposition* of his thought, but no change in the thought itself. They treat of the question of the future of the kingdom of God (in the epistles to the Thessalonians) before bringing into light the ground upon which salvation is founded (in the epistles to the Galatians, Corinthians, and Romans); and it is not till after he has completed this second task, that Paul reaches the point at which he can set forth in all its grandeur the person of Christ, and in all its beauty the institutions of the Church which is His body (in the epistles to the Colossians, Ephesians, and Philippians). Having thus gone through the cycle of Christian theology, he occupies himself in his latest writings with questions of a practical nature; he urges the establishment of the ministry in the churches, and the necessity of good works (in the pastoral epistles). But does it follow from this that he did not from the first admit the duty of holy living, or the necessity of establishing a ministry in the Church? The epistles to the Thessalonians and the book of the Acts prove the contrary.[1] Or were his views on salvation and its conditions not settled till after his stay at Thessalonica? It is easily proved that they date even from his call to the apostolate, and are contemporaneous with it. Or, lastly, did Paul arrive only by degrees at the idea of the divinity of the person of Christ?—But it can be proved, and it has been proved to wearisomeness, against Baur, from the epistles of the first groups, that all the ideas which he developed later on this subject, were present to his mind even from the beginning of his ministry.[2]

What are we to conclude from this? That from the very first the new heavens displayed themselves in their fulness, with all their constellations, above his head, and that he surveyed them with his eyes, but only reproduced them by degrees, if I may venture to use such an image, upon his astronomical chart; in other words, he only unfolded the contents of the revelation he had received, in

---

[1] Acts xiv. 23 ; 1 Thess. v. 12.

[2] Jesus Christ *Divine* in nature (Rom. i. 3 ; viii. 32); *God* (Rom. ix. 5) ; the Jehovah of the ancient covenant (1 Cor. x. 4) ; Creator of the world (1 Cor. viii. 6).

his writings, in proportion as the practical needs of the Church called him to do so. The elements of the evangelical idea which unfolds itself by degrees in the long series of his epistles, were all present to his mind in a more or less rudimentary state, as the immediate result of the three days which transformed his whole life and thought.

In order to prove that the apostle's ideas had undergone a change, certain passages are specially alleged which seem to imply a different view as to the nearness of the return of Christ. Even were this granted, it would prove nothing in favour of the thesis against which we are contending; for a question of time is quite a different thing from one of dogma. Jesus Himself, while upon earth, knew not the day of His advent. But is the fact really so? Does not St. Paul write in one of his later epistles, just as he might have done in the earlier: "The Lord is at hand"?[1] And in one of the earlier, does he not write, just as he might have done later: "We beseech you that ye be not troubled . . . as that the day of Christ is at hand"?[2] The fact is, that in St. Paul's view, as in that of Jesus Himself, the normal attitude of the faithful servant is the constant *waiting for his Master's return*. The only real change which we can observe with certainty respecting his predictions on this subject, is that some time before his martyrdom he leads us to suppose

---

[1] Phil. iv. 5.   [2] 2 Thess. ii. 2.

that the Lord's return will not precede his death, but that his death will precede this return. [1] Now this is not a change in his *ideas* with regard to Christ's return; it is only a modification in his view of the relation in which that return would stand to the completely accidental event of his own death. We do not see how either dogma or morality is concerned in that. St. Paul never pretended to know beforehand the date of his death. [2]

There is another assumption widely prevalent,— that Paul imported into his Christian views many ideas which had belonged to his past Judaism. The doctrine of the two Adams, of predestination, etc., are quoted in proof of this. [3] To this again we must in the first place oppose the psychological argument which we urged against the former theory. The profound and complete transformation which St. Paul underwent, must have taken effect upon his thought, as well as upon the whole of his life ; and the temptation must have been greater for him to reject the elements of truth contained in his former way of thinking which he had now repudiated, than to retain any false or

---

[1] 2 Tim. iv. 1—6.

[2] If he seems to class himself (1 Thess. iv. 15 : *we which are alive* . . .) among those who shall remain till the coming of the Lord, he places himself, on the other hand, in 1 Cor. vi. 14, amongst those "whom the Lord will raise up by His power ;" which clearly proves that in both cases the *we* is to be taken in a collective, not an individual sense.

[3] M. Sabatier, *Revue Chrétienne*, p. 38.

doubtful ideas which had belonged to it. It is not difficult to explain the necessary connection between his idea of the two Adams and the light which on the day of his conversion fell upon the contrast between the state of man by nature and his new condition in Christ. Besides, the ideas which he may have learned upon this subject in the school of the Rabbins, were drawn from the preparatory revelation contained in the Old Testament, and they grouped themselves like scattered particles of truth around the perfect revelation which had now been granted to him. Assuredly none of his former ideas passed into his apostolic preaching without having received the stamp of that new creation which had taken place within him.

We must say the same of the dogma of predestination. Whatever he may have heard upon this subject, in the Jewish schools, had been purified and made more precise by its application to Christ and to the Church, before it was admitted into his teaching. There is no trace in Paul of a fatalistic predestination. Human free-will and responsibility are always presupposed, and often asserted by him; and as to Rom. ix. and x., we will undertake to prove that they contain precisely the strongest protest against that fatalistic predestination, of which Israel audaciously made use as a reason for not receiving the gospel.

To the Christian theology of the apostle, as well

as to his moral life, we may apply those great words :
" If any man be in Christ, he is a new creature :
old things are passed away ; behold, all things are
become new."

The first point upon which the light of revelation
fell, after the question of salvation had received its
full solution in the consciousness of the apostle, was
the person of the Saviour. He had seen Him in
His Divine glory, even with his bodily eyes, with such
intensity that he was struck blind by the brightness
of that sudden apparition. It is from this moment,
doubtless, that we must date the impression which is
conveyed in those words in the epistle to the Colossians : " In Him dwelleth all the fulness of the
Godhead bodily." None of the subsequent visions of
the apostle, not even that in which he was carried up
into the third heaven, can so well account for the use
of this word *bodily*,—especially from the pen of Paul,
who has so exalted an idea of the spirituality of
Christ, and who goes so far as to say : " The Lord
is that Spirit."

St. Paul had probably up to that time shared the
rabbinical opinion, according to which the Messiah
was to be man elevated to his highest power.
Perhaps—but this is less probable—he was already
initiated into the idea which forms the foundation
of all the later cabalistic speculations, according to
which the Messiah was to be the apparition of the
archetypal man, of the celestial model after which

the terrestrial Adam had been created.[1] But the contemplation of the Messiah in the person of Jesus glorified, raised him at once to a higher idea; he recognised in Him the apparition of a Being divine in essence. This is clear from all his great epistles —Galatians, Corinthians, Romans.[2] If he did not at that time develop this thought, because he was then wholly occupied with the question of grace and of the law, he nevertheless clearly proclaimed it. The exegetical necessity which compels us to apply the adoring exclamation, (Rom. ix. 5,) "God over all, blessed for ever," to Jesus Christ, has been proved in a manner which may well be called definitive, in the classical dissertation of M. Schultz.[3] And if we reflect upon the distance which, in the Jewish mind, separates between the Creator and the creature, we shall perceive that Paul's thought could not have passed over it by mere speculative impulse.

Doubtless the Old Testament might have already started him in the right direction, since it gave hints in many passages of the divinity of the future Messiah; and one passage in the last of the prophets expressly represented the advent of this Personage as the supreme theophany.[4] But it was probably only by degrees that St. Paul learned to put together these

---

[1] Baur asserts that Paul never got beyond that idea.
[2] See note, p. 264.
[3] *Jahrbücher für deutsche Theologie*, 1868.
[4] *i.e.* apparition of God ; cf. Mal. iii. 1.

scriptural proofs. It was the truth already possessed by him which drew his attention to them—not the converse.

We must, besides, take note here of a difference to which Neander has already drawn attention. James had known Jesus from childhood, Peter had accompanied Him in His ministry, Paul did not know Him by sight till He appeared to him in glory. When we meditate upon these differences of circumstance, we cease to wonder at the manner in which each speaks of Christ,—especially at the fact that the Divine attributes are continually applied to His person in the writings of St. Paul.

It is in his later epistles that he has set forth directly his manner of thinking upon the person of Christ. He represents Him as voluntarily exchanging His condition as "in the form of God"—His Divine manner of existence—for "the form of a servant;" then submitting Himself in this human condition to the profoundest abasement; and finally raised again, as man, to the full height of Divinity, of which, by becoming incarnate, He had emptied Himself.[1]

---

[1] Phil. ii. 6—11. We do not understand how M. Sabatier can see in that expression of St. Paul, "the form of God" (of which Christ emptied Himself), no higher meaning than that of "an *empty form* which was to be filled—that is to say, spiritually realised"—by His holy life (*Thèse sur St. Paul*, p. 224). This expression must necessarily indicate a state neither more nor less real than that other of the "*form of a servant*," which constitutes its antithesis. Now this latter is evidently taken in the most real

One of the most important of St. Paul's views in this province of thought is the union of the natural and the moral creation, produced by means of the link between them in the person of Christ, who is the common Head of both. These two processes are part of the carrying out of a single and connected plan,[1] in such a manner that in nature as in history, in humanity as in the Church, everything has its spring and origin in the same starting-point, Christ; and leads up to the same goal, Christ, the "Alpha and Omega," according to the expression of the Apocalypse. This, according to St. Paul, is the foundation-principle of a new wisdom in Christ, a wisdom of which He reserves the full exposition for *them that are perfect*, and of which the design which God decreed from all eternity *for our glory*, forms the main substance. For the

---

historical sense. But who could maintain that in that passage from the same apostle, " Who being rich, became poor . . . . " (2 Cor. viii. 9), the word *rich* is to be taken in a purely ideal, but the word *poor* in an historical sense? Besides, the Greek word *morphe* does not admit of being used in the sense of an *empty form*—a simple *idea*. It always indicates a form that is *organic*, and consequently living and full of reality. Men may deny, if they will, the real pre-existence of the Lord, but at least let justice be done to the plain sense of texts. No more can we, as to the words which follow, accept the forced sense which the author with whom we are arguing wishes to give them. The context clearly shews St. Paul's thought:—" In becoming incarnate, Jesus did not come, as He might have done, to make a display of His Divine condition; instead of presenting Himself here below as God, He appeared simply as man, and in the form of a servant."

[1] 1 Cor. viii. 6; Eph. i. 8—10; Col. i. 15, 20.

Church being one with her Head, when He is glorified, she is glorified with Him. And the supreme position which belongs to Christ in the universe becomes necessarily ours also.[1]

It is to this general view of the person of Christ that we must attach the idea which St. Paul forms for himself of *Nature*. M. Sabatier has asserted that St. Paul had not realised, as Jesus had, the conception of Nature. But this implies, it would seem, that he who says so has never read the magnificent passages in Rom. viii., in which the apostle pictures to us Nature subjected in its whole being to that condition of frailty and of corruption into which it has been brought by our fall; and joining his groans to those of the children of God, and of the Holy Spirit Himself, who fervently long for the renewal of the external world as the crown of the spiritual renewal of humanity by Jesus Christ. Nature, to the mind of St. Paul, is what in our days it has become to science, in consequence of the discoveries of geology—a living whole, which is in process of self-transformation, not a dead thing, imprisoned in the grip of mathematical laws; the scene of a continuous progress; consequently the prelude to a work still more magnificent, which is one day to evolve itself out of her, like a child from its mother's womb.[2] This furnishes the basis for a true philosophy of nature.

---

[1] Col. i. 26—28 ; I Cor. ii. 6, 7 ; xii. 26, 27 ; Rom. viii. 29, etc.

[2] Rom. viii. 22 : "The whole creation groaneth and *travaileth in pain together*."

The *history* of humanity is grasped by St. Paul with equally profound insight. The universality of the fact of sin is proved by the universality of the fact of death. But over against this universality of corruption and condemnation is set the equal universality of justification and of life. The two are summed up in the two personalities—that of Adam and that of Christ. As by our birth we are involuntarily connected with the former, so by a free act of faith we have the power to unite ourselves to the latter, and to find in Him, not only the equipoise to the evil which we suffer in Adam, but a surplusage of grace infinitely surpassing the transitory effects of the primeval and collective sin of the race.[1]

Within the compass of history so understood, arises the problem of the mysterious people of Israel, elected of God, and yet, in the end, rejected by Him. What an inconsistency! What a moral impossibility! Must we not despair of the truth of the gospel, if it can only be maintained at the cost of holding to the untenable assumption of God's faithlessness to His chosen people? St. Paul addresses Himself to this formidable problem, and treats it under all its aspects in the famous dissertation, Rom. ix.—xi. As against the idea of an election imposing itself upon the Divine will as an obligation from which there is no escape, the apostle asserts the sovereign liberty of God, who can reject even the elect nation, if it should cast away the indispensable condition of its election—faith ; and can

---

[1] Rom. v.

call to Himself individuals even belonging to non-elect
nations, if they should fulfil this moral condition of
election—faith (ix.). He proves that the former of
these two cases has been realised in Israel, since, instead
of allowing themselves to be *led by the law to Christ*,
they made use of the Mosaic system for *establishing
their own righteousness*, and obstinately rejected the
offer of salvation with which God pursued them in all
countries by His messengers (x.). Then he unfolds
at last, before his readers, this grand perspective :—
When, by the very means of this rejection of the
Israelitish people, free access into salvation shall have
been opened to all other nations; and when, like the
prodigal son, they shall have re-entered their Father's
house, then the mercy thus shewn to them will turn
into a source of repentance and conversion to proud
Israel—that elder son who went out of the house
because his brother was received back into it. In this
manner both the theocratic nation and the undisci-
plined Gentile world—the two spiritual halves of
humanity—after having each of them passed through
their time of disobedience and unbelief, will finally
unite in the acceptance of a common salvation, and
will arrive, by widely different roads, at the glorious
goal fore-ordained in the counsels of God. For " God
hath concluded them all in unbelief, that He might
have mercy upon all. Oh the depth of the riches
both of the wisdom and knowledge of God !" (xi. 32,
35.) Such is the *coup d'œil* cast by St. Paul upon the

march of the religious development of humanity. No grander conception has ever been propounded with regard to this aspect of the philosophy of history.

Modern thought is still in doubt upon the true idea of *the State*. Some recognise the Divine element which is at the root of this institution ; but they are too often inclined to make a theocracy of it, and place it under the yoke of the clergy. Others refuse to oppose the modern instinct, which demands, as the most precious of all kinds of liberty, that of conscience and worship ; but they generally fail to recognise the Divine principle which is at the root of the State, and see in civil society only the result of a contract originating in motives merely utilitarian. St. Paul's well-balanced thought hits the truth exactly between these opposite errors. On the one hand, the work assigned to the State is limited by him to the purely *psychical* and terrestrial sphere ;[1] but, on the other hand, he attributes, without hesitation, to it within this domain, a Divine origin and object. God has willed the existence of the State as well as of the Church. Conscience, and not interest only, requires of a Christian that he should be in all respects a faithful citizen.[2] Thus do we find sketched in broad outlines the true idea of the State, and the only solid basis upon which the philosophy of right can be founded.

---

[1] Rom. xiii. 1 : " Let *every soul* be subject unto the higher powers."

[2] Rom. xiii. 1—6.

It may be said that upon every subject upon which the apostle brings his thought to bear, he sheds a ray of light from heaven.

Finally, what are we to say of this man who, besides being the founder of churches which, in twenty-five years, conquered the Roman empire—the thinker who illumines, without losing his way for a single moment, domains of thought the most varied and the most obscure—the writer who, during ten months of an apostolic career, to a rare degree burdensome and hampered with difficulties, contrives to compose those three master-pieces, the two epistles to the Corinthians and that to the Romans—writings of which each sentence is like a cut diamond ; what shall we say of this man when, together with all this, we find in him the most watchful of friends, who can even remember to recommend his youthful fellow-labourer not to neglect to take a little wine—a man so considerate to his colleagues, that he delights in giving, even to the lowest of his helpers in the common work, a place of honour by his side—the tenderest of brothers, who, with his own hand, commends an unfaithful slave, whom he has " begotten in his bonds," to his former master as his *own self, his own bowels !*

If it be true that a man is great in proportion to the greatness and to the multiplicity of the contrasts which he combines in his own person, there is perhaps no one upon earth who can be legitimately compared to St. Paul.   A man gifted with vast intuitions as well as subtle analytic power, of the profoundest mysticism together with the most unfailing good sense, combining with the genius of speculation and of practice—that is to say, with all the faculties of the intellect—all the graces, all the amenities, the tendernesses, and all the deep-seated passions of the heart—we understand how Christ had need of such an instrument for carrying out the greatest work after His own, and how, not finding it offered to Him willingly, He should have taken possession of it by main force.

Whilst the other apostles walked, Paul flew, across the world ; and what is perhaps most admirable is that, without forcing them, or allowing himself to be in the least interfered with by them, he succeeded in preserving intact the link of fraternity and of mutual co-operation which united him with them. The preservation of this bond between them was the crowning work of the love of Christ, which bore sway in those hearts, and which made all their wills converge upon one sole end—His glory.

4

THE APOSTLE JOHN

In the intellect of St. Paul the dialectic powers predominated over the contemplative, which however, as we have seen, were not wanting in him. In John, on the contrary, the faculty of intuition preponderated to such a degree as to leave scarcely room in his mind for the labour of reasoning. John did not reason—he *saw*. Accordingly, he did not dispute ; he simply affirmed or denied ; resting his assertions solely upon their intrinsic truth, which ought to be perceived at once by every sincere mind. To this primary contrast between the two men, there was added another relating to the tendencies of their characters. Paul was of a practical turn, and very wise in the management of affairs ; John's nature was dreamy, rather poetical than practical, more inclined to the ideal than to outward activity. Accordingly, he did but little ; there is no creation in ecclesiastical matters due to his apostolate. The world in which his mind moved was that of supersensuous realities. His mind and will tended to the centre of things, not to their circumference.

When such natures are stirred by a tender and loving heart, their affections easily take a character somewhat passionate and exclusive. They so entirely identify themselves with the object of their love, that they retain no other life, and towards all who are net of their mind they indulge a degree of intolerance which sometimes amounts to violence. Such a person John seems to have been before he underwent the influence of the renewal worked in him by the Spirit of Christ. It was he who imperiously silenced the man who allowed himself to cast out devils in the name of Jesus without having taken his place among His disciples. It was he who demanded that fire should descend from heaven upon the Samaritan village which shut its gates against Jesus. Nothing can be more different from the real John than the idea which men commonly make to themselves of that apostle. Instead of a soft, pliant nature, we must rather picture one of ardent, trenchant, *brusque*, abrupt character, whom Jesus well described by that epithet, *son of thunder* (*Boanerges*), which He gave to him as well as to his brother James. Like the lightning which issues suddenly with a crash from out of the silent, motionless clouds, so did love or hate burst forth from these two youths, true representatives of the Semitic mind.

We have recognised in Peter, in James, and in Paul, the ruling aspirations which found their response in the gospel. We shall not, we think, be mistaken if we say that the profound necessity which filled the soul of John from the first was the desire for the infinite. The name of "*mal de l'infini*" [1] has been given to that nameless desire which consumes sensitive and dreamy natures until they have found the object of their aspirations. From St. John's writings we can perceive that this was the necessity of his nature which opened his soul to the gospel. It is not without significance that the word *life* is the dominant one in his writings. In life we see the natural vanity and

---

[1] Literally, a thirst for infinity—akin to home-sickness.

emptiness of finite existence, saturated with the richness of infinite being. It is the heart of the creature quenching its thirst with peace, with holiness, with strength, by immediate access to the supreme fountainhead. It is man lifted to God, and God living in man. This seems to have been the ideal of John from his youth. This was that spiritual good which he found in Jesus, which he obtained for himself through Him, and which established between his Master and himself the close intimacy characterised by the expression, *the disciple whom Jesus loved.*

It does not seem, then, that John arrived at faith by means of any conflict or moral revolution. He had not, like James, to overcome a jealousy provoked by any rivalry during childhood. Neither did Jesus meet with open resistance in him, as in St. Paul, from the effects of prejudice and pride. From the first moment of his conversing with Jesus, John was drawn to Him by an irresistible attraction, and surrendered himself to Him with all his soul. Faith, in him, resulted from an immediate intuition, due to that inward teaching from God of which he so often speaks in his writings. He recognised in Jesus the Messiah, with all that that name signified to his mind, that is to say, as the supreme Good. The pious instructions of his mother, Salome, had brought him under the teaching of John the Baptist ; the invitation of the forerunner led him with the same facility into the arms of Jesus. He had no gloomy darkness, or mists of any kind, to traverse. He walked on from light to light, till full noonday shone upon him in all its brightness.

Hence arises a great difference between his evangelical intuition and that of St. Paul. In the mind of the latter, the idea of *salvation* predominates; in St. John, that of the *Saviour*. It is in the fact of deliverance that Paul finds the liberator; in salvation itself, that he discovers the author of salvation. In the mind of John, on the other hand, the person of the liberator takes precedence; salvation to him is only an emanation from the Saviour, Jesus Himself communicating Himself to the soul.

If he describes to us the person of Christ, who is to him the gospel itself, as *the Word made flesh*, do not let us believe that he borrows the idea thus expressed from the speculations of his age. The most that can be said is that he takes from these the imperfect form of words which he needs for expressing his thought. This latter was formed in him by the contemplation of his Master, and the daily listening to His words. He drank at the fountain of that one life in which he recognised the true Life worthy of the name ;—more than that, he heard Him who so completely realised his ideal, say, "I am the bread of life, which came down from heaven to give life unto the world ;" and he exclaimed, in consequence of that experience, and on the strength of that testimony, "The life which was from the beginning with the Father was mani-

fested, and we have seen it."[1] Divine truth, which is
the light of the soul, grew within him as he listened to
Jesus ;—more than that, he heard Him say Himself,
" I am the Truth ;" and immediately he exclaimed,
" Truth came by Jesus Christ. . . . He is the *light of
life*.[2] Here is the simple origin of this theorem, which
is of a religious, not at all of a metaphysical, character
—the Word made flesh—of which men have sought
the source in Philo and even in Plato.   From the
point of view of Jewish monotheism, a man could not
be *the truth* and *the life* for the human soul, except
so far as he was the revelation of God Himself, and
partook of His essence,—so far as he was His living
image, the reflection of Him in the eternal mirror of
the Divine consciousness, the adequate expression,
co-eternal with Himself, of His mind and being. The
Old Testament had already consecrated the term
word to designate the all-powerful manifestations of
the Divine will. Jewish theology had, long before
the time of St. John, applied the expression, *the Word
of the Lord*[3] to all the visible signs of the action of
Jehovah in the external world. The term *Word*, of
which John makes use to designate the Divine aspect
of the person of his Master, does not therefore even
require to be explained by the philosophy of his age.

---

[1] John vi. 48, 51 ; 1 John i. 1—3.

[2] John xiv. 6 ; viii. 12 ; i. 17.

[3] *Memrah di Jehovah*, in the Chaldaic paraphrases of the Old
Testament.

The Bible, and the teaching of the Jewish schools
which flowed from it, are sufficient to account for it.

A contemplative and reserved nature is the soil in
which poetical or philosophical geniuses grow. The
philosophic faculty, which consists in the power of
ascending rapidly from each individual fact to its
general principle, is evidently the child of contemplation; and the poetical mind, which is quick at
discovering at once the concrete image in which the
abstract idea may be clothed and embodied, presupposes the habit of surrendering oneself to a meditative reverie, of which the only aim is to fix more
firmly in the mind the idea with which it is pre-occupied,
and to give it a body. The first of these faculties
comes out most conspicuously in his gospel; the
second in the great biblical poem, the Apocalypse.
In the former, every manifestation of the person of
Jesus is contemplated from the point of view of its
eternal and spiritual significance. Reading this narrative with attention, we feel the Divine Word throbbing
in every fibre of the flesh of the Son of man. Each
of His miracles is like the illumination of some one
of the aspects of His dignity as the Son. The various
effects which are seen produced around His path,
however accidental they may seem at first sight, are
all referred to their distinctive principles, whether in
the direction of good or evil; and beyond the secondary
causes we can always discover, in the two domains of
light and darkness, the higher cause, God or Satan.

From this we understand why it is that his polemics against heresy, which are naturally not found in the gospel, but which develop themselves in the first epistle, should be summary and affirmative, not analytical or discursive ;—thundering, such as befit the son of thunder.

The poetic faculty of John blossomed in the Apocalypse, which is the complement of his gospel. We do not understand how it is possible to do what is, however, so often done—to oppose these documents the one to the other. If they differ in respect of language, the reason is easily perceived. The influence of the Old Testament is perceptible from one end of the Apocalypse to the other; for that book is, in fact, but the reproduction at the close of the New Testament of all that part of the prophecies of the Old Testament which had not been fulfilled by the first advent of Christ. With respect to its drama, it corresponds exactly, as we shall see, with that of the gospel history. It is poetry completing narrative, prophecy finishing history. Just as, in the gospel, John is ever mounting up from the particular event to its originating principle, from the terrestrial Jesus to the eternal Word, so in the prophetic picture does he bring into view those supreme principles from which things proceed coming down into their ultimate consequences, the mysterious powers which govern the history of the world making their appearance at length upon the stage of the world in their most concrete form.

As to the conflict between the law and grace which occupied so large a part of the life of Paul, it is to John a storm that has blown by. There is not a trace in his writings of that antagonism which plays so important a part in the writings of the apostle of the Gentiles. Faith, in John's view, is not the belief which has to be *completed* by works, as in James; nor yet the cause which *produces* works, as in Paul, It is work itself—the supreme work, the act of taking direct possession of Christ—that is, of salvation, of life. "What shall we do that we might work the work of God?" the Jews ask of the Lord. "This is the work of God," Jesus answers, "that ye believe on Him whom He hath sent."[1] Faith is the work of works. To believe is to give oneself up; and to give oneself up is the apogee of the whole moral activity of man. This is the point we must reach before we can perceive the profound harmony between Paul and James; faith is only faith in so far as it is a work, and works are only works in so far as they are faith. Jesus had beforehand formulated this concordat between the two. All the storms which succeeded the passing away of the Master had not stifled, in the memory of John, those sweet accents which once fell from His lips, putting an end to all controversy, and bringing into harmony all the different aspects of truth.

The practical work of John was next to nothing.

---

[1] John vi. 28, 29.

To lay foundations was not his gift. All that he could do in this external sphere was to labour at maintaining in existence that which his colleagues had created. This was the work he did in Asia Minor, amongst the churches that had been founded by St. Paul in his third missionary journey. There,—the last remaining depositary of the immediate personal knowledge of the Lord, the most intimate confidant of His thoughts, the living reflection of His words and of His person,—he wore, as Polycrates, the Bishop of Ephesus, says, in his poetical language, the tiara of the high priest, with the gold plate and the inscription, *Holiness to the Lord;* thus presenting in his own person an example of the summit of the Christian life already reached—Christ's perfection realised in the believer—and thus bringing up the Church of the firstborn into a relative consummation, to serve as a type of that of all subsequent ages. John completed the work begun by his predecessors. He placed the crown upon the building of which they had laid the foundation. This glorious office which he fulfilled is clearly seen in his three principal writings. By his gospel he has consummated the knowledge which the Church possesses of Christ; by his first epistle, her knowledge of the holiness of the believer ; and finally, by the Apocalypse, the light granted to her with regard to her own life—to her great final conflict, and the triumph which is to follow. Christ, the Christian, the Church—all are irradiated in the

writings of John with a sublime splendour like that
with which the setting sun colours the Alpine heights.

Glory, as the ultimate goal ; *good works*, as the path
by which the believer attains to glory ; *righteousness*,
as the threshold which has to be crossed before
entering upon this course of the practice of virtue ;
and finally *life*, as the inmost essence of these different
elements of salvation,—these are the four aspects
under which the supreme Good granted to man in
Jesus Christ presented itself to the minds of the four
principal apostles.

When we are contemplating a journey which we are
about to undertake, the first thing which presents
itself to our minds is the end to be reached ; next
come the questions relating to the route to be followed ; then we decide upon the point from which to
start ; and finally, we take in at a glance the whole
undertaking before us, while considering the principal
thought which inspires it.

Entering upon the course along which the Church
was to travel, Peter fixes his eyes upon the proposed
goal, that is, the promised glory ; this was the point
of attraction, the originating spring of the movement.
James simply sketches the route—holiness, without
which no man shall see the Lord. Paul points out
the entrance into that route—personal justification,
reconciliation with God, the alone Good, apart from
communion with whom man can do nothing. John,
lastly, contemplates this whole work under the form

of a divine life communicated to man through the medium of righteousness, with the view to producing holiness, and in prospect of the final glory.

Observe this remarkable fact : that these four conceptions of salvation correspond more or less with the four aspects under which the person of Christ is set before us in the Gospels.

Long since it has been noticed that there is a close relationship between the gospel of Matthew and the epistle of James.   In both these writings, salvation in Jesus Christ is represented as the fulfilment of the law.   Raised to its full spirituality by Jesus, the Divine law sheds itself abroad in the heart as a power of holiness, by the influence of the glorified Saviour, and becomes there the health of the soul's salvation. Let any one read over again the Sermon on the Mount and the epistle of James, and see whether this is not the fundamental thought common to both.

Paul occupies, in the epistolary canon of the New Testament, exactly the place that Luke does in the evangelical canon.   In both these authors, the principal subject is the act by which the sinner enters into the state of grace before God.   This consists, on God's part, in the gratuitous gift of forgiveness ; on the part of man, it is faith.   Let any one read the three parables of the lost sheep, the lost piece of money, and the prodigal son, in Luke xv., and he will be driven to the conclusion that Paul, in his epistle, has developed nothing else, and in his missionary action has realised nothing else, than the thought of Jesus as it is expressed in these three pictures.

The analogy between Mark and Peter is perhaps less striking. The point of similarity between them is rather to be found in the intermediate position which these two men occupied between the representatives of the two preceding points of view. Nevertheless, the idea of Jesus as the Messiah and Son of God, which runs through the gospel of Mark, connects itself closely with that of the kingdom of glory which occupies the mind of St. Peter in his epistle. To both these writers, Jesus appears as the Jewish Messiah raised to the dignity of the Son of God, and the Church as the Jewish theocracy glorified.

With respect to John, the idea of life which fills his epistles pervades also the whole of his gospel ;—not that he has imported it by his own authority into this latter. The disciple did not allow himself to refashion the Master after his own image. It is, on the contrary, his spirit which has taken the impression of his Master's image. It is because he had heard Jesus say, as the gospel tells us, " I am the bread of life," or, " He that believeth on me, out of his belly shall flow rivers of living water," that in his epistle he sets Him forth as the Eternal Life made visible, seen and tasted by faith.

And now we are in a position to appreciate the part to be played in the life of the Church in all ages by these four historical and doctrinal expositions of the salvation to be found in Christ. Jesus, in His last prayer, said, as He contemplated His apostles assembled around Him : " Father, I pray Thee for all them which shall believe on me through their word." It is then the preaching of the apostles which is made by Jesus the necessary, and in itself sufficient, intermediary agent between His manifestation on earth and the belief in Him of all mankind. He that believes, does so only because he receives the testimony and the preaching of the apostles : he comes to the living Jesus only through their instrumentality. Jesus only reveals Himself to a soul by making use of that fourfold representation of His person and of His work, which is contained in the New Testament, and which is its normal and complete revelation. It is by means of this Divine dispensation, so full of wisdom, that the Church is saved from all false mysticism ; and all pretension to any action of the Holy Spirit independently of this written revelation is thereby branded beforehand as false. " I am glorified in them," said Jesus, in speaking of His apostles ; for His glory as the promised Messiah, as the Saviour of all men, as the Son of God, as the eternally Beloved of the Father, had been revealed to them ; they were the depositaries of it for the whole world. Now it is precisely this glorifying of Jesus in the minds of the Twelve which has, as it were, concentrated itself in those four groups of evangelical or apostolic writings to which we have just been drawing attention in the New Testament. The glory of Jesus is there set forth as the Saviour, perfect from all points of view, and He can only be similarly glorified in us by the use of the same means. Every revelation of Christ in after-ages is but a reproduction of the direct and primordial revelation preserved in these four groups of canonical books.

From this we may estimate the value of this four-fold portraiture of Christ, which the Church possesses in the New Testament.

But that which we feel constrained to bring into prominence above all, in concluding this work, which has brought before us four individualities so different and so marked in character, is the greatness of Him who had so powerfully subjugated to Himself all the four, and pressed them into His service. Two of these, Paul and John, were of the elect of the world, although gifted with very different qualifications. The former would have played a brilliant part in the Synagogue as he did in the Church, and his name would certainly have remained impressed upon the rolls of history, even had it not been inscribed there as that of the apostle of the Gentiles. That would probably not have been the case with John, notwith-standing the undeniable eminence of his talents. The natural reserve of his timid and modest character would have hindered him from ever placing himself prominently before the world. He would have been the leader of a small band of elect minds and spirits, who would have grouped themselves around him, like Banus, to whom, in his youth, the historian Josephus attached himself. But what must not He have been, who had so absolutely subjugated to Himself these two minds, that there was not in their whole being a single fibre which did not throb for Him, or in their minds a single thought which was not a radiation from His own! The most subtle dialectician whom the spirit of humanity ever produced, devotes his whole sagacity to the work which had been conceived by this Master; and at the same time one of the most remarkable mystic geniuses of all time, recognises, thenceforth, no other object of intuition than the person of this same Master.

James and Peter are natures certainly much less highly gifted. But perhaps the spiritual greatness of Jesus is more triumphantly shewn in their poverty than in the riches of John and of Paul. It is not to their own gifts that we can attribute the work accomplished by them. All that they effected—it was Jesus, to whom they ever bore witness, Who effected it. Their intellectual gifts contributed nothing to it; and to them applies in the highest degree St. Paul's image, when he compares Jesus to a treasure displaying its glories in an earthen vessel. For the rest, this is what the Father willed when He gave to Jesus such men for His apostles, and Jesus fully recognised it. "I thank Thee, O Father, because

Thou hast hid these things from the wise and prudent, and hast revealed them unto babes."

Thus this same Jesus, who had the art of making the great, such as John and Paul, play lowly parts, had also that of making lesser men, such as James and Peter, great,—great in such a way as to surpass even the greatest personages of history. And it is hard to say by which of the two—by the influence He exerts over great souls, or by the works He effects through the instrumentality of the simple— He most displays His own greatness.

5

ESSAY ON THE APOCALYPSE

THIS work upon the Apocalypse is the *pendant* to
the Essay on the Song of Songs which concludes
our first volume.

There is a close relationship both in substance and
in manner between these two works, and it is not
without reason that the one has been called the *Apo-*
calypse of the Old Testament, the other the *Canticle*
of the New. In both writings there appear, personified, and as if acting on the visible scene of the
world, the high and invisible powers which govern
on the one hand the development of the life of Israel,
and on the other the history of the Christian Church.
In each of the two it is by the help of poetic language
that the author renders perceptible to the minds of
men the action of these hidden forces, whether for
good or evil.

But the two works do not belong to the same kind
of poetry. We have seen that the Canticle only
becomes intelligible when we agree to consider it a
dramatic composition. Like the book of Job, the
Apocalypse belongs rather to the *epic* class of poetry.
It is the epopee of the supreme conflict between God

and Satan, the possession of humanity being the prize of the battle.

Perhaps some reader will ask whether the notion of a *poem* is compatible with that of prophecy, particularly when prophecy takes the form of a vision. Is not the prophetic picture, as well as the thought which is revealed in it, the creation of the Holy Spirit? The marriage between the Divine Spirit and the intellect of man is the profoundest of mysteries, and I do not presume to attempt here to fathom its depths. But do we not know that in those lower spheres to which the notion of inspiration is applied in the æsthetic meaning of that word, its mightiest breath does not at all exclude the labour of reflection? Music is certainly the art of all others in which it would seem that the creative power ought to be most free from all restraint; yet it is the one of which the results are subjected to the most rigorous laws—those of rhythm and of the scale. Does not the rich intuition which forms the primary substratum of all poetic work continue to exert its influence upon all the labour of careful and detailed thought, by which the author lays out the plan of his poem, makes up its details, and determines its form, even to the rhyme and the measure of the verse? Preaching, even when most inspired, is not therefore the less elaborated; and the beauty of its form, which is the object of our admiration, is due to no other inspiration than that which cal'ed forth its general conception.

The more sublime a thought is, the more does it aspire, in the mind of him who has conceived it, to give itself a form worthy of it.

These analogies prove, it seems to me, that there is no contradiction between the Divine origin of the prophecy of the Apocalypse, and the labour of thought in the writer who, in drawing it up, gave it its shape. To say it is prophecy *or* poetry, is to propose a false dilemma. The vision is the simultaneous result of the Divine inspiration and the imagination of man, co-operating in a way that cannot be defined. The essential point here is, that while in other domains the intellect lends its powers as the unbiassed organ of the Divine thought, in this the imagination offers itself the docile instrument of prophetic revelation.

The apocalyptic vision is the last form in which prophecy in the Old Testament clothed itself. It appears for the first time in a complete form in Daniel. It consists of a series of visions, forming a whole, of which the essential subject is the final stage of development of the history of humanity, and of which the aim is to prepare the people of God for passing victoriously through the terrible struggles which must precede that final term.

This kind of writing having once been introduced by Daniel, it was imitated in the following centuries by the authors of divers fictitious Jewish writings, as the *Sibylline oracles* and the *fourth book of Esdras*, for example.

The Apocalypse of John sums up in a picture of the same kind all the prophetic contents of the teaching of Jesus and of the apostolic revelations; and as Daniel had his spurious imitators amongst the Jewish people, so has John had his in the Christian Church. It is enough to mention the *book of Enoch*, of which the Christian character seems now well established, the *Testament of the Twelve Patriarchs*, and the Christian portions of the so-called *Sibylline books*.

From the beginning of its history, humanity has lived in a state of expectation, of disquieting fears, and of glorious hopes. "The seed of the woman shall bruise the serpent's head,"—this prophecy contains already an indication of the formidable struggles which are impending, and of the assured final victory. This expectation concentrated and purified itself in the heart of the people of Israel, which was ever attracted towards the future, and whose fervent aspirations were met on their upward way towards heaven by the prophecy which was descending from thence to meet it. Through Jesus this divine aspiration became that of the Church; and the book of the Apocalypse is the precious vessel in which this treasure of Christian hope has been deposited for all ages of the Church, but especially for the Church *under the Cross*.

The more deeply the Church plants in the earth the stakes of her tent, and establishes herself at her ease here below, the more does the Apocalypse become to her a foreign and even repulsive book. The more, on the other hand, tempestuous winds shake the curtains of her temporary dwelling-place, and threaten to break their cords, the more does she feel the value of this marvellous book, which teaches her to look up continually towards the Bridegroom whose return she expects. This is indeed her proper attitude in all times, whether those of prosperity or of persecution. Did not the Lord say to the believer: "Be like unto men that wait for their lord when he will return from the wedding"?[1]

A. The Plan

The first part of our task is to study, without any prejudice in favour of any particular interpretation, the *plan* of the prophetic vision.

The general idea of the book stands out clear from its beginning to its end—Christ will return. The Gospels had given the history of His first, the Apocalypse describes, in the language of prophecy, His second coming. The salutation of John to the Churches is so worded as to convey this idea: "Grace be unto you, and peace, from Him which is, and which was, and which *is to come* . . ." (v. 4). This salutation is immediately followed by the words which, properly speaking, form the opening of the book: "Behold, He

---

[1] Luke xii. 36.

cometh with clouds; and every eye shall see Him, and they also which pierced Him. . . . I am Alpha and Omega, the beginning and the ending, which is, and which was, and which *is to come*, the Almighty." The last word of the book corresponds with the first : " He which testifieth these things saith, Surely *I come* quickly; Amen. Even so, come, Lord Jesus !"

Did not the Lord declare in the assembled Sanhedrim, and at the very moment when His death was about to put an end to His presence upon earth: " I say unto you, Hereafter shall ye see the Son of man sitting on the right hand of power, and coming in the clouds of heaven " ?[1] In that notable saying, Christ's return in glory, as King and Judge—this latter is the idea implied in the symbol of the *cloud*—is closely connected with the fact of the Ascension. The reason is that in fact from this moment the office fulfilled by Jesus in the world's history is that of establishing, by the instrumentality of preaching, and of the Holy Spirit whom He sends forth from the seat of His glory, His kingdom in the earth, and of successively overthrowing all the obstacles which oppose themselves to its progress. His glorious appearing, when the close of this period of His working has been reached, will not be His *coming*—for that began to take place from the time of His ascension—but His *Advent*. The coming of Christ takes place during the whole of the present age ; it will only be consummated in the event

---

[1] Matt. xxvi. 64.

which is specially called the *Parousia,* or Advent. Accordingly, the sigh of the Church, and of the inspired bard, who prays in her name, is not, Come *soon,* but more exactly and literally, Come *quickly.* This expression refers, properly speaking, not to the nearness of the arrival, but to the rapidity of the journey, though the former is the necessary result of the latter.

This coming of Christ, from the time of the Ascension to that of the Parousia, is therefore the true subject of the Apocalypse, just as His first coming, between the fall of man and the Incarnation, was the true subject of Old Testament prophecy. "Behold, He shall come," said the last of the prophets, at the highest summit of ancient revelation, speaking of the Messiah-Jehovah.[1] The history of the world, in its essential character, is summed up in these three sayings: He is coming; He has come; He will come again.

It is upon this idea that the whole plan of the apocalyptic drama rests. In every journey we contemplate as distinct from one another, the starting-point, the journey itself, and the arrival.

The *starting-point* in the *coming* of the Apocalypse is the state of the Church at the time the author receives the vision. We find it described i.—iii.

The *journey* consists in all the preparations which

---

[1] Mal. iii. 1.

lead up to the final appearing of the Lord. They are described iv.—xix. 10.

Lastly, the *arrival* is the Parousia itself with all its consequences. From xix. 10 to the end of the book.

We do not here distinguish the first part from the preamble (i.) or the third from the conclusion (xxii. 6—21).

PART 1: REVELATION 1—3

In the first chapter, which is the preamble of the first part and of the whole book, the Lord appears to John clothed in all the insignia which serve as emblems of the different aspects of His glory. He is surrounded by seven golden candlesticks, symbols of the seven churches which are about to be mentioned by name ; and He holds in His hand seven stars, figures of the pastors of these churches.

It is from this picture of the glory of the Lord that the emblems by which He describes Himself in His messages to the seven churches are drawn. These emblems represent the qualities in virtue of which He will have power to do all that He announces to them.

The seven messages are contained in ch. ii. and iii.

The seven churches to which they are addressed are all situated in Asia Minor, but they are deliberately selected from among the churches, very much more numerous, of that country. There is, in fact, no mention made of Miletus, nor of Colosse, etc. What was the principle of this selection? It is not difficult to discover.

The first, Ephesus, is described in such a manner that praise and blame are almost equally balanced in the message from the Lord; though the rebuke expressed in verses 4 and 5 stands out as the dominant note of the epistle.

In the second church, on the contrary, Smyrna, praise predominates. There is no serious rebuke, no threat, but a marked recognition of the fidelity which is the general characteristic both of the community and of its pastor.

On the other hand, the tone of menace and rebuke preponderate again in the third epistle, addressed to the church of Pergamos, and is emphasized with even greater force than in the letter to Ephesus.

The Lord addresses, no doubt, words of rebuke to the fourth church, Thyatira; but the faithful members of that church receive unmitigated praise, and are the subjects of a magnificent promise.

The fifth church, Sardis, is openly accused of being *dead*, while having the *reputation of being alive;* and the call made to her to *repent* is developed in a tone severe and urgent.

No church receives richer praise than Philadelphia, the sixth. It seems as if she had but one step to make in advance, to obtain her admittance into the bosom of the Church triumphant.

Lastly, the seventh, Laodicea, is the one of which

the state is described in the darkest colours, and
whose future seems to be most compromised. She is
threatened with immediate rejection: "Because thou
art lukewarm . . . I will spue thee out of my mouth."
There is here more than an expression of indignation
—it is one of disgust. Laodicea has fallen as low as
a church can fall, while still bearing the name of a
church.

The law, then, according to which the seven churches
have been disposed in this picture seems to be this:
the numbers 1, 3, 5, and 7, indicate the different degrees of the dominion of sin over the Christian life in
a church,—its graduation in evil. The numbers 2, 4,
and 6, indicate, on the contrary, the different degrees
of the victory gained by the work of God over sin,—
its progress in good.

We are now in a position to seize the general idea
of this picture. It contains the portraiture of all the
shades, and, in a manner, the statistics of all the
spiritual states, either of good or evil, in which Christianity on earth may find itself. The Lord chose, in
order to characterize these seven degrees, the churches
of the country in which John lived, which embodied
most perfectly these seven types. The number *seven*
indicates here, as it always does, a totality. But the
idea of the book is that of a *simultaneous*, not that
of a *successive*, totality, as those think who see in these
seven churches the portraiture of the principal phases
of the history of the Church. One may, doubtless,

by taking up this latter stand-point, succeed in bringing out some ingeniously conceived points of harmony, but they always have a somewhat arbitrary character. Besides, the subject itself of this first part is against such an interpretation. It is the *starting-point* of the Lord's progress which should be here indicated ; this starting-point is the state of the Church at the time of the vision, and not the unrolling of its future history, which is contained rather in the subsequent visions.

We find, for the first time, in this arrangement of the messages to the seven churches, that alternation of bright and dark pictures which is to form one of the most striking characteristics of the whole book. The author has taken pains expressly to indicate his intention by an outward sign. He has introduced into the four epistles with odd numbers, and into those only, the formula, " Repent," followed by a threat in the event of obstinate hardness of heart. [1]

Is it not most remarkable that the churches thus reprimanded and threatened are, with the exception of one, Pergamos, entirely effaced from the map of Christendom, whilst the three which are the subjects of the Lord's promises have lasted through the ages, and are flourishing even to this day ? [2]

---

[1] ii. 5 (Ephesus); 16 (Pergamos) ; iii. 3 (Sardis); 19 (Laodicea).

[2] Ephesus, Sardis, and Laodicea are now nothing but heaps of ruins, while Smyrna is in possession of many churches of all the Christian creeds ; Thyatira numbers more than three hundred

PART 2: REVELATION 4—19:10

Here we have a picture of the *progress* of the Lord down the ages, to come and take possession of His heritage, the earth. He has for this end a war to wage. Just as Israel resisted the solicitations of Jesus during His life on earth, so will the Gentiles resist the pressure exerted upon them by the action of Jesus glorified. The conflict which the heavenly King will have to maintain with the intractable Gentiles will comprehend three principal phases, described in the Apocalypse under the image of the seven seals, the seven trumpets, and the seven vials.

The *seal* is the emblem of an event still hidden, but divinely decreed. The *trumpet* is something more than the mere revelation of an event that is to happen in the future; it is a manifestation of will which calls for a speedy realisation. Lastly, a *vial* poured out is the image of a decree as identified with its execution. There is, therefore, an evident gradation from one of these emblems to another.

A progression may also be remarked in the effects which result from the three orders of phenomena thus represented. The events designated by the seals bring about the destruction of the fourth part of the inhabitants of the earth; those announced by the

---

houses inhabited by Christians; and in Philadelphia, Christian worship is celebrated every Sunday in five churches. (See Keith on the fulfilment of prophecy.)

trumpets, the third ; and the vials destroy the half of the remainder.

There is, lastly, a gradation in the *idea* which governs each of these three series of events. The seals signify the first assault of the heavenly King against the fortress of rebellious heathenism ; the trumpets, the final summons to submission and repentance ; and the vials are the chastisements which come upon men hardened in rebellion ; or, to make use here of an historical analogy which naturally presents itself, the seals answer to the first miracles of Moses before Pharaoh, the trumpets to the ten plagues, and the vials to the catastrophe of the Red Sea.

In the apocalyptic vision, these three series of chastisements, by the help of which the Lord of glory aims at overcoming the resistance of the pagan world, are unfolded as follows :

The fourth chapter is a vision of the glory of God. His throne is supported by four *living creatures*, and twenty-four *elders* fall down before it. These are the representatives of *Nature* and of the *Church*. The former represent the forces of nature, which, in the ancient religions, sat upon the throne, personified in the pagan deities, but which, in the monotheism of the Bible, play a more modest part, and are employed in bearing up the throne of God,—that is to say, in establishing His kingdom. They are represented by the four living creatures which are supposed to be the *chefs d'œuvre* of the animate creation,—the lion, the bull, the eagle, and man. The twenty-four elders represent the Judæo-Christian and the Gentile Church, twelve for each of these two moieties of the primitive Church, in conformity with the types of the twelve patriarchs, the twelve tribes, and the twelve apostles.

The fifth chapter pictures the glory of the Lamb,— Jesus sacrificed and risen again. In His hands is a roll made up of seven leaves, and sealed with seven seals; this book contains the Divine decrees which are about to be put into execution with regard to the world. These two circumstances,—that the Lamb is entrusted with it, and that it is He who successively breaks its seals,—evidently signify that it is He who is to be the executor of the designs of God; accordingly, He is represented as possessing the *seven eyes* and the *seven horns;* that is to say, the fulness of omniscience and of omnipotence, without which He could not accom plish this divine work.

In the sixth chapter the opening of the first six seals takes place.

First seal : A white horse appears, whose rider is armed with a bow, and adorned with a victor's crown. This is an emblem of the *gospel,* which, through the instrumentality of preaching, is about to extend itself victoriously through the earth.

Second seal : A red horse, whose rider is armed with a sword, and who is none other than the angel of *war.*

Third seal : A black horse, whose rider holds a pair of balances in his hand, with which he measures

out to men their daily portion of wheat and of barley;
—the angel of *famine*.

Fourth seal : A pale horse, with two riders, Death
and Hell;[1]—an emblem of contagious sickness—of
pestilence.

Fifth seal : A scene in the invisible world ; the cry
of the martyrs whose blood has been shed unjustly,
and who demand the appearing of the Judge of the
world. White robes are given them until the time
shall arrive when they shall be joined by the martyrs
whose blood has yet to flow for the name of Christ.
It is the announcement of the *last persecutions*, but
also of the glory which those already enjoy who have
made of their life on earth a sacrifice to the Lamb.

Sixth seal : A great earthquake shakes the con-
tinents and seas; the earth trembles to its foundations;
it seems to the dwellers upon it as if the stars were
falling. They cry out in terror, as if the last day was
come. This is the expression of that presentiment of
the end of the world which seizes men in the great
catastrophes of nature.

How can we fail, as we study these six pictures, to
be reminded of the words of Jesus in the prophecy of
the destruction of Jerusalem, and of the end of the
world? (Matt. xxiv. 7,) "Nation shall rise against
nation, and kingdom against kingdom (second seal),
and there shall be *famines* (third seal), and *pestilences*
(fourth seal), and *earthquakes* (sixth seal) in divers

---

[1] The place of departed spirits.

places ;" words to which we must add (ver. 14), " And the gospel of the kingdom shall be preached in all the world, for a witness unto all nations (first seal) ; and then shall the end come." Does not even the fifth seal, the only one which at first sight does not seem to be taken from one of the expressions in this discourse of Jesus, rest upon these words : " They shall deliver you up to be afflicted, and shall kill you"? (ver. 9.)

The opening of the seventh seal is prepared for by two scenes, of which the serene and luminous character is contrasted with the dark pictures which precede it (vii.). A hundred and forty-four thousand members of the people of Israel, twelve thousand from each of the twelve tribes, are sealed with the seal of the living God ; that is to say, marked out to continue His, in the midst of that general apostasy which is about to invade the earth, and to absorb even the Jewish nation itself. It is impossible to interpret, as many wish to do, these hundred and forty-four thousand as signifying the Christian Church—the spiritual Israel. What purpose would be answered, in this figurative sense, by the enumeration by name of the twelve tribes of Israel ? Besides, the contrast evidently intended between this scene and that which is to follow, leaves no doubt as to the author's meaning.

In fact, after this scene referring to Israel, we are led on to the contemplation of a second ; a multitude *which no man can number, of all nations, and people, and kindreds, and tongues,* who triumph before the throne of the Lamb. This is the Christian Church. Its members are not counted; for this innumerable multitude comprehends the elect, not of one nation only, like the hundred and forty-four thousand, but of *all nations.* The foresight of her own triumph is to inspire the Church with courage to face the formidable crises which still stand between her and the object of her hope.

The seventh seal is broken (viii.). Its contents do not consist of any particular event, but of all that is still left unfulfilled of God's plan;—the seven trumpets, and the great events which they are to herald. Heaven prepares by a solemn silence, and a redoubling of prayer, for the conflicts which are coming on.

First trumpet: Hail, mingled with fire and blood, brings barrenness upon the earth. This is the aggravation of the judgments of the third seal (famine).

Second trumpet: The sea is smitten; its inhabitants perish; commerce is interrupted. Nothing consequently can diminish the terrible effects of the preceding calamity.

Third trumpet: The waters are corrupted over the whole earth; a terrible mortality seizes mankind; this is the pendant of the fourth seal (pestilence).

Fourth trumpet: After the earth, the sea, and the fountains of waters, the air takes its turn. It becomes dark, and the inhabitants of the earth are deprived of a part of the light of the sun and of the stars.

There is nothing to indicate that these plagues are to be understood in an allegorical sense. They are the convulsions of Nature in process of dissolution.

The last three trumpets are distinguished from the preceding ones by a special name, *the three woes* (ix.).

Fifth trumpet (first woe): From out of the bottom-less pit, the dwelling-place of the devils,[1] issue a cloud of evil spirits, represented under the image of locusts, of brilliant and attractive colours, but armed with the sting of a scorpion, and who for five months (the time during which in the East the plague of locusts lasts— May to December) throw into a kind of delirium— not of joy, but of deep sadness—mankind crushed under the weight of its struggle against the Almighty. It is as if the inhabitants of the earth were subjected to *possession* on a great scale, after the likeness of the single instances of the kind which we find in the gospel history. The fifth trumpet corresponds to the fifth seal in this respect, that both scenes belong to the invisible world, one in the celestial sphere, the other in the world of darkness.

Sixth trumpet (second woe): An invasion of foreign nations coming out of the East, leaves nothing in the earth but ruin and disaster.

And yet, notwithstanding all these calamities,—last appeals from the Divine holiness to the conscience of man,—men do not come to themselves. They continue to live in their idolatrous and corrupt practices. The

---

[1] Luke viii. 31.

Apocalypse, in fact, does not recognise any conversion of the pagan world between the time of the primitive Church and the epoch of the Parousia.[1] It sees the abominations of idolatry lasting on to the end.

Just as the opening of the seventh seal had been preceded by a twofold consolatory scene, guaranteeing the fidelity of a part of Israel and the final triumph of the Church, so is the seventh trumpet preceded by an episode which, if we are not mistaken, has specially in view (like the first of the two scenes in chap. vii.) the destiny of Israel in the crisis which is coming on. In order clearly to indicate that we are here dealing with a scene by itself, and, as it were, isolated in the midst of the great apocalyptic drama, the author makes it the subject of a special *little book*, inserted within the great one (x.). John is to *eat* it. This represents the most complete spiritual assimilation. This nourishment is to strengthen him for taking up again the great prophecy relating " to peoples, and nations, and tongues, and kings " (x. 11).

The contents of the "little book," which are at once joyful and bitter, are comprehended in xi. 1—13.

An angel, holding in his hand a rod, is employed in measuring the temple at Jerusalem, "with the altar and them that worship therein." This emblem corresponds with that of the seal set upon the

---

[1] Rev. ix. 20, 21 : " And the rest of the men . . . repented not of the works of their hands, that they should not worship devils and idols of gold and silver. . . . Neither repented they of their murders. . . ."

hundred and forty-four thousand. Just as those were sealed to mark them for ever as the heritage of God, so is the temple measured as destined to remain His domain for ever. But the court without the temple was not to be measured, it is said, because it is "*given unto the Gentiles*," for a period of forty-two months, or three years and a half. The event here spoken of cannot be a *material* seizure of this court by the Romans ; for if so, would not the taking of the temple accompany that of the court in the midst of which the temple stands ? The temple, together with the court, is therefore here the emblem of the Jewish nation. One part will remain faithful to its God—that represented by the temple measured by the angel, with the altar and its worshippers—and the other part, carnal Israel, will give itself up to the spirit of apostasy which will carry captive the Gentiles. This is the court which the Gentiles will tread under foot. The worshippers around the altar are none other than the hundred and forty-four thousand who were sealed in order that they might be preserved, and whom we soon come upon once more in the final struggle. All the rest is an Israel thenceforth emancipated from the fear of Jehovah, and confounded with the pagan nations.

This twofold Israel, the carnal and the spiritual, is once more established as a nation. It has its capital at Jerusalem ; for it is impossible not to take this name in its literal sense, in view of the explanation (ver. 8) : "the great city, which spiritually is called Sodom and Egypt, where also our Lord was crucified." In the midst of this restored Israel arise *two witnesses* for God, two preachers of repentance, who, dressed like the ancient prophets, and endued with their power and with their miraculous gifts, prepare the conversion of the nation. But the beast, that is, the Antichrist— this is the first time of his appearance ; and as he is not properly introduced into the apocalyptic picture till chap. xiii., we perceive clearly here that this "little book" is an anticipation in the course of the great prophecy—the beast, we say, kills these two men, who smite the earth with all kinds of plagues, and thus rids himself of his two most formidable adversaries. The inhabitants of the earth rejoice, but their joy is short-lived. The two witnesses for the truth rise again on the fourth day, and are glorified in presence of their enemies. At this moment an earthquake destroys the tenth part of the holy city, seven thousand persons perish, and the remnant of the Israelites give glory to God.

This is the picture of the conversion of the Jewish nation, in the sense in which St. Paul said : "And so all Israel shall be saved."[1] As this event is the principal fact in the future development of the kingdom of God, it is contained, for this reason, in a

---

[1] M. Reuss and M. Renan recognise, as we do, in this verse, the announcement of the general conversion of Israel to the gospel.

special book ; and as the mention of it at this point of the vision is a prophecy within the prophecy, the author indicates this by using in general the future tense : " I *will give* power unto my two witnesses to prophesy ; . . . . they *shall be clothed* in sackcloth ; . . . . when they shall have finished . . . ." etc.

The seventh trumpet (xi. 15), or third woe, has reference to the appearing of the Antichrist. The preceding verse (14) is intended to take up the thread of the general vision, which had been interrupted by the intercalation of the little book. Compare this verse, " The second woe is past, and behold the third woe cometh quickly," with ix. 12, which preceded the sixth trumpet: " One woe is past, and behold there come two woes more hereafter."

We shall see that it is the reign of Antichrist which brings upon men the last calamities, represented by the seven vials ; hence it follows that these latter are included in the seventh trumpet, just as the seven trumpets formed the contents of the seventh seal. There is great art in this way of picturing history as a series of periods, each of which arises out of the last term of the period which precedes it. In this simple image is expressed one of the profoundest laws of the progress of the world.

The preparation for the appearing of Antichrist (xii.) is as follows. (This event on earth is the result of a revolution in heaven.)

A woman, in whom we recognise the symbol of the

kingdom of heaven—the word kingdom is feminine in Greek, *basileia*—is on the point of giving birth to a son, no longer the Messiah in a state of humiliation, who was the child of the Jewish theocracy in the days of Herod, but the Messiah who is to *rule the nations with a rod of iron* (ver. 5),—that is to say, the Messiah as King and as Judge.   Satan, who from the high position which he occupied in the celestial regions up to the time of his last fall, still rules the Gentile nations, watches for the moment in which the son of the woman will appear, in order to devour him. But Michael, the champion of God, the defender of monotheism, watches and fights.   Satan is thrown down from the position which he is still holding, and cast upon the earth ; and he it is who, in order to avenge himself, calls forth from the depth of the seas, that is, from the midst of the nations, Antichrist—his instrument for waging a final conflict against Christ.[1]

The appearing of Antichrist is described in chap. xiii.   He is a universal ruler.   As *the beast*, who represents him in the vision, combines in himself the characteristics of all the animals previously described by Daniel, so will the empire of this last representative of the power hostile to God in the earth include in itself all the kingdoms which existed before it.   It will at length realise that universal monarchy towards which a secret instinct impels mankind.

---

[1] The true reading of xiii. 1, seems to be : " And he stood (not I stood) upon the sand of the sea."

It is, no doubt, indicated by the vision contained in the little book (xi.) that the beast is to reign in Jerusalem, but not that his throne will be there at first. Chap. xvii., in which his capital is characterised by the *seven hills*, proves that Rome is the place in which his empire is to be founded.[1]

But the seven heads, which figure the seven mountains, are also *seven kings*, it is said (xvii. 10); that is to say, according to Daniel's manner of writing, seven *kingdoms;* and this explains to us the reason why the beast unites in himself the insignia of all the preceding monarchies (xii. 2).   To this power, of which Rome is to be the centre, all the empires which have succeeded each other in history contribute their share.

One of these heads has received a deadly wound (according to xvii. 10, we may suppose that it is the fifth); but this wound, contrary to all expectation, is suddenly healed, and this marvel astonishes the whole earth, and brings all its inhabitants to worship the beast. We see here, therefore, one of the earlier forms of the anti-Divine power on the earth, which, after having been put down by an act of the Divine power, reappears suddenly in the person of the Antichrist himself, in such a manner that the kingdom of the latter seems to be only the restoration of that ancient power.   This is one of the most important features

---

[1] "The seven heads (of the beast) are seven mountains" (ver. 9).

of the apocalyptic vision. We must be satisfied here with having pointed it out distinctly.

The object of the enmity of the beast is God and His tabernacle (xiii. 6); and next, all the inhabitants of the earth who refuse to bend the knee before him, and to blaspheme God and heaven. The Church is declared outlawed (ver. 16, 17). This is the time of the last persecutions announced in the fifth seal.

The Antichrist has an auxiliary, a second power represented under the image of a beast "*which had two horns like a lamb, and spake as a dragon.*" According to xix. 20, this is the *false prophet.* Here again we find ourselves in presence of the very text of the discourse of Jesus in Matt. xxiv. In ver. 24, we read these words : " There shall arise false Christs and false prophets." The Lord adds : " And shall shew great signs and wonders, insomuch that if it were possible they shall deceive the very elect." These expressions are almost literally reproduced in Rev. xiii. 13, 14, and applied to the false prophet. In this diabolical work, Antichrist represents political despotism, and the false prophet spiritual error.

This dark picture of the reign of Antichrist is followed (as is always the case in the Apocalypse) by a scene adapted to strengthen the believers who might be shaken by prospects so terrible. In chap. xiv. the Lamb passes in review before Him, on Mount Sion, those hundred and forty-four thousand faithful Israelites who are to form the strength of the Church

during this supreme calamity. In fact, they form
henceforth part of the Church, and are the *élite* of her
army (xiv. 4). The conversion of Israel to the gospel,
foretold in the "little book," is therefore now completed. Accordingly, the development of the mission
to the heathen takes a new step forward. The *ever-
lasting gospel* is proclaimed to all the inhabitants of
the earth (ver. 6). Men are warned by faithful servants against all concessions which they might be
tempted to make to the power of the beast (ver. 9—
12); they are reminded of the glorious and immediate
rewards of fidelity (ver. 13). Lastly, the visions which
follow, of a harvest and of a vintage (ver. 14—20)
typify the time, now nigh at hand, in which God will
gather in His own, and will trample His enemies in
the winepress of His wrath.

Chapters xv. and xvi. describe the pouring out of
the seven vials, that is to say, the extremest punishments of God, upon the throne and empire of the
beast. Antichrist had promised to mankind a new
golden age under his rule; but he promised without
God. Christ now wields His own sceptre, and smites
with repeated blows the nations who have been led
astray. It is the history of the plagues of Egypt over
again. A noisome sore consumes the flesh of the
subjects of the beasts (first vial). The waters of the
sea are corrupted, and all the inhabitants of the ocean
perish (second vial: an aggravation of the second
trumpet). A similar judgment smites the rivers and

fountains of waters (third vial ; compare the third trumpet). A burning sun scorches the inhabitants of the earth (fourth vial). These four vials constitute a first series of plagues, after which the author remarks that men only blasphemed with so much the greater audacity the name of the God who had sent these plagues upon them.

A thick darkness comes upon the kingdom of the beast, as before upon the kingdom of Egypt (fifth vial) ; men gnaw their tongues in their rage, rather than confess their faults. The Euphrates is dried up, to open the way for a new invasion of the Eastern nations, whom three unclean spirits summon to the last battle against the Eternal (sixth vial ; compare the invasion described under the sixth trumpet). Lastly, an earthquake of unprecedented violence falls upon Babylon, the capital of the beast, and the other cities of that empire (seventh vial ; compare the similar phenomenon described under the sixth seal).

Many reasons may incline us to think that these plagues let loose upon mankind when subject to Antichrist are the same as those which in chap. xi. are attributed to the power of the two witnesses preaching repentance in Jerusalem (xi. 5, 6), those two prophets of whom it is said (ver. 10) that they *tormented them that dwell on the earth.* And this explains the presence of the beast in Jerusalem (chap. xi.). Antichrist has perceived the origin of the punishments which desolate his empire,—the power and the prayers of those two men who exercise at this time, with regard to the world, a ministry similar to that which Moses and Aaron fulfilled in old time with regard to Egypt; and he goes to Jerusalem, in order to annihilate this centre of resistance to his universal power. With regard to the earthquake which follows the murder of the two witnesses, and which is the signal for the conversion of the Jewish nation, it may perfectly well be identical with that of the seventh vial, which introduces the destruction of Babylon. But what is the result of all these chastisements? "And men blasphemed God" (xvi. 21). There comes a time when all that should convert man, only hardens him. Then it is that society, and individual men are ripe for judgment.

The vision in xvii. and xviii. refers to the fate of Babylon. We note here an unexpected change in the conduct of Antichrist with respect to his capital. Before, the beast had carried Babylon upon his seven heads, but now becomes violently hostile to it. Together with the ten auxiliaries who had assembled around him, Antichrist pillages Babylon, and burns it with fire (xvii. 16, 17). What is the meaning of this sudden antagonism, and why does the beast now turn against his ancient dwelling-place? There is a mystery here in the apocalyptic vision, which we shall endeavour to clear up.

All God's enemies receive in succession their judgment. Babylon has just undergone hers at the hands

of the very same power which had before exalted her.
The time has arrived when Antichrist in his turn must
receive the reward he has deserved.

PART 3: REVELATION 19:11-22

In the midst of the reign of the beast, heaven
opens, and the Messiah appears upon a white horse,
the emblem of victory. He calls Himself the *Word
of God*; His armies follow Him ; that is, the believers,
clothed in white—the symbol of holiness. Antichrist
and the false prophet are cast into the lake of fire ;
those whom they have led away in their revolt perish.
Then Satan, the tempter, is imprisoned in the bottom-
less pit for a thousand years. This period is the time
of Christ's reign amongst men. The gospel sheds
upon society all its beneficent effects ; the faithful
dead who have risen again take, from their higher
spheres, an active part in this perfected manifestation
of the kingdom of God upon earth. The second
petition of the Lord's prayer is fulfilled ; the kingdom
of God is come.

But the reintegration of earth into heaven is not
yet consummated. At the end of this period, Satan
is unloosed ; a long time of spiritual and social prosperity has prepared the way for a last crisis. It breaks
forth, and the result is the complete overthrow of the
Evil Spirit. Satan is now cast headlong into the lake
of fire, where the beast and the false prophet await

him. The universal resurrection and the last judgment take place, and are followed by the appearing of
the new heaven and the new earth. In the midst of
this transformed universe appears the New Jerusalem,
the society of the elect, whose perfection is magni-
ficently described in this one sentence: " The length
and the breadth and the height of it are equal." It
follows from this that it forms a perfect cube. What
is the meaning of this image, which, taken literally,
sounds absurd ? The cubical form was, as is well
known, that of the holy place in the temple at Jerusalem. The meaning of this emblem is, therefore, that
the whole city is henceforth the same as was the holy
place—the place of the immediate manifestation of
God. This is the reason that John sees no temple
there. It is itself, taken as a whole, the perfect
temple. Accordingly, all creatures who have not yet
shared in the redemption, come thither to be healed
(xxii. 2).

In the second part of chap. xxii., the angel who is
the interpreter of the revelation returns to John and
to the actual state of the Church and of the world at
the time of the vision. He calls upon the Church to
grow in holiness even unto perfection, and upon the
world to ripen, by ever-growing defilement, for the
judgment. Then John adjures the copyists who shall
reproduce this prophecy to respect scrupulously its
text ; and making himself the organ of the aspirations of the Church, he calls upon the Lord to hasten

His coming : "Lord Jesus, come quickly." The Lord replies : "Yea, I come ;" and this last word expresses the essence of the history from the time of the vision up to that of the *Parousia*.

A. The Vision

After this analysis, no one will be tempted to dispute the unity of this book, or to see in it, as has been sometimes done, a compilation of collected documents. The idea which dominates the whole is the conflict of Jesus glorified with the Gentile world. This conflict develops itself through a certain number of phases which succeed each other in an evident gradation up to the end. The unity of the vision is made manifest also by a number of details ; for instance, by the fact that the seven promises made to the churches in the epistles of chaps. ii. and iii. find their realisation in the splendours of the New Jerusalem, described at the end of the book.

But, some may ask, is it possible to allow that a vision of such length, and composed with so much skill, is the result of Divine revelation ? Should we not rather see in it a human composition somewhat artificial, and of a character altogether poetical ? This question is closely connected with that of the authorship of the book. But let us, first of all, call to mind some analogies in the Old Testament—the vision in Isaiah liii., where the whole picture of the sufferings and the triumph of the servant of Jehovah passes before the eyes of the prophet ;—Ps. ii. and cx., in which the seer contemplates the elevation of the Messiah to the throne of God, His conflict with the assembled nations and with their kings who conspire against His power ; lastly, His victory (as a royal priest, reigning after the manner of Melchisedec) over the principal enemy from whom He conquers His heritage, the ends of the earth.   But the most striking instance is offered us in the series of visions with which the book of Zechariah opens.   In nine pictures presented to the inward eye of the prophet, in the course of a single night, he beholds the Lord protecting Jerusalem after its rebuilding, the casting down of the heathen monarchies who had oppressed it, the help of God assured to the labours of Joshua and Zerubbabel for the complete restoration of the people of God, renewed corruption and renewed captivity, and finally the appearing of the Priest-Saviour, upon whose head, contrary to the law of Moses, and to the fundamental charter of Israel, is to be placed a kingly crown. (Zech. i.—vi.)   Such precedents approximate very closely to the vision of the Apocalypse.

Shall it be said that though we, weak human creatures as we are, are enabled, by the magic power of speech, to awaken in the mind of one, or in those of even thousands of listeners, a whole world of ideas, which an instant before were quite strange to them, God, on the other hand, " *the Father of the spirits of all flesh*," cannot call forth, when it pleases Him, in the depths of the human soul, a succession of pictures.

which shall be the expression of His own thought? Of course such a fact is not to be conceived as an isolated act ; it can only be one step in a great process of the same nature,—that is to say, of a work of education and of Divine revelation ; but is it not just in this way that it presents itself in the history, and is pictured for us in the Scriptures? The great apocalyptic vision which we have just gone through is the crown and the highest development of the organism of the Divine revelations.

But that which authorises us above all in attributing the character of a revelation to the vision we are studying, is that, according to our conviction, the book in which it is transmitted proceeds from that disciple whom Jesus had admitted more deeply than any other into the inmost secrets of His thought.

B. The Person

Who is the person, named John, who twice over designates himself as the author of the Apocalypse ?[1] Is it one of the believers in Asia Minor, one of the presbyters, for instance, of the Ephesian church, as has been sometimes supposed, and therefore quite a different person from the apostle John ? But in that case, would he not have designated himself in a more definite manner, especially since it is certain, from the writings of the Fathers, that John, the disciple whom Jesus loved, ended his ministry and his life amongst

---

[1] i. 4, and xxii. 8.

the churches of Asia Minor, and that a confusion would therefore be inevitable? The author who, in addressing those churches, and, at that time, designated himself simply by the name John, must either have been John the apostle, or have intended to pass for him. Now we think we may put aside at once the idea of an imposture. The spirit of falsehood is incompatible with the Divine breath of holiness and of truth which pervades every page of the Apocalypse.

This conclusion, drawn from the book itself, is confirmed by the unanimous conviction of the churches of the second century, and of their principal doctors. We will only draw attention here to two testimonies of special importance. The first is that of Justin Martyr. In a public discussion with a Jew named Trypho, which he held at Ephesus less than fifty years after the death of St. John, and of which he has given an account in a work which has been preserved to us,[1] he says: "One of our body, named John, *one of the twelve apostles of our Christ,* in the revelation which was made to him, has predicted that the faithful *shall spend a thousand years in Jerusalem.*" Justin had visited a number of churches, and in this passage he expresses their sentiments, and not his own only.

The other testimony which we must quote, of later date than that last mentioned by thirty years, but which nevertheless has an even greater weight, on account of the circumstances of the life of the man

[1] *Dialogue with Trypho the Jew.*

from whom it comes, is that of Irenæus. " *John, the disciple of the Lord*," he says, "beheld in the apocalyptic vision the sacerdotal and glorious advent of the kingdom of Christ." And when speaking of the number of the beast (xiii. 18), he says : " This number is to be found in all the ancient and correct manuscripts, and even those *who have seen John* declare that this number is that of the name of the beast." Irenæus had, in his childhood, received Christian instruction from the venerable Bishop of Smyrna, Polycarp, who was himself a disciple of St. John. The testimony of such a man, of whose honesty also there can be not the least doubt, carries a weight which none can fail to recognise.

We are not ignorant of the objections that have been urged to the view which we are defending.

John does not give his name in his Gospel ; why, then, should he do so in the Apocalypse ? Because the Gospel is a history, and the Apocalypse a prophecy. The Hebrew historians do not give their names, the contents of their narratives being matter of public notoriety ; but all the Hebrew prophets do so, because their names are the only guarantee for the reality of the revelation which they claim for themselves.

If John was the son of Zebedee, could he speak of himself as he does in xxi. 14, when he relates that the names of the twelve apostles were engraved upon the foundations of the New Jerusalem ? Yes, because he did not attribute this dignity of apostleship to his own merit, but to the gratuitous gift of his Lord and Saviour.

But is not the spirit of the Apocalypse as grossly Judæo-Christian in its character as the Gospel of John is the contrary ?   The difference is in the form of the book, not in its substance. The Apocalypse speaks in a language of imagery and figures.   There is but one way of making it into a judaising document—that is, by failing to recognise the spiritual sense of this language, and taking all this imagery literally.   Nothing can be conceived more absurd than this process in some cases. We have just seen that the height of the New Jerusalem was equal to its length and to its breadth ; and we had no difficulty in discovering the idea conveyed under this image. As the image literally understood would be startling, grotesque, and absurd,—a city wall twelve thousand stadia, that is to say, 450 leagues, in height !—so, understood allegorically, it conveys a sublime idea.   Baur, the great adversary of the authenticity of the Gospel, but the not less zealous defender of that of the Apocalypse, has said that the Gospel was nothing but "a spiritualised Apocalypse."   One could not do more complete though unintentional homage to the fundamental harmony that exists between the two books.   The Apocalypse, spiritually understood (as it should be whenever it describes the kingdom of God), is therefore *identical with the Gospel.*

It is further said : All the wrath of John *the evangelist* is reserved for the Jews—call to mind the conflicts between Jesus and the inhabitants of Jerusalem in the fourth Gospel—while that of John, the author of the Apocalypse, is for the Gentiles. But this contrast arises precisely from the fact that the two documents are but two moieties of one and the same whole. The idea of the complete work is the conflict of the Messiah with *the world*. The Gospel describes the first act in this drama—the conflict of the Messiah, during His earthly ministry, with His people Israel. The Apocalypse describes, prophetically, the second act of the same drama—the conflict of Jesus glorified with the Gentile nations. These two subjects, considered from a logical point of view, are mutually exclusive, just because they complement each other, and make up in reality but one whole.

But John was a gentle and kind man ; how can we attribute to him the sanguinary threats and the terrific pictures of the Apocalypse ? The character of the apostle John, as commonly represented, is a pure fiction, as we have endeavoured to prove in the preceding essay. The Lord characterised His chosen disciple quite otherwise when He called him a *son of thunder ;* and it is this surname which we must call to mind when picturing to ourselves the author of the Apocalypse. Is it not the same St. John who, at Ephesus, on entering a bath-house with Polycarp, and understanding that a false teacher, called Cerinthus, was there at the time, exclaimed sternly: " Let us depart hence, lest the house should fall in upon the heretic and us."   This is he who, in the Apocalypse, beholds, in the spirit, our ancient universe falling in ruins upon mankind in its rebellion.   His charity is not weakness ; according to the Bible expression, it has *truth for its girdle.*

The only serious objection that can be urged against the authenticity of the Apocalypse lies in the difference which is observable between its style and that of the fourth Gospel.   The latter is free from Aramaic expressions, the former is saturated with them.   But this difference is to be explained by that which exists between the style of narrative and that of prophecy. In the Gospel, John speaks simply the language which is natural to him—a kind of Greek, in which we easily recognise Jewish thought clothed in Hellenic forms. In the Apocalypse, in which he imitates and copies, so to say, the prophets of the Old Testament, he is obliged to appropriate their style, and does not succeed in conforming it to the requirements of the Greek language, to which that style was completely foreign. On the whole, a profound study of the two documents discovers, in the style of them both, such deep-seated and significant analogies, that men belonging to the critical party which is the most opposed to orthodoxy have attempted to demonstrate from this very fact the identity of authorship of the two documents.

We have answered the principal objections ; let us

now look into some of the indications by which we perceive that the two writings do, in fact, proceed from one and the same mind.

Such are the correlation between the personages who play a part in each of the pictures :—in the Gospel —Jesus, the Jews, and the disciples ; in the Apocalypse —Jesus, the Gentiles, and the Church (or the Bride). In both cases are presented to us—first, the object of faith, and, next, the personifications of unbelief and of faith.

Next, notice the correspondence between the progressive steps of the two narratives ; in both a conflict increasing in intensity, ending in the defeat, externally, of the cause of God, and in its ultimate triumph by means of that very defeat ; the end always seeming to be approaching, and yet always retiring into the distance again. The formula of postponement, which is of such frequent occurrence in the Gospel, " For His hour was not yet come," is not less exactly applicable to the apocalyptic drama.

Then we find the same preponderance of the law of contrast in both documents: a continual alternation between the dark and the bright pictures, between the scenes of faith and those of unbelief.

Notice, again, two other points of detail. Jesus is designated by two names in the Apocalypse—the *Lamb* (through the whole course of the prophecy) and the *Word of God* (xix. 13). Now we know that of these two names the former is only to be found in the

writings of Peter and of the fourth evangelist, who had
heard it from the lips of their master, John the Baptist ;
and the latter is never, in the whole of the New Testament, given to Jesus, except in two other of the writings of St. John, his gospel and his first epistle.[1]

We do not think, then, that we can be wrong in
maintaining that when criticism wishes to impose
upon us the alternative of John the apostle, the author
of the Gospel, or John the apostle, the author of the
Apocalypse, it is strangely mistaken. Even if Christian
antiquity did not attribute both these works to the
beloved disciple, a thorough study of the two must, it
seems to me, lead to that conviction.

C. The Date

The question of the exact date of the composition of
the Apocalypse has no necessary connection with that
of its authorship ; for the two principal dates between
which there can be a doubt, are both of them comprehended within the lifetime of the apostle John. These
are, as we shall see, the time of the short reign of
Galba, in 68, and the reign of Domitian, from 81 to
96. This latter date is the one indicated by Christian
antiquity. Irenæus says, speaking of the interpretation of the number 666 which is the mark of the beast,
" If it had been intended to reveal clearly the name of
the personage designated by this cipher, at that time,
it would have been indicated by him to whom the

---

[1] John i. 36; 1 Pet. i. 19; John i. 1 ; 1 John i. 1.

revelation was granted.   For it is not in a long past
age that this vision was seen, but almost in the present
generation, towards the end of the reign of Domitian."
This testimony is clear and precise ; there is nothing
in it which savours of the vagueness of hypothesis, or
of the uncertainty of exegetical calculation.   Irenæus
professes, moreover, in more than one place, to have
received his teaching from the lips " of the presbyters
who lived with John in Asia Minor up to the time of
Trajan."   In these words he refers more particularly
to Polycarp and Papias.

The other date, that of the year 68, is a result of
the exposition which most of the critics of our day
give to the Apocalypse.   According to them, the
beast, or Antichrist, represents the Roman emperor
in the collective sense of that word.   The seven
heads are the first seven emperors ; and as the
author says (xvii. 10) that the sixth "is now," we
conclude from this that he must be writing in the
reign of Galba, that is, in the second half of the
year 68 ; since, from the point of view of the Roman
historians, the emperors succeed each other as follows :
Augustus, Tiberius, Caligula, Claudius, Nero, Galba.
Nero, the fifth, is signified by the head which received a deadly wound (an allusion to his tragical
end).   The sixth is Galba ; Otho and Vitellius
are left out, as not having really reigned.   The
seventh head is the expected successor of Galba ;
and the eighth, which is identified with the beast

itself, is none other than Nero risen again, whose
reappearance is thus announced by the author, in
accordance with a legend which was current at that
time, and of which some ambitious persons took
advantage in their attempts to play the part of a
pseudo-Nero.

We will examine this interpretation considered in
itself later on. At present we are treating only of
the date at which the book was composed ; and
enquiring which of the two dates proposed is the
more probable,—that indicated by tradition, or that
which modern science thinks it has discovered.

1. Let us consider first the *condition* of the churches
in Asia Minor. They had been founded by St. Paul
between 55 and 58, and, therefore, ten years before
the date at which, according to the interpretation
now prevalent, the Apocalypse was written. Now
let us weigh well the rebukes addressed to them in
the seven messages contained in chaps. ii. and iii.
Ephesus has *fallen from her first works.* Sardis has
a name to live, but *is dead.* Laodicea is *lukewarm,*
and ready to be *spued out of the mouth* of the Lord.
No respite is promised or announced ; if they do not
repent, the Lord will come and will remove their
candlestick. Is that, then, a condition to which the
churches founded by St. Paul could have been reduced,
after not more than ten years of existence ? If it
were only a question of the breaking out of some
heresy, as in the case of the Galatians, or of a return

to certain vicious habits, as at Corinth, there would be nothing in this difficult to understand. But that which is described is a falling away so complete, that the evil seems to have reached its consummation—death. Luther is reported to have said that a religious revival lasts for thirty years. The revival which has taken place in our own day began about the year 1817, and has not yet, after more than fifty years, spent its force ; and yet we are to believe that those "powers of the world to come," those graces of the " first love," which the ministry of St. Paul had called forth in the most flourishing churches of the world— those of Asia Minor—had exhausted themselves in ten years ! Do I say in ten years ? Why, in 63, Paul writes to the Ephesians and to the Colossians ;— in 63 or 64, Peter writes also to all the churches in Asia, Bithynia, etc. ; not a word that escapes from either apostle would lead us to suppose that the slightest loss of energy had supervened in the religious or moral life of these churches. And we are asked to believe that all at once, in the year 68, only four or five years later, John could address to them the language we know so well ! We venture to say that this is a complete moral impossibility; and if the modern interpretation can only be maintained at the cost of an improbability so gigantic, it seems to us sufficiently condemned by that fact alone.

2. The ecclesiastical *organisation* which is pre-

supposed by the Apocalypse is no less incompatible
with so early a date as the year 68.   It is well known
that in the constitution of the apostolic churches, the
communities were governed by colleges of *presbyters*,
who were also called *bishops*. These two titles, of
which one proceeded from the Synagogue and the
other was of Greek origin, described precisely the
same office.[1] It is only towards the end of the
apostolic age that the presbyteral authority concen-
trates itself in the person of a head of the flock, who
takes specially the name *bishop*.   The epistle of
Clement of Rome, written probably in the reign of
Domitian, at the end of the first century, and the epistles of Ignatius, which date from the reign of Trajan,
at the beginning of the second century, are the first
monuments in the patristic writings of that form of
the ministry which we meet with in the Apocalypse :
" Unto the *angel* of the church of . . . . write."   This
name, as of a person—*angel*—as well as the fact of
the responsibility which is laid upon the functionary
so designated by the rebukes and praises addressed
to him by the Lord, will not allow us to take this
expression to mean a collective or abstract being, nor
an angel properly so called—the invisible patron of

---

[1] Cf. Acts xx. 17, " He called the *elders* of the church,"
with ver. 28, " Take heed therefore . . . to the flock, over the
which the Holy Ghost hath made you *overseers* " (ἐπίσκοποι) ;
Titus, i. 5, " I left thee . . . . that thou shouldest ordain
elders . . . ." with ver. 7, " For a *bishop* must be," etc.
Lastly, Acts xiv. 23, with Phil. i. 1.

the flock. It can only mean a bishop, such as we find in all churches from the end of the first century. The Apocalypse brings before us the period of transition from the primitive presbyterian constitution to the monarchic organisation which is universally admitted to have prevailed in the second century. This point of detail therefore just as positively excludes the date 68 as it agrees naturally with that indicated by Irenæus.

3. An ecclesiastical *usage*, to which allusion is made in another passage, leads to the same result. It is said (i. 3) : " Blessed is *he that readeth*, and *they that hear*, the words of this prophecy." These expressions presuppose two things : first, that the writer is speaking here of reading in public, in an official manner, in a congregation gathered for worship, and not only of any one reading privately and to himself. This is indicated by the opposition between the singular, *he that readeth*, and the plural, *they that hear*. Moreover, the use of the present tense, *he that readeth*, implies, especially in Greek, an habitual, often-repeated act. Now the regular reading of the apostolic writings as a part of worship could not have been begun so early as the year 68. I may here appeal to M. Reuss, one of the inventors of the modern exposition, who says : " During the whole of the remainder of the first century, and during at least a third part of the second, the apostolic writings had not yet been made the subjects of an official, repeated, and so to

say, liturgical reading."[1] This assertion certainly goes
beyond the truth ; men did not wait till the year 130
before they began to read in public the writings of
the apostles, thus filling up the void left by the loss
of their personal ministry ; but at any rate we shall
be right in admitting that this custom did not exist, as
a received form, before the destruction of Jerusalem in
the year 70, and that consequently the Apocalypse,
which implies the use of that custom, cannot have
been composed in the year 68.[2]

4. We find in this book one *expression* so foreign to
the style of the other New Testament writings, that it
would of itself lead us to the same conclusion—that
is, the word *Lord's day* applied (i. 10) to Sunday. It
is well known that the apostolic writings of a date
anterior to the destruction of Jerusalem never speak
of this day except as the *first day of the week*.[3] The
expression, *the Lord's day*, is of purely Christian
origin, belonging to the ecclesiastical and technical
language of the later times of the apostolic age, when
the Church had broken off all connection with the
Synagogue. Accordingly, we find it only in the
writings of the second century. The date indicated

---

[1] *Histoire du Canon des Saintes Ecritures*, p. 14.

[2] M. Renan, another defender of the modern interpretation,
understands this passage exactly as we do: " Allusion is here
made to the reading in the Church by the *Anagnostes.*"
(*L'Antéchrist*, p. 360.)

[3] 1 Cor. xvi. 2 (in the year 58) ; Acts. xx. 7 (some years later
at least).

by Irenæus is the only one compatible with the use of this expression.[1]

5. Again, the name given to *the Jews* in the Apocalypse will not allow us to suppose that this book was written before the great judgment of God upon Jerusalem. They are called (ii. 9, and iii. 9) *the synagogue of Satan*. What Christian author—especially what Judæo-Christian writer, such as the author of the Apocalypse must have been—would have allowed himself to brand with such a name the chosen people, before God had finally broken with them? Call to mind how the whole Judæo-Christian Church, according to the Acts, took part in the worship of the temple up to the year 60; read over again the epistle to the Hebrews, which was written in the year 67 or 68, with the object of consoling the Christians of Jewish origin for their loss of the worship of the sanctuary—a loss so deeply felt that it became to them even a temptation to apostasy; . . . . and yet we are asked to suppose that one of these same Hebrew Christians could at that very time have given to his compatriots the name of a Satanic assembly! No, nothing but an event of so decisive a nature as the destruction of Jerusalem and of the Jewish nation can explain so novel a manner of speech with respect to the ancient people of God.

---

[1] A comparison with iv. 2 will not allow us to explain i. 10 in the sense which has been proposed: "I was in the Spirit on the day of the Lord,—that is to say, at His advent."

6. Lastly, let us notice a striking coincidence between one feature of the apocalyptic vision and the special form taken by the persecution under Domitian. In that of Nero, the Christians had been at once delivered up to execution. It was not so under Domitian. Many persons of eminence were, according to the historians of that time, transported into islands far away in the sea.[1] The banishment of the author of the Apocalypse to Patmos is exactly an instance of this kind of punishment.

According to all these indications, we have no hesitation in saying that the Apocalypse belongs to the end of the first century of the Church. Judging from the several features which we have now pointed out, it marks the transition between the state of the primitive churches as they had been founded by the apostles, and that of the episcopal churches of the second century.

D. The Interpretation

We come now to the most important and most difficult part of our task,—the interpretation of the book. The number of the expositions of the Apocalypse is almost past calculation ; and it is not even easy to classify all these essays, which start from the most opposite points of view, and arrive at the most

---

[1] Eusebius mentions particularly—quoting from the heathen historians—an instance of a Christian lady, Domitilla, who was transported to the island of Pontia (or, according to Dion Cassius, Pandateria).

diverse results. In a general way we may say that these expositions may be referred to three different systems : 1. That which we may call the *modern* interpretation, though we find some traces of it in ancient times, but it has only prevailed decidedly since the year 1836, when four learned men discovered at the same moment [1] the meaning of the number 666, which established in their view unanswerably the truth of this interpretation. From this point of view the book is wholly determined by the passing circumstances of the time in which it appeared. 2. The *traditional* exposition, which sees in the apocalyptic vision, in a manner more or less general or detailed, a picture of the destinies of the Church from the first century till the return of Christ. 3. A mixed system, of which M. de Pressensé has sketched an outline,[2] and which endeavours to effect a combination between the two preceding points of view by the help of the supposition that it was the particular circumstances of the time of its composition which awoke in the mind of John the vast intuitions that are contained in his book.

The assurance with which the former of these two forms of interpretation adjudges to itself the honours of victory[3] obliges us to examine its claims very

---

[1] Fritzsche, in Rostock ; Hitzig, in Zurich ; Bénari, in Berlin ; Reuss, in Strasburg.

[2] *Histoire des trois premiers siècles*, vol. ii., p. 315, *sqq.*

[3] Reuss, *Histoire de la théologie biblique*, vol. i., p. 429, *sqq.* ; Réville, *Revue des deux Mondes*, October, 1868 ; Renan, *l'Antéchrist*, p. 341, *sqq.*

closely. If we are brought to perceive the falsehood of its first assumption—the application of the vision of Antichrist to Nero, supposed to be risen from the dead—the whole theory falls to the ground at once together with it, and the intermediate system attempted to be established by M. de Pressensé, which supposes its relative truth, falls also with it. We shall then be able to take our stand at the second point of view—that which the Church has instinctively admitted ; and to seek in some application, ancient or modern, of the picture which forms its centre— that of the Antichrist—the key of the sanctuary.

The following are our principal objections to the interpretation which sees in the apocalyptic vision an amplification of the popular legend of the re-appearance of Nero, returning as a persecutor of the Church, and at the same time an exterminator of ancient Rome :—

1. This exposition, as we have seen, supposes that the Apocalypse was written in the reign of the sixth emperor, and at the moment at which men were expecting the advent of the seventh,[1] consequently under Galba, in the latter half of the year 68. Now we think we have discovered some sure indications that the Apocalypse dates from a much later period of the apostolic times.

2. The legend of Nero's reappearance is supported

---

[1] xvii. 10 : " Five are fallen, and one *is*, and the other is not yet come." The eighth is to be the last—Antichrist himself.

by the fact of the attempts of some false Neros who
endeavoured at that time to seduce the provinces, and
to gain possession of power. We find traces of it also
in the Sibylline books, the earliest in book iv., which
seems to have been composed soon after the eruption
of Vesuvius in 79; that, at least, is the latest event to
which the author alludes at all clearly. There is also
some allusion to the reappearance of Nero in books
v. and viii. But all that is here spoken of is a *return*
from the far East, where he was thought to have been
concealed, and not a miraculous cure such as that
supposed in Rev. xiii., nor even an escape from the
bottomless pit, or Hades (xvii. 8); that is, a resurrection,
properly so called. Moreover, the description which
the pretended Sibyl gives of Nero, in book iv., seems
to refer, not to Nero himself, but rather to the pseudo-
Nero who, immediately after the eruption of Vesuvius,
raised the standard of revolt in the East, in the reign
of Titus, and perished miserably.[1] If this be so, this
picture has nothing in common with the meaning
usually attributed to the description in the Apocalypse
and its application to the real Nero. With regard to
books v. and viii., they belong to too late a date (the
reign of Hadrian) to enable us to draw any safe conclusion from them respecting the ideas which were
prevalent in the first century. We should have then
to admit that it was the author of the Apocalypse
himself who invented and set afloat the fantastical

---

[1] Hengstenberg, *Die Offenbarung*, vol. ii., p. 75.

idea of a miraculous cure, or of a resurrection, of Nero after his suicide. Is this supposition reconcilable with the lofty and holy spirit which reigns throughout the whole book, particularly in the seven epistles at the beginning, and in chap. xxii.? Augustine and Lactantius consider that belief as an instance of a kind of delusion into which none but men in delirium (*deliri*) could fall;—and we are asked to believe that this is the fundamental idea of the Apocalypse!

3. According to this exposition, very few years would have sufficed to convict the whole apocalyptic prophecy of falsehood. The successor of Galba was only to reign for a short time (xvii. 10); then Nero, the head with the deadly wound, was to reappear, and play the part of Antichrist. But what, on the contrary, did really happen? Vespasian succeeded Galba, and reigned for ten years; then came Titus, who, it is well known, was by no means a Nero. The risen Nero was to reign three years and a half as Antichrist, to establish the universal monarchy, to per-secute the Church, to destroy Rome, and to kill the two witnesses in Jerusalem. The temple, finally, was to be miraculously preserved at the time of the taking of the capital. But we ask, once more, what did really happen? The hour fixed by the pretended prophet struck, and nothing of all this took place; Rome remained standing; no divine witness appeared at Jerusalem; the city was destroyed, and the temple with it; and the false Neros, one after another, failed

so totally in their attempts, that soon afterwards the
wretched game which had been suggested by this
name came to an end. Lastly, the empire still stood
firm, and the second successor of Galba was by no
means that last Roman monarch whom the appearance of the glorified Christ was suddenly to suppress.
And we are asked to believe that this prophecy—a
tissue of mistakes, or, it would be more correct to say,
of impostures, and in excuse for which only one ex-
tenuating circumstance could be pleaded—that the
brain which gave it birth was under the influence of
delirium—was the work of St. John, of the beloved
disciple of the Lord, of the apostle with whose
holy life of calm activity in Asia Minor we are acquainted through the narratives of the Fathers, and
through his gospel and epistles! No, certainly, say
Lücke, Neander, and other religious writers who
adopt, as to its essential features, the modern system
of interpretation, it is not to the apostle John that we
attribute such a book, but to some eminent Christian
of his time, of the same name with the apostle. But
then how could it have happened that a book, against
which the charge of delusion had been so clearly established by the events of the years which followed
upon its appearance, instead of losing all credit, should
have gained so much in the respect of the contemporary generation, and of those which succeeded it, that
in the second century we find it universally attributed
to the apostle John? It rises in the estimation of the

Church just in proportion as facts pronounce against it the sentence of degradation!

4. We are well acquainted with the ideas of St. John respecting the Antichrist through his first epistle; and they in no respect resemble that which he would have conceived of that personage if he had for a moment entertained the notion of him as a Nero risen from the dead. The Antichrist of John's epistle is at the same time a collective being and a spiritual principle. "Even now," he says, "there are many Antichrists." These persons, he adds, "went out *from us*, but they were not of us." Antichrist is "the liar that denieth that Jesus is the Christ." "Every spirit that confesseth not that Jesus Christ is come in the flesh (the truth of the incarnation) is not of God; and this is that spirit of Antichrist whereof ye have heard that it should come, and even now already is it in the world."[1] What connection is there, we ask, between these false teachers who go out from the Church without having really belonged to it, and the Emperor Nero? We should have then to admit that between the date of the composition of the Apocalypse and that of his epistle, John had completely changed his ideas upon this fundamental point; and that, after having had to recant his doctrines, the apostle could have retained his self-respect before the whole Church!

5. It is probable that the apostles had often con-

---

[1] ii. 18, 19, 22; iv. 3.

versed together, when they met at Jerusalem, upon a
subject which occupied so important a place in the
hopes and fears of the Church. Now we know the
ideas of the chief among them upon this subject. St.
Paul has set them forth in 2 Thess. ii. He says first
that the Antichrist will be the representative of the
great *apostasy* which is to take place before the return
of Christ. This expression implies that he will come
forth, with all his adherents, from out of a *holy* society,
consecrated to God. Only in such circumstances can
any one be an "apostate." Will it be from the midst
of Judaism or of the Christian Church that this
defection will take place? Paul does not tell us. It
seems that it will invade simultaneously both these
divine kingdoms, of which one is but the extension of
the other; and we recognise here, consequently, the
fact pointed out by John—the Antichrist already
come, come forth out of a religious and even Christian
society. Next, Paul declares that the *mystery of
iniquity doth already work*, which has no meaning if
applied to an individual such as Nero, and can only
refer to a spiritual principle working for a certain time
within the hearts of men, before it breaks forth as an
actual phenomenon in history. This is exactly the
idea we have just been discovering in John: "Even
now are there many Antichrists," and "Even now
already is it in the world." Finally, St. Paul declares
that there is a power which he calls "*he that*," or "*that
which letteth*," (in one place it is masculine, in another

neuter,) which hinders as yet the manifestation of the
Antichrist. Whenever the apostles or the prophets
make use of expressions of that kind, which have a
character of mystery about them, we may be sure that
they allude to the political powers of the time. We
cannot then but agree completely with the view of
M. Reuss, who understands this *withholder* to be the
Roman power, and the man of sin, or Antichrist,
whose coming forth is for a time restrained, to be
the false Messiah of Judaism, that principle of carnal
Messianism which has been the soul of that nation's
life ever since (to use the language of the Song of
songs) they preferred the glories of Solomon to the
invisible Shepherd, Jehovah, and the empire of this
world to the kingdom of God. It is this principle
which impelled them to say in the presence of Jesus,
"We have no king but Cæsar," but which ever seeks
to give birth to a Cæsar of its own, a Jewish Cæsar
who is to crush the Roman Cæsar. About half a
century after the composition of the second epistle to
the Thessalonians, Barcochba, the *son of the star*, attempted to play the part to which St. Paul alluded,
and the *withholder* did not fail in his mission. The
Roman legions annihilated this false Messiah, because the time of Antichrist's appearing was not yet
come. But this time may and will come at last.
And then the world will know what is meant by the
Antichrist or counter-Christ; for there shall be no
longer any Roman legions to keep back his coming.

This is St. Paul's idea of the man of sin, or Antichrist.
But if so, how could the Roman imperial power, the
principle which, according to St. Paul, is still hinder-
ing the manifestation of Antichrist, be, according to
John in the Apocalypse, the Antichrist himself? We
should have to admit that the two apostles had never
conversed together on this subject, and that the most
contradictory ideas prevailed in the primitive Church
respecting it. This hypothesis is undeniably very improbable, and we have ascertained one fact directly
opposed to it in the harmony which exists between
the first epistle of John and the second to the Thessalonians.

6. The strongest proof in favour of the application
of the beast to Nero is certainly that which is drawn
from the explanation of the number 666 (Rev. xiii. 17).
It is supposed that this number is the sum which
is obtained by adding together the letters which
form the word Antichrist when taken as ciphers.[1]
Now the letters of the two words in Hebrew, *Neron*,
Cæsar, added together, give precisely the sum 666.[2]
There is even a special point worthy of notice.
Irenæus mentions manuscripts in which the reading
is six hundred and sixteen instead of six hundred

---

[1] It is well known that the Hebrews and the Greeks have no
special signs for numerical figures, and that they make use, for
that purpose, of the letters of the alphabet.

[2] נ (N), 50 ; ר (r), 200 ; ו (o), 6 ; נ (n), 50 ; ק (k), 100 ; ס (s),
60 ; ר (r), 200.

and sixty-six. Now, if we admit the Latin form
of the name indicated (*Cæsar Nero*, without the
final *n*), we reach precisely the number 616, since in
Hebrew the letter *n* is equal to fifty. We will not
object to this calculation that in a Greek book
we should expect the name and title to be rather
in Greek than Hebrew. As the Apocalypse bears,
from one end of it to the other, the character of a
Hebrew prophecy, it would not be impossible that
the author should have wished at once to reveal and
to disguise his thought under a form borrowed from
that language. Neither will we insist upon the inaccuracy of translating the Greek text, as M. Renan
does, "it is the number of *a* man ;" whereas it really
means, it is a man's number ; that is to say, human,
calculable in the manner of men, just as in xxi. 17,
" the measure of a man " does not mean that of any
individual man, but the measure *of man* (human), as
opposed to that of *an angel*. But what is more important is, that in order to arrive at the number 666,
it is necessary to cut out the second letter of the
name Cæsar, which represents the *e*, and which in
Hebrew is a consonant, and therefore forms part of
the body of the name itself. M. de Vogüé has
proved by a Nabathean inscription of the year 47,
that the name Cæsar used to be written in Hebrew
with four letters (*k e s r*), and not with three only
(*k s r*), which agrees with the inscription on the
Asiatic coins where we find this name (NERON

KAISAR).[1] It is said, it is true, that in the Talmudic writings, and in some inscriptions of the third century, the word Cæsar is reduced to three letters by simply cutting off the *e;* and that in the word Cæsaræa, the second letter, which ought to be *ai,* is abridged into *e,* which leads to its suppression as a consonant ; and that consequently it may be omitted in the same way in the name *Cæsar.* But in the word *Cæsarea,* this abbreviation arises naturally out of the lengthening of the name, just as in the word *aromatique,* the letter *o* loses the circumflex which it bears in *arôme ;* or as in the word *suprématic,* the *e* becomes short, while it is long in *suprême.* Does it follow from that that we might write, *aromc, supréme?* This example, therefore, proves nothing ; and as to the inscriptions of the third century, they scarcely prove anything, particularly in the face of the instance quoted relating to the orthography which was received in the first century. The true sum of the letters of the name *Cæsar Neron* is therefore 676, not 666.

The subsidiary proof which has been drawn from the other reading, 616, turns, when examined more closely, into an insurmountable objection. If the application of this number to the name of Nero was so well known that the copyists in the West, who knew the name under this form *Ncro,* had intentionally modified the number 666 in order to make it agree with their orthography, how could an inter-

---

[1] See M. Renan, *l'Antéchrist,* p. 447.

pretation so widely prevalent have been totally
unknown to Irenæus, who had occupied himself
specially with this question, and who quotes all the
attempts which had been made in his time to solve
the mystery ?[1]   Above all, when once the mistake
of the prophecy had been so completely unveiled,
how could the credit of the book survive such an
ordeal, and even grow still greater ?

The inadequacy of this explanation of the number
of the beast is so evident, that two of its most recent
defenders find themselves obliged to make the following concessions.   M. Renan thinks that the second
letter in the name Cæsar has been cut out because the
number 676 would " look less well " than 666, which is
made up of a threefold repetition of the same figure.
Is not this allowing that this number has a symbolical
value independently of the letters of which it is the
sum, and of the name which it represents ?   On the
other hand, M. Volkmar[2] perceives in the cipher $\chi\xi\varsigma$[3]
(*ch*, 600 ; *x*, 60 ; *st*, 6) that since the first and third
letter are the abbreviation of the name Christ, and the
second is the emblem of the serpent, the enemy of Christ,
this cipher indicates, by its very form, that it has an em-
blematical sense—Christ destroyed by His adversary.[4]

---

[1] It is well known that he mentions the Greek words *Lateinos*,
Teiton, and others, of which the letters make 666.

[2] *Commentar zur Offenbarung Johannis*, pp. 18, 215.

[3] The number 666 is thus written in the Greek text (xiii. 18).

[4] This idea, first proposed by Heumann, had already received
the approval of Herder.

The irrefragable proof which was believed to have
been found in this calculation in favour of the modern
interpretation, does not then give it so firm a support
as is supposed. Accordingly, men such as De
Wette, Lücke, Bunsen, who cannot be suspected of
partisanship, and who have even adopted in a general
way the application of the apocalyptic vision to Nero,
reject this explanation of the number of the beast,
and prefer one of those mentioned by Irenæus—
Lateinos, for instance, or some other.

M. de Pressensé's attempt to accommodate this
interpretation to a broader and higher view of the
apocalyptic vision seems to us to break down under
the following dilemma : Either the various features
of the picture, and the number 666 in particular, refer
to Nero, and if so, how can we transform this historical
personage, so clearly described, into a final Antichrist
still to come ? or else all these features refer directly
to this latter, and then where is the necessity for still
giving an integral place in the vision to the absurd
legend (which belongs besides to a much later date) of
Nero risen again ?

M. Düsterdieck has endeavoured to give a different
application to the modern system of interpretation.
According to him, the head mortally wounded and
then miraculously healed, does not signify Nero, but
the imperial power of paganism, which, after Nero,
seemed on the point of perishing, until Vespasian
restored it by delivering the Roman people from

anarchy, and substituted the family of the Flaviani
for that of the Cæsars which had become extinct with
Nero.   The sixth head, then, which *now is*, would not
be Galba (whom the prophetic vision omits, as well
as Otho and Vitellius), but Vespasian himself, undeɪ
whose reign the Apocalypse would have been composed at the beginning of the year 70.   The seventh
head, who was only to reign for a short time, would
be Titus, for whom, owing to the dark character of
Domitian, it was easy to foresee an early and violent
death.   And the eighth, who is at the same time the
beast itself, would be Domitian, whose advent to
power the Christians were already dreading.   The
number 666 answers accordingly, in the view of the
commentator, to the word *Lateinos*.   Most of the reasons which we have urged against the application of
the Apocalypse to Nero equally forbid our applying
it to Vespasian ; and this interpretation is even less
plausible, since, instead of alluding to past or present
events, the Apocalypse would in that case rest its
assertions upon historical previsions of so uncertain a
nature as the possibility of the murder of Titus by his
brother Domitian, and the approaching advent to
power of the latter as the last emperor.   Who would
have ventured to build a prophecy upon such a calculation of probabilities as this ?

The course of criticism we have now been pursuing
conducts us necessarily, by its negative results, to a
third system of interpretation,—that which sees in the

Apocalypse a general view of the fortunes of the
Church until the complete setting up of the kingdom
of Christ. But here again three paths open before us,
which lead to very different issues. According to one
system of interpretation, we should take the Apocalypse to be a picture, more or less detailed, of the
history of the world from the time of Jesus Christ,
not only from a religious point of view, but also with
reference to the great events which have marked the
phases of political and social development. Thus
Bossuet and Hengstenberg—two writers who must
certainly be surprised to find themselves in agreement
—seeing in the image of the beast a figure of the
Roman empire, understand by its mortal wound the
fall of that empire, brought about by the establishment
of Christianity; according to which, the healing of the
wounded head must signify the foundation of the
holy Roman empire by Charlemagne, and the reign
of a thousand years would prefigure neither more nor
ess than the Christian society from that time up to
the present day. The present crises would signify the
end of this happy state of things, and would prepare
for that final conflict which in the Apocalypse is represented under the image of the invasion of Gog and
Magog at the end of the millennium (xx. 7—9). The
Romish Church has certainly no right to complain of
this interpretation as developed by Hengstenberg,
which identifies its reign with the most brilliant period
of the apocalyptic vision. But what can we make,

from this point of view, of the resurrection of the head with the deadly wound ?   Did, then, Roman paganism come to life again in the holy Roman empire of the middle ages ?   And further, what can we make of the first resurrection, which is to precede the millennium ? And how can we recognise the slightest real analogy between the picture of the millennium as painted in the Apocalypse, and the state of the world and of the Church before the Reformation ?   We can, certainly, get out of all difficulties by the help of subtle explanations ; but our sense of truth protests.

The case is the same with the expositions of the bishops of the middle ages, who interpreted the beast of Mahomet; and with that of the persecuted sects of the same period, who saw distinctly pictured in it the image of the papacy; and, once more, with that of the Romish writers, who took it for a representation of the empire in its fierce struggles with the papal authority. All these expositions establish, with more or less of ingenuity, certain points of contact between some features of the apocalyptic picture and that historical phenomenon upon which the pre-occupied mind of their authors has chosen to fix its attention.   But the impossibility of finding an application for a number of other features soon forces upon the impartial reader the conviction that these explanations are but a kind of *jeu d'esprit*, and that they do not correspond in any way with the idea really contained in the vision.

We affirm the same of the application, drawn out

into the most minute details, of the history of the
Church up to our own time, which has been so often
attempted, especially by the Anglo-French school.
The most distinguished representatives of this method
are Faber, in England, Bengel, in Germany, Gaussen
and M. de Rougemont, in French Switzerland.[1] How
can we feel any confidence in this method of interpretation when we see, for instance, one and the same
vision—that of the locusts with the tail of a scorpion
(ix.)—interpreted by some of the Arabian invasion in
the seventh century ; by others, of the incursion of the
Persians under Chosroës ; by a third party, of the introduction of the Talmud among the Jews ; and by others
again, of the establishment of monasticism ?   Is not
the arbitrariness which gives birth to such a method
of interpretation most glaring? and can we help ask-
ing ourselves what object the Holy Spirit could have
had in view, in writing, according to the malicious
expression of M. Réville, "a history of the Church in
riddles " ? If this vision is intended to serve as a
guide to the caravan during its march, must it not be
made more intelligible ?   If it is not to be understood
until the end comes, and when the goal shall have
been reached, of what use will it be then ?

M. Darby has felt the force of this, and has sug-

---

[1] M. Henriquet, pastor at St. Fay, has just published a new
exposition from this point of view. It gives us pleasure to
announce this work, " *L'Apocalypse brièvement expliquée par
l'Ecriture et l'Histoire.*"

gested quite a different method,—the second one in this system. According to him, the Church having apostatised from the apostolic times, and not being destined to be restored till the Lord's return, the whole of that period of infidelity is omitted in the prophecy; and the apocalyptic vision, which begins in chap. iv., and which represents the last days, is found, by reason of that omission, following immediately upon the picture of the apostolic church in chaps. ii. and iii. Thus it is that the last conflicts and the last victories of the Church find their places quite naturally at the end of the apostolic age. Far, then, from having to look for the fulfilment of the seals and trumpets in the past, as in the preceding system, we are rather to see in them an image of the crises which shall immediately precede the coming of the Antichrist. This method has some attractions in it. It agrees well with the passages in the New Testament which seem to announce the near approach of the *Parousia*. And moreover, by placing the fulfilment of these pictures in the future, it has the advantage of greatly facilitating the task of the interpreter. But is it the real idea of the book? And when it is said, in chap. iv., "After this I looked, and behold a door was opened in heaven," is it not more natural to believe that the heavenly picture about to be unfolded before the eyes of the seer is immediately connected with the earthly picture of the seven churches which he had just been contemplating?

Between, then, those who see in the Apocalypse a detailed photographic picture of the whole history of the Church and of the European states since the time of Jesus Christ, and those who admit into this vision a complete blank between the first ages and the end of the world, we must once more endeavour to steer a middle course. We know none but Auberlen,—that religious *savant* so early removed from the Church of which he was one of the brightest lights,—who has attempted this method ; and even he seems to us to have leaned a little too much to one side, that is to say, to that of those who discover in the apocalyptic vision a greater number of historical indications than it contains in reality. We, for our part, are persuaded that the intuitions of the prophet did not wander for a single instant into the domain of political history, and that they have reference solely to the great conflicts which constitute the religious progress of humanity. If, in order to explain an apocalyptic detail, it is found necessary to make use of any source of knowledge other than the Bible itself—to be in possession, for instance, of data foreign to the prophecies of Jesus and of His apostles, with regard to the latter days, we may conclude that the method which has been followed is an erroneous one, and will lead only to the discovery of ingenious but arbitrary points of coincidence. It is with the Apocalypse as with the Song of songs. It can only hold its ground as part of the canon, on the condition that it refers solely, with regard to its fundamental ideas and to its details, to the sphere of the kingdom of God.

Let us endeavour to give, from this point of view, a brief outline of its principal pictures.

It begins, as we have seen, with a description of seven churches in Asia Minor, which, taken as a whole, present a complete picture of the Christian Church at the time of the vision.   Christendom, as represented by these seven churches, is therefore the real audience to which the author addresses himself.

The six seals (for the seventh has a place by itself) represent, not each of them a special event, but categories of judgments by which God in all ages supports the preaching of the gospel. This we perceive clearly by the words of Jesus, to which these seals refer, and of which they are but a paraphrase: " There shall be wars, and famines, and pestilences, and earthquakes, in divers places ; but the end is not yet." Out of each word in this sentence the vision makes a picture. M. Darby perfectly describes these plagues when he calls them "the governmental measures" adopted by Providence.[1] The application of these general measures lasts till the moment at which the trumpets begin to sound. The vision of the seals refers therefore to all that period of the history of the Church which may be called preparatory ;—this is the time of God's calls to the Gentiles. The first seal

---

[1] The Old Testament had already enumerated these plagues in the same sense—Ezek. v. 12 ; vi. 11, 12, etc.

signifies *all* the preachings of the gospel, the second *all* the wars, the third *all* the famines, the fourth *all* the contagious sicknesses, the fifth *all* the persecutions, the sixth *all* the earthquakes, which have visited the earth, or will visit it, until the concluding phase, and for which the trumpets are to give the signal. It is, then, in the vision of the seals that we must place the whole history of the Church up to our own day; a history of which we must not, as will be seen, seek for the details either in the seals or the trumpets, but which, on the other hand, could not be altogether omitted. It is evident that the practical application of all these pictures is in this way very easily made, and that the use of the Apocalypse for purposes of edification gains infinitely by the adoption of this method. Curiosity is the only loser.

The two pictures in chap. vii., which precede the opening of the seventh seal, alike represent two abiding facts in the religious history of mankind. The act by which the angel seals the hundred and forty-four thousand Jews signifies that in all ages, from the time of the dispersion of the chosen people until that of the fulfilment of the task which will be committed to them in the latter days, God preserves in the midst of them a faithful few, who, even under the pressure of the surrounding heathen nations, will not abandon Jehovah and His law, and will remain obedient to His commands. M. Renan does not understand the continued existence of Judaism after the coming in of Christianity. " In one sense," he says, " after the birth of Christianity, Judaism has no longer any *raison d'être*. It is like a walking skeleton which has survived the blow which has smitten it. . . . . There is no stranger sight in history."[1] It is true that the obstinate existence for two thousand years of this wandering and homeless people is a great problem in history for those who do not believe in Providence ; but faith knows that God holds in His hands the key to this enigma. And He makes it shine before our eyes in the Apocalypse. It is not for nothing, nor even for a trifling reason, that this nation subsists, and that the miracle of its history is perpetuated before our astonished sight. There are amongst them more than *seven thousand* men who, even to this day, have not bowed and will not bow the knee to Baal. God holds them in reserve for a great and sublime destiny.

In the second picture we behold the abundant fruits of apostolic evangelisation, and then of Christian preaching in all ages. Faithful men *from all nations, and kindreds, and people, and tongues,* enter, like a triumphant army, the celestial abodes. These innumerable troops are like a contingent furnished by the Gentile churches to the victorious retinue of the Lamb. Some have had the boldness to maintain, on account of their incalculable numbers, that these Gentiles are but as a vile *plebs,* compared to the hundred and

---

[1] *L'Antéchrist,* pp. 544, 545.

forty-four thousand Israelites who are divinely sealed;
as if these redeemed Gentiles were not clothed in white
robes; as if they did not carry palms in their hands;
as if the Lamb did not lead them unto living fountains of waters! The hundred and forty-four thousand, on the contrary, are not yet even members
of the Church. They do not appear as forming part
of the army of the Lamb, till chap. xiv. 1—5. This
picture, painted with such enthusiasm, would suffice
to prove the admiration and lively sympathy which
the author of the Apocalypse felt for the work of Paul
in the Gentile world, and to put an end to all idea of
an opposition of principles and of tendency between
him and the apostle of the Gentiles.

Chap. vii. establishes, then, the fact that, up to the
time of the last phase, there will exist in Israel an
elect few, faithful to God and to the law of their
fathers, and in the Gentile world a multitude of souls
washed in the blood of the Lamb, and ready to reign
with Him.

The sixth seal, as we have seen, is only, if we may
so speak, the *container* of the seven trumpets. The
disciplinary measures of a more general kind, with
which God has hitherto enforced the preaching of the
gospel, are about now to give place to a system of
measures of a more decisive nature, and which are to
constitute an *ultimatum* offered by Him to the heathen
world which is hardening itself instead of being converted. It may be asked in what way this intuition

corresponds with the history which exhibits to us, on the contrary, the Gentiles entering in a body into the Church, and receiving Christian baptism. This official *Christianisation* of the heathen nations is not recognised by the vision; for it is not a reality in the sight of God. This so-called Christianity is in most cases no more than a varnish spread over a substratum which remains none the less heathen. Divine revelation could not recognise a fact of so equivocal a nature.

The six trumpets—for the seventh is isolated from the six preceding ones—are the preparation for the decisive ordeal which is to be brought in by the Antichrist. They remind us of the trumpets of the priests, which, after having during six days shaken the walls of Jericho, caused them to fall on the seventh. They are signals for the dissolution of the ancient social order, and then for the establishment, followed by the ruin, of the empire of the Antichrist. Convulsions accumulated in the four domains so often united in prophecy, the earth, the sea, the rivers, and the air (from the first to the fourth trumpet); next, convulsions in society, which is undermined by a diabolical visitation (fifth trumpet), and of which an invasion of savages overthrows the foundations (sixth trumpet),—these are the judgments which prepare the way for the last adversary. It is upon the ground of these ruins that he is to build his throne.

And let us not say that such an accumulation of plagues, of physical misfortunes and social catas-

trophes, is improbable or unheard of. Against such
an assertion I appeal to the striking picture which M.
Renan has drawn of the state of the world at the time
to which he refers the composition of the Apocalypse,
about the year 70 of our era. " Never," he says,
" had the world been seized with such a trembling-
fit; . . . . the earth itself was a prey to the most
terrible convulsions : the whole world was smitten
with giddiness. . . . . The planet seemed shaken to
its foundations, and to have no life left in it. . . . .
The conflict of the legions (amongst themselves) was
terrible ; . . . . famine was added to massacre ; . . . .
misery was extreme. . . . . In the year 65, a horri-
ble plague visited Rome ; during the autumn there
were counted thirty thousand deaths. . . . . The
Campagna was desolated by typhoons and cyclones ;
. . . . the order of nature seemed to be overturned ;
frightful tempests spread terror in all directions.
But that which produced the greatest impression
was the earthquakes. The globe was undergoing
a convulsion analogous to that of the moral world ;
it was as if the earth and mankind were taken with
fever simultaneously. . . . . Vesuvius was preparing
for the terrible eruption of the year 79. . . . . Asia
Minor was in a chronic earthquake. Its cities had to
be continually rebuilt. From the year 59 onward we
find scarcely one year unmarked by some disaster.
The valley of the Lycus, especially, with its Christian
towns of Laodicæa and Colosse, was laid waste in the

year 60, etc."[1]   And why, we may ask, should not
times such as these return, and with a redoubled intensity in proportion to the nearness of the approach
of the dissolution of this our old world, and the birth-
throes of a new earth ?   And, as we have just seen, we
cannot separate, in such periods of commotion, the
physical world from the moral; the two domains are
connected together by mysterious affinities ; and just
as Palestine followed, in its cycles of desolation, the
fate of Israel, so is the earth similarly related to man.
Is not humanity that "soul of the world" of which
men used in ancient times to dream ?   And is it not
so that in this great whole, as well as in our own
persons, nothing can take place in the soul without
something to answer to it in the body, and nothing in
the body which does not react simultaneously upon
the soul ?

The last signal—that of the seventh trumpet—is
preceded, as the opening of the seventh seal had
been, by a scene of an encouraging tendency—that
of the two witnesses (xi.).   This episode refers, as
did the former of the two which prepared for the
seventh seal, to the destinies of the Jewish people.
This subject is so important that it is treated here
in a little book which forms, as it were, a parenthesis
in the great book.   It is the announcement (already
anticipated in the prophetic vision itself) of the
conversion of Israel.   The faithful Jews, together

---

[1] *L'Antéchrist*, p. 326, *sqq.*

with the hundred and forty-four thousand, (cf. chap. vii.,) are seen prostrated in the holy place before the golden altar (the symbol of Judaism) in an ideal temple; for the material temple is no longer in existence. They are awaiting the new revelation which is to carry them on a step farther, into the most holy place. The mass of the people are given up to the Gentiles, who tread them under foot. The author here reproduces the exact words of Jesus: "Jerusalem shall be trodden down of the Gentiles, until the times of the Gentiles be fulfilled." John does not, any more than Jesus, use the expression *to tread under foot* in a literal sense. The subject in his mind is that of the moral domination of the Gentiles over Israel, and of the *apostasy*, becoming ever more and more general, of that ancient elect people, in abjuring the divine principle of their national existence, and basely seeking to identify themselves with the heathen nations amongst whom they were scattered. Thus, whilst the elect part of the nation, by their unshaken fidelity, prepare themselves for a sacred mission, the mass of the people —these constitute the outer court given up to the Gentiles—degrade and materialise themselves more and more to the level of the heathen. In the midst of this defection appear—as did in ancient times Enoch in the midst of the degenerate children of Seth, Moses before Israel corrupted by Egyptian idolatry, Elijah amongst the ten tribes who had become almost completely *paganised*—the two witnesses, whose preaching, as well as their dress and acts of power, preach repentance to Israel. It is at Jerusalem that this scene takes place. Israel has therefore regained its own land; and finds itself once more in possession of its capital. For, as we have seen, it is impossible to interpret otherwise than literally this expression: "The great city . . . . *where our Lord was crucified*" (xi. 8). If the author had intended to describe Christendom, and the spiritual crucifixion of the Saviour in the midst of her, he would have used the present or the future tense—*is* or *will be* crucified; and not the past—"*was* crucified." But—and this is surprising—the beast now appears upon the scene, though his coming has not yet been described. The reason is that the contents of the little book constitute a special prophecy within the great one. We shall see later on why the Antichrist thinks it expedient to leave Rome, his capital, and to take up his abode at Jerusalem. The two witnesses are killed by him, but they come to life again miraculously. The city is smitten with an earthquake, and one part of the inhabitants are swallowed up in it. The remainder of the people, and particularly those who have been specially reserved for these supreme moments, give glory to God, and are converted to Him. Accordingly, we shall find in chap. xiv. the hundred and forty-four thousand surrounding the Lamb, between

the time of the advent and that of the destruction
of the Antichrist.

This picture is well adapted to encourage the
Church in presence of the terrible conflict she is
about to be called upon to sustain. She knows now
beforehand that she will have within humanity
itself a powerful ally—that is, the people of peoples,
of which the elect part will occupy a central place
in the Christian army, and form a kind of body-
guard of the Lamb.

Now that the Church has been reassured as to
the issue of the conflict, she can listen without fear
to the sound of that seventh trumpet, which is to
call forth the Antichrist from out of the seas—that
is, from the midst of the nations.

But his appearance is preceded by a combat waged
in heaven between Michael, the champion of God, the
representative of monotheism—that is the meaning
of his name, *"who is like unto God?"*—and Satan, the
seducer of men, who entices them into idolatry, into
that worship of imaginary beings which is, at bottom,
only the adoration of Satan himself and of his angels.
"The things which the Gentiles sacrifice, they sacrifice to devils," says St. Paul (1 Cor. x. 20). What
is then the meaning of this combat? It represents
the final conflict between monotheism and paganism,
and the fall of the latter. In one sense this conflict
takes place upon earth. It is the voice of the
preachers of the gospel which overthrows the temples

of the idols. But the reference here is to an event belonging to a higher than a merely terrestrial sphere. The power obtained by Satan over the spirit of the nations, through the fascination of idolatry, is a phenomenon which results from the elevated position which he still occupies in the supernatural sphere—*in the heavenly places*, as says St. Paul (Eph. vi. 12). Jesus, when He saw His disciples returning from their first evangelising expedition, in which they had healed some demoniacs, led them to contemplate the sublime significance of these first victories, when He said to them: "I saw Satan fall like lightning from heaven." These isolated facts formed in His view a pledge of the future destruction of idolatry by the evangelic messengers who should carry on the work of the disciples. This saying of the Lord is the text of the vision in Rev. xii., just as the words of Jesus, quoted above, had formed the subject of the vision of the six seals.

Satan loses his place in the celestial spheres from whence he had been still ruling over men's hearts, and making himself worshipped as God. He is cast down to the earth; that is to say, his reign in the sphere of religion comes to an end. The diabolical superstitions of paganism disappear from human society. But a certain degree of power is still left to this enemy in the terrestrial sphere. Only he cannot exert it directly; and just as evil spirits require the body of those who are possessed, as a medium for

their action, so Satan needs a man wholly given up
to him, to enable him to realise the plans of vengeance which he is revolving in his heart. "Thou
hast robbed me of my heathens," he seems to say
to Christ, as he casts upon Him a look of hellish
defiance; "but wait—I, on my part, am about to
rob Thee of Thy Christians." And the coming of
the Antichrist is the means which he employs for
realising this threat.

What will become of the Church under these circumstances? The end of the vision in chap. xii.
tells us; and chap. xiii. will confirm it. She will
disappear temporarily from off the face of the earth,
at least as far as the kingdom of the Antichrist shall
extend. But she will find a place of refuge prepared
for her by God—a land of Goshen, into which the
perfidious solicitations of the Antichrist cannot pursue
her. And Christ, the King and Judge, whom she
has just brought forth, but whose reign is still post-
poned for a time—until the Antichrist shall have
realised his own—is withdrawn temporarily into
heaven, awaiting the day when He shall appear to
substitute Himself definitively for the diabolic monarch
whose advent was to precede His own.

This vision of the woman in travail has often been
made to represent the Jewish Church giving birth to
the Messiah. But what meaning could there be in
such a return—in the middle of the prophecy—to a
period long since passed away, and one so perfectly

well known? This vision is not retrospective, but prospective. This is, moreover, sufficiently proved by the *three years and a half* during which the exile of the woman lasts, and which answers to the *forty-two months* of the reign of the Antichrist, and to the *twelve hundred and sixty days* during which the two witnesses preach. These three periods are really one and the same, applied successively, under these three forms,—to the Church during the time of her emigration,—to Israel during the days of its future, purely national, restoration,—and to the Antichrist during the time of his domination.

The Antichrist, the subject of the signal given by the seventh trumpet, appears in chap. xiii. What is this personage to be?

His very *name* tells us. Antichrist means counter-Christ, or anti-Messiah. This name, then, with the idea represented by it, is Jewish in origin and in character. The Anti-Messiah, as well as the Messiah Himself, is necessarily a product of Judaism.

The apostle Paul confirms this idea. We have seen that his doctrine lays it down very decidedly that the *man of sin* realises in himself the spurious Jewish Messiah, set up by carnal Israel, in opposition to the Messiah of God. This personage will be the Israelite, who shall consent to that act of felony to which Jesus would not consent—that of doing homage to the sovereignty of the prince of this world, in order that he might receive from his hands universal empire. Satan will fulfil to him the promise which he made to Jesus : " If thou wilt worship me, I will give thee all these kingdoms, and the glory of them ; for that is delivered unto me." Further, St. Paul has taught us that that which kept back in his time the manifestation of this principle, ever latent in the heart of every Israelite not purified from above, was the Roman power, which put an immediate stop to the acts of ambitious self-will of the Jewish people, and was able to curb the leaders who arose from time to time and undertook to stir them into insurrection. We have also seen how far this description of the man of sin drawn by St. Paul resembles the manner in which John speaks of the Antichrist in his first epistle. In both of them this personage represents a religion opposed to the gospel, and at the same time a political power. These two characteristics in combination belong naturally only to a Jew.

We can easily understand from the very *nature of things* how it should come to pass that as it was from the Jewish nation that there issued the most perfect fruit of humanity, so from it also there should proceed the worst that it will ever produce. *Corruptio optimi pessima.* "The Jewish nation comprehends within it both extremes," says M. Renan. "Nothing can equal in wickedness the wickedness of Jews ; at the same time the best of men have been Jews. You may say of this race whatever good or evil you please, without danger of overstepping the truth." In blas-

phemy, as well as in adoration, the Jew is the foremost of mankind; and one of these peculiarities
always goes with the other. To blaspheme with
energy is not within the power of every man. In
order to do so, a character by nature religious is
needed. The Roman will never excel in that art,
precisely for the reason that to him the things of faith
are in their nature foreign and indifferent. We of
the other western nations are more or less in the
same case. He must spring from a holy race, that is
to be impious with fervour and force. It is only
an apostate who can blaspheme with all his heart.
Hence the unquestionable superiority of the Jew
in this region. No one can form any idea of the
hatred which a materialistic and antichristian heart
can feel towards the gospel, till he has seen it
gleaming in the eyes of a Jew; and to understand
what the words *curse* and *blaspheme* really mean,
one must have heard profane irony poured from
the lips of a child of Israel. Our Gentile Voltaires,
let them try as they may, are in comparison but
lambs when the object is to revile Christ and His
Church. None but Israel could have given birth to
Judas; and it alone, accordingly, is in possession of
the frightful privilege of a capacity for opposing to
Jesus Christ the rival who, during the time marked
out, shall hold seriously in check the kingdom of God
on earth.

Moreover, *history* has demonstrated the truth of all

that we are now saying. It testifies to the persecuting hatred of the Jews as soon as they had possession of power. "You curse us in your synagogues," says Justin to Trypho the Jew,—"us who believe in Christ. Only you have not the power to touch us, because those who now govern the world (the Romans) prevent you. But whenever you have been able, you have not failed to do it." And in his first *Apology*, the same author writes to the emperor concerning the Jews thus: "As soon as they have the power, they carry us off and torture us. In the war which Barchokeba has just been carrying on at the head of the Jewish people, it was the Christians alone upon whom the extreme penalties were inflicted, when they would not deny and blaspheme Jesus the Christ." And what a painful feeling of the furious hatred of this people against the gospel is expressed in that passage of St. Paul: "Who both killed the Lord Jesus, and their own prophets, and have persecuted us; and they please not God, and are contrary to all men; forbidding us to speak to the Gentiles that they might be saved, to fill up their sins alway." [1]

Finally,—and this is the decisive point,—the picture drawn in the Apocalypse of the Antichrist can, it seems to us, only be explained when we apply it to a Jew. What is this beast which *was*,

---

[1] 1 Thess. ii. 15, 16.

which *is not*, and which *shall be?* (xvii. 11.) What
is this head *wounded to death*, which had preceded
that which was reigning at the time in which John is
writing, and which was to be miraculously *healed*
in order to play, as the eighth head, the part of
Antichrist? There are only two possible interpre-
tations of all these mysterious characteristics. Either
we must see in them traits intended to point to
Nero risen again,—that is, to an absurd fable,—or
we must interpret them of Israel ; of its destruction,
nearly two thousand years ago, and of its final restoration, when it will form that last monarchy of which
the Anti-Messiah will be the head.   We have already
refuted the former of these explanations.   The latter
alone, we are convinced, answers to the idea of the
apocalyptic vision.

We can prove from the fourth Sibylline book,
written about the year 80, that it was even at that
time the custom to include in one vast and com-
prehensive *coup d'œil* the whole past history of mankind, and the succession of the great monarchies
which had marked its phases. According to this
poem, six out of the twelve successive races of mankind belong to the Assyrian age, two to the Median,
two to the Persian and Greek, one to the Roman ;
and the twelfth and last is that of the times of the
Messiah.

All intuitions of this kind evidently rested upon
Daniel's prophecy. The author of the Apocalypse

himself gives us a proof of the connection which exists between his picture of the Antichrist and that of this ancient prophet, when he attributes to the beast the form of a leopard, the feet of a bear, and the mouth of a lion. These three animals represented in Daniel the Grecian and Persian monarchies and the Babylonian empire. John intends us therefore to understand that the empire of the Antichrist will combine in itself all the powers which these different nations had in succession possessed.

But did the Jewish nation ever really occupy such a position in the series of the ancient kingdoms, that John could lawfully make of it one of the seven heads of the beast, in the sense which we attribute to this symbol? From the standpoint of political history we might answer in the negative; but from that of the religious history of mankind—which is that of John—the truth of this intuition needs no demonstration. Did not Israel, by the hand of Herod, declare war against the Messiah, even from His birth? And did it not, by means of the Sanhedrim, seek to suppress His kingdom? The conduct of Israel towards the infant Church was the same as that of Egypt towards Israel in its cradle; and it is not without reason that St. Paul, in Rom. ix., applies to this nation all the scriptural passages relating to Pharaoh.

According to this, the first four heads of the beast are the following States: In the Old Testament times,

Egypt, which endangered the existence of Israel when still in its infancy; *Assyria* and *Babylonia,* which put an end to its existence as an independent nation; *Persia,* which held it in bondage until the time of its own humiliation; and *Greece,* with its principal representative, Antiochus Epiphanes, the true Antichrist of this former period, the persecutor properly so called. But as there had been four heads hostile to the Divine power during the times of Israel, there are also four during the *times of the Gentiles,* which have carried on war against the Church. The first is *Israel* itself, numbered henceforth among the *nations of the earth* (the *Gojim*) and deprived temporarily of its title of the people of God. Did not the Jews pronounce sentence of degradation against themselves with their own lips when they exclaimed: "We have no king but Cæsar"?[1] Accordingly, John calls them, in the epistles to the seven churches, *the synagogue of Satan.* Israel is, then, the fifth head; and it is not difficult therefore to understand what the apostle means by the *deadly wound* with which one of the first five heads has been smitten. Who could fail to recognise in this fatal sword-thrust (xiii. 14), proceeding from an unknown hand, the destruction of the people of Israel by the Roman sword in the year 70, and their dispersion among the heathen? Israel, which had been the first of the nations, disappearing suddenly from its place

---

[1] John xix. 15.

among them—this is the beast " that *was*, and *is not*, and *yet is*," and which, the prophecy adds, shall be again. It is this Israel, humanly speaking annihilated, which will come to life again, to give the final expression to the revolt of mankind against God the Creator.

If the fifth head represents Israel, what are the two powers represented by the sixth and seventh? " Five are fallen," says the angel, " and *one is*." This expression gives us the desired answer. The sixth head (the second in relation to the Church) is the *Roman* power which is reigning over the world at the time in which St. John is writing. This apostle is therefore here quite in accord with St. Paul when the latter recognises the actually existing imperial power as the force which still keeps back the breaking forth of the Jewish Messianic principle. The seventh head (the third Antichrist of the times of the Gentiles) consequently, quite naturally, represents the power upon which will devolve the work of making a clean sweep of the Roman dominion, and thus of preparing the way for the advent of the final antichristian power. St. Paul indicates it with sufficient clearness, 2 Thess. ii. 7. In order that Antichrist may come, it is necessary that " he who now letteth (Rome) shall be taken out of the way." This destruction presupposes some one to execute it—a power who shall sweep away the last remains of the Roman empire. The agent indicated by this passage in St. Paul is no other than the seventh head of the apocalyptic vision. What is this head? One might take it to signify the barbarous nations whose invasion put an end, in a certain sense, to the empire. But the barbarous monarchies have rather continued, than replaced or destroyed the Roman power; the existing European states formed themselves out of the materials of the Roman edifice. They are like the ten toes of the statue in Daniel's vision, and still form a part of the colossus. Roman civilisation remains mistress of the world. It is these remains which a violent force, and one, as the vision says, of transitory duration,[1] is to sweep away, like a devastating torrent. Then will the Antichrist appear, the eighth head, and at the same time the beast himself, issuing this time not only from the *sea* of nations, but from *the abyss*—in virtue of the diabolical inspiration which animates him. He will present himself to mankind, in their disorganised and desperate condition, as their saviour, and in order that he may accomplish the work of their social restoration, will only ask to be recognised as the incarnation of the Infinite Spirit.[2] And to the surprise of the whole world, the power which will keep him in check will be found to be that Israel which had been, it was thought, erased for ever from the catalogue of the nations, which scarcely even retained its place

---

[1] Rev. xviii. 10.

[2] 2 Thess. ii. 4 : "He as God sitteth in the temple of God."

in statistics, and which will reissue suddenly from its grave as what it really is, the foremost among the nations, the one to which belongs, for good or for evil, the sceptre of the world.

There exists in the heart of this people a pledge of this future which belongs to it, in the indestructible hope which they carry with them of hereafter *possessing the world*. This is the secret of their mysterious vitality. We are not to look for an explanation of their strange preservation in any external circumstances. They live because they will to live; they will to live because they feel themselves called to reign, and specially gifted for this high vocation. But they are to fulfil this mission after a diabolical, before doing so after a divine, fashion. It is nearly always so in the history of mankind. Divine ideas do not generally appear embodied in facts under their true form, till after they have appeared as caricatures. Guessing in some way at the order of the day of the Divine government, the devil forestalls God, and casts an ape upon the earth just at the moment at which God is about to create a man. Thus will the Jewish Antichrist precede the advent of the Christ.

Will it be asked in what way this is to come to pass? Are we to believe that this people with their bowed backs and trembling knees, whose only wish seems to be to dissemble before the Gentiles, are to become some day their masters? I beg permission to answer this objection by a personal recollection.

As I was conversing one day with a rabbi of the most extreme opinions, I said to him at last, " Shall I tell you what I think? It is you that are destined one day to become the rod in God's hand to chastise us." I expected this would astonish him a little. But he answered at once with a frigid smile, "And shall I tell you what I think? *We are so already.*" He was right, and he evidently knew more about it than I did. The whirlwind which is now carrying the world captive is the inspiration of the Jewish spirit. Jewish finance dominates society from Europe to the United States. As a careful observer remarks,[1] " There is not one of us who does not already, whether consciously or not, do homage to this power." With the sceptre of finance, the Jew dominates also the politics of the world. M. de Rothschild was the third party with the President of the French Republic and the Emperor of Germany in concluding the last peace. It is the Jewish mind which is guiding the religious and moral movements of society in our day. Journalism and the lesser literature belongs to it almost entirely, especially in Germany; and in places where, as in France, things have not perhaps as yet gone so far, every one nevertheless pays court to the Jew. M. Renan is perhaps alone among free-thinkers in not kissing the hand in adoration of this rising sun. Together with the Voltairians or materialists in all countries—what are these little shades of difference

[1] Osman Bey, *La conquête du monde par les Juifs.*

to him ?—the Jew, through the thousand voices which
are everywhere at his disposal, cries to the world,
" Fraternity! Toleration!" And in secret he is
forging the chains with which he is preparing to load
these miserable Gentiles, who are looking down upon
him in their folly. More and more are they the representatives of his race who shine in art, and who take
precedence in science. Ere long it will fall to him to
offer to the unchristianised masses that moral refuge
of which they will be feeling the need. After having
favoured and brought about the triumph in every place
of the antichristian tendencies of the day, he will
boldly proclaim the fall of the Christ of the Gentiles.
Was it not the sole mission of Jesus and of Christianity
to spread abroad amongst heathen nations the worship
of the God of Abraham? This work is now accomplished. The gospel has laboured well in the cause
of Judaism. Its task is fulfilled. Let it now give
place, and let Israel reap the fruit of its labours! The
latest self-accommodation of Providence to the ido-
latries of the Gentiles—the adoration of Jesus—has
but to give way, and mankind will have reached its
goal—it will at last have become Israelite! Such is
the hope of the Jew, and this it is which encourages
him in his labours. One must be blind not to see
the work which has been already done, and that which
is in preparation. As the author whom I have just
quoted says,[1] "Although not visible, the colossus is

---

[1] Osman Bey, pp. 32—44.

none the less real, like the atmosphere, which is present everywhere, though hidden from our eyes. There needs but one more cataclysm,[1] and then he will be manifested to the nations, saying, " Worship me, and I will give you happiness."

The Antichrist has an acolyte represented under the image of a second beast, having *horns like a lamb*, and called, later on, *the false prophet*. M. Renan gives up in despair the task of explaining this personage in the vision. The reason is easy to see. These lamb's horns are evidently the symbol of a religious influence which places itself at the disposal of the political power of the Antichrist. Now, what fact analogous to this can be discovered amongst the surroundings of a risen Nero, or even—for it would seem that this is the real idea of M. Renan with regard to the Antichrist of St. John—what false prophet can we find amongst the band of deserters who were the companions of the pseudo-Nero in that island of the Archipelago in which he had taken refuge? To us, it seems clear that a Jewish monarchy could not exist without a clergy at its command ; and that by the side of the new Solomon there would infallibly be found a complaisant high priest, willing to place his piety, his pantheistic wisdom, and even his tricks and pretended miracles, at the service of this false Messiah. May we not believe that we are actually witnessing the first noiseless steps of the approach of this power,

---

[1] Which will be precisely that of the seventh head.

when we hear it said that even now there is a tendency
to give to the decrees of the grand Rabbi of Jerusalem
an universal authority in the Judaism of the whole
world ?[1] This is the new infallibility which is silently
substituting itself for that of which the claims are in
our day disturbing the world ; and the Jerusalem infallibility will be more formidable than the Roman.
Whilst the monarch will exert his despotic power over
the bodies of men by his legions, he will exert it over
their minds, through the priest-prophet who will celebrate the mysteries and the worship of the beast.

It is said that the beast will begin by carrying
Babylon away with him ; then, that he will cast her
into the fire, and deliver her over to be pillaged by the
ten kings, his allies. Babylon is certainly the capital
of the universal monarchy which the Antichrist is to
found. And since the author describes her sitting upon
seven hills, it is clear that she represents Rome. It is
then in Rome that, during the first period, the Jewish
monarch is to take up his residence. This sovereign
will make himself the guardian of humanitarian civilisation, of social cosmopolitanism ; and the great
religious capital of past times will be at the outset
the centre of his empire. But the taking up of this
position will be but a stroke of policy intended to
give security to his first steps, and to lay the foundations of his power. How could a Jew ever forget
the death-blow which his nation had received at the

---

[1] Renan, *L'Antéchrist*, p. 547, note.

hands of Rome, or overlook his opportunity of revenge? The hour of vengeance, long expected, has
now struck. God made Rome His weapon to punish
Israel; now He will make Israel His weapon to
execute judgment upon Rome. It is the old antagonism between the Jews and the heathen, the profoundest antithesis of history, which is now reaching
its supreme crisis. Rome is reduced by victorious
Israel to a condition like that of Nineveh, or of
Babylon. After this act of vengeance, the Antichrist
will, as we saw in ch. xi., take up his residence in
Jerusalem, his natural capital. It is a repetition of
the fate which Rome underwent for the first time
when Constantine abandoned it for Constantinople,
and transferred the seat of monarchy to the East.
It is here that we must place the conflict between the
beast and the two witnesses, and the conversion of
the Jewish nation politically restored.

The reign of Antichrist will last three and a half
years. The interpretation of this number has been
sought in chronology; but it is rather in the symbolism of numbers that we must look for a key to its
meaning. The number *seven* represents a whole;
three and a half, the half of this whole. This number,
then, signifies simply that in the midst of its development, and during the strongest stage of its growth,
the power of the Antichrist will be suddenly destroyed.
Instead of completing his course, he will come to an
end like a tree that has been struck by lightning·

"The Lord Jesus," says St. Paul, "will destroy the
wicked one with the spirit of His mouth."[1]

It remains to explain the number 666, the mark of
the Antichrist. Observe, first, that in the Greek it is
written, not with the same figure three times repeated,
but with three letters of different shapes, the mutual
relation of whose values (*six* hundreds, *six* tens, *six*
units) is not at first sight clear. This is why John
speaks of a calculation that must be undertaken to
find the *value* first, then the *meaning* of the number
represented by these letters ($\chi \xi \varsigma$)[2]

Next we must observe that these three Greek
letters have a peculiarity which is not reproduced in
our numerical writing. The first letter, χ (*ch*), whose
value is 600, and the third, ς (the final *s*) equivalent
to 6, make up, in Greek, the abridged form of the
name Christ (*Christos*);[3] the middle letter, ξ (*x*), which
as a cipher signifies 60, is, in virtue of its form and of
the sibilant sound with which it is pronounced (*chsi*),
an emblem of the serpent.[4] Now, as the name which

---

[1] 2 Thess. ii. 8.

[2] The reading of certain MSS. which give *in extenso* the
number six hundred and sixty-six, is only a paraphrase of the
cypher in three letters. This is proved by the fact that the MSS.
which give this reading present it in the three forms—the masculine (*Alexandrinus*), the feminine (*Sinaiticus*), or the neuter.
The true form has been preserved in the *Vaticanus*.

[3] It is in this form that this name is generally written, whether
in the ancient MSS. or in the ancient Greek inscriptions (Didron
Iconographie Chrétienne, p. 178, and elsewhere). The two letters
are joined by a hyphen placed above them, X̄C.

[4] The antique majuscule form of this letter (Σ) in an in-

John commonly gives to Satan in the Apocalypse is the *old serpent*, in allusion to the story of the temptation in Gen. iii., one is naturally disposed to see in these three letters, so arranged, a figurative sign of the *Satanic Messianism*, substituted for that of the *Divine Messianism*, or Christianity.

And let not this interpretation be charged hastily with puerility. We have here, as the text says, a *mark*,—a kind of graphic decoration, intended to serve as a coat of arms, an official seal, a stamp engraved upon metals or coins, perhaps even as an amulet, in the kingdoms of the Antichrist, and which was to be openly worn, in some form or other, by all his adherents, as M. de Rémusat observes, in his interesting work on the Christian Museum at Rome: " The imaginations of Asiatics are by nature inclined to delight in imagery. Faith, amongst these nations, *has its officially sanctioned designs*, just as moderns have their coats of arms.[1]

We have a very striking proof of the truth of the fact brought out by this writer in the many gems, called by the name of *abraxas*, which are brought to light in our day, and which were probably used as amulets. They proceed from very ancient religious sects. Sometimes they bear a simple inscription, at other times a symbolical figure is attached to the

---

scription of Melas is just the same as the Greek minuscule form (ξ).

[1] *Revue des deux Mondes*, 15th June, 1863, pp. 864, 866.

inscription—very frequently that of a serpent coiled up. M. Didron gives us one which represents the ruler of the world, under the image of a dragon with his tail folded back ; on his right is the image of the sun, and on his left that of the moon : exactly as in the symbolical cypher of the Apocalypse, the first and last letters of the name *Christos* are separated by the ξ.[1]

This form of the mark of the beast reminds us of an ancient Christian sect, which in all probability was the parent of that to which is attributed the invention of the abraxas—the *Ophites*, or *serpent worshippers*, whose origin is to be traced as far back as to the first century of the Church. In our time the Ophites are regarded as the earliest *Gnostics*—a name which signifies *those who know,* and by which was designated, in the primitive Church, a large philosophico-religious party. The serpent in Genesis was, according to the Ophites, the saviour of mankind, the champion of liberty, of intelligence, of progress ; and the invisible being represented by him must therefore be the truly good God ; whilst Jehovah, his adversary, was the jealous god, the spirit of evil. It seems to me that John alludes to speculations of this kind when he speaks, in the epistle to the church of Thyatira, of the doctrine of *those who have known, as they say, the depths of Satan.* We may trace also to these doctrines, as its origin, the blasphemous exclamation, "Accursed

---

[1] *Iconographie Chrétienne*, p. 39.

Jesus!" which St. Paul puts into the lips of certain
fanatics of his day.[1] The mark chosen by the beast
is nothing more than the summing up in a picture of
this whole class of ideas as found historically existing
in the age of the Apocalypse, and in the countries in
which it was composed.

There is a singular various reading of the passage
in the first epistle of St. John, relating to the Antichrist. The ordinary text has: "Every spirit that
confesseth not that Jesus Christ is come in the flesh is
the spirit of Antichrist." But these words are quoted
by Irenæus, Origen, Augustine, etc., in this form:
"Every spirit which *dissolves* or analyses (λύει) Jesus
is the spirit of Antichrist." To "dissolve" Christ is
precisely the act which is figured by the three letters
of the name of the beast. In the place of the hyphen
which ordinarily unites the two letters of Christos, is
substituted the emblem of the serpent, which separates
them.

But the text does not speak only of the *mark* of
the beast; it also draws attention to the *number* of his
name. This number, when we give the three letters
their numerical value, is, as we have seen, 666. What
is the meaning attributed by John to this number?
Seven, we know, is the emblem of a divine totality.
If, therefore, the plenitude of the Divine essence, as it
is revealed in the gospel, was to be expressed in a
number, it would be by a 7, and by a 7 three times

---

[1] 1 Cor. xii. 3.

repeated ; for the number 3 designates the complete cycle of the phases through which a being arrives at his perfection. *Six*, as the number nearest to seven, expresses an aspiration—but a powerless aspiration—after the plenitude of life and strength figured by seven : and if ever there should present itself here below an impious trinity, daring to usurp the office and the honours of the Divine Trinity, it could not be represented, in the symbolical language of numbers, more fitly than by the number 6 three times repeated.

Now the case we are supposing is exactly that which presents itself at the point of the apocalyptic drama at which we have now arrived. As God transmits, in heaven, His power to the Son, and the Son exerts it in the Church through the Holy Spirit who glorifies Him, so has Satan just transmitted his power to the false Messiah, who, in his turn, exerts it in the world through the false prophet, whose influence is altogether at his service. Remember, to complete this comparison, that Satan is called the *god* of this world, that the Antichrist wishes to be its Lord, instead, and in the place of, the Son, and that the false prophet is the personification of the spirit of falsehood, whose work it is to exclude the Divine *Spirit*. After this, the mystery of the number 666 seems to us to be cleared up. John sees in this cypher the symbol of a threefold powerlessness—that of the dragon to equal God, that of the beast to equal Christ, and that of the false prophet to equal the Spirit. The last and final effort of the creature to make himself God does not reach its aim ; and the very mark of the Antichrist contains in itself already the unconscious avowal of his defeat.

No poor act of arithmetical calculation, therefore, has to be gone through in order to discover the meaning of this number. We are here, as in the whole of the Apocalypse, in the region of symbolism, not of arithmetic. Otherwise, as Hengstenberg observes, a cunning Jew would be better able to interpret this sacred book than a believer whose soul is illumined by God.

As to the opinion, held by some to this day, which finds the meaning of this number in chronology, by combining it with that of the twelve hundred and sixty days translated into as many years, how are we to harmonise it with the expression, " the number of *the name* of the beast " ?

M. Renan gives up the point of explaining in any way the name *Armageddon*, applied to the field of battle in which the coming in of the Christ is to destroy the beast and his army. It is the name of a place in Palestine celebrated in the history of the Jews ; it designates *the hill of Megiddo* in the vast plain situated at the foot of the chain of Carmel, where so many important battles were fought in ancient and modern times. If, as John has announced, the Jewish anti-Christian monarchy, after having established itself at Rome, is to have its seat in the East, at Jerusalem

—the rival of Rome—then the choice of this field of battle, the normal one of Palestine, has nothing surprising in it.

Are we to see in the victorious apparition of the Christ, described in chap. xix., an event purely spiritual, or a visible phenomenon ? Jesus compares it to the lightning which shines instantaneously from the one end of heaven to the other ;[1] the latter view is the only one compatible with this expression. On the other hand, it follows from His use of this image, that Jesus had no thought of a permanent and visible abode of His glorified Person on the earth, whether at Jerusalem or elsewhere, as the Millenarians[2] in all ages have thought. The *Parousia* will be, on the contrary, like the stroke of the red-hot rod, which is to startle mankind absorbed in fleshly living, and to prepare the way for the mighty reaction whence the plenitude of the spiritual blessings of the millennium is to proceed. Living in a higher sphere, but near at hand, the faithful who will have been glorified at the advent of the Lord[3] will be in communion with the earthly Christendom, just as the risen Christ was in communion with His disciples until the ascension. This will be the time of the complete development of spiritual worship and of Christian civilisation, in which, as in the middle ages, but under the effects of the

---

[1] Luke xvii. 24.

[2] The advocates of the idea of a visible reign of Jesus on the earth for a thousand years.

[3] 1 Cor. xv. 23.

shining forth of a more intense and pure light, science, art, industry, commerce, will lend their resources to the Christian spirit to enable it to incarnate itself completely in the life of man.   Then will be fulfilled the image of the *leaven which leaveneth the whole lump*. The number *a thousand* is symbolical, like all numbers in the Apocalypse.   It represents a complete development which nothing external to itself will interfere with, or abridge—an era which shall expand itself at ease in the latter days of history.

It does not seem to us that the apocalyptic vision of the *reign of a thousand years* contains a single feature which overpasses the conception of which we have just sketched the outline.   It is that perfect state of things which Ezekiel had already described in the last nine chapters of his prophecy, under the image of an ideal temple.

We do not think we are called upon to pursue this rapid and too incomplete sketch, beyond this point, which is the real *dénouement* of the apocalyptic drama. To reach this concluding stage of our course, we have not had to appeal to any other data than those which are furnished by sacred history and biblical revelation. The great antagonism set up by God Himself, which forms the foundation of the development of His kingdom amongst men—that between the Jews and the Gentiles—has been our key to prophecy, as it is the key to history, which has been shewn by St. Paul in Rom. ix.—xi.

About the year 90, near the first secular jubilee of the new creation, John, lifted as it were upon a rock from whence to command a view far into the past and into the future, beholds, as Moses did before him on Sinai, the visions of God. Behind are the traces of the torrents of blood shed by Nero; before him the sea of fire [1] of a new persecution, with which Domitian —that monster who might well be compared to a Nero risen again—threatens the Church. The eight emperors who have just succeeded one another on the throne of Cæsar, appear to him as types of the eight phases of the anti-divine power in the history of mankind. In Rome triumphant, and Jerusalem in ruins, he sees the two poles between which the destinies of our race oscillate; in the *times of the Gentiles*, and in the ordeal to which these nations are now subjected, he sees the *pendant* and the complement of the *times of Israel*, and of the ordeal now brought to a close through which that people had to pass. The issue of one of these two ordeals does not seem to him less tragical than that of the other. The heathen will go on hardening themselves. Paganism will no doubt fall; but Satan will turn this victory to his own profit. The Gentile Church will be apparently destroyed, as was once Jesus at Golgotha; but the faithful Israel will maintain the kingdom of God in face of the pagan rebellion, as the Gentiles had before maintained it in face of the obduracy of the Jews; Israel divided will be at once the

---

[1] Rev. xv. 1—4.

great power of the Lamb, and His supreme adversary, uttering the final word of humanity in two opposite directions—that of the flesh and that of the spirit— under the form of Antichrist, who makes everything give way to his power, and under that of Christ, who returns from heaven to overthrow his throne. . . . . Is not this really the history of the Church, not in its details, but in its *essence*? Did not John behold at Patmos the work of the Redeemer, as Moses on Sinai had beheld that of the Creator?

Between these holy and vast intuitions, and the puerilities of the apocryphal apocalypses—grotesque imitations of our own, such as the book of Enoch or the fourth book of Esdras—there is a distance like that between the sublime simplicity of our gospel narratives and the religious and moral monstrosities of the apocryphal gospels.

The Apocalypse is the crown of the New Testament and of the whole Bible.

If the Gospels are principally intended to lay the foundations of faith, and the Epistles to enkindle love, the Apocalypse gives food to hope. Without it we should perhaps see in the Church only a *place across which believers pass* in order to attain, individually, to salvation. But by its help we recognize in her a body which develops and which struggles, until with all its members it attains to the full stature of Christ.

The Apocalypse at the same time closes the scheme

which was opened by Genesis, and concludes Holy
Scripture. It shews us the *dénouement* of the drama
which was inaugurated by the victory of Satan over
the first man—the fulfilment of that ancient promise
which is the summary of all those which follow: " The
seed of the woman shall bruise the serpent's head."
By the aid of the first chapters of Genesis, we assist
at the birth-throes of the present order of things in
nature and in history. The last chapters of the
Apocalypse give us the picture of the convulsions
which are to bring about its dissolution, and to
prepare the birth of the new heavens and the new
earth.

What a grand whole! What book can be compared
to the aggregate of the books of the Bible? How can
we fail to recognise in this beginning, middle, and end,
the finger of God, and exclaim with Jacob at Bethel,
" The Lord is in this place, and I knew it not! This
is none other but the house of God!" Each time,
then, that we take up this volume, we may say with
St. Paul in sacred ecstasy, " I hold in my hands the
thought of God."

BIBLE STUDY AIDS by Frederic L. Godet

The works of Frederic L. Godet (1812-1900) are classics in the field of Old and New Testament studies. With the blend of the scholar's mind, the pastor's heart and the reformer's courage, this author refutes the stance of rational and mythical interpreters to staunchly defend the historic Christian faith, using principles as valid today as when they were first recorded. Scholarship, thoroughness and reverence characterize Godet's writings.

STUDIES IN THE OLD TESTAMENT. In this in-depth study of the Old Testament, the author masterfully handles the higher-critic's objections and arguments while discussing in a scholarly manner these subjects: Angels, God's Plan to Develop Life on Earth, The Six Days of Creation, The Four Greater Prophets, The Book of Job, and Song of Songs. 350 pp.

STUDIES IN THE NEW TESTAMENT. In a most interesting and instructive manner, this work covers the key elements of the entire New Testament. Godet's insight is profound and his teaching is weighty and suggestive as he deals with: The Origin of the Four Gospels, The Person and Work of Jesus Christ, The Four Principal Apostles and The Book of Revelation. 408 pp.

STUDIES IN PAUL'S EPISTLES. The author maintains a level of careful scholarship, critical sagacity and practical piety. Godet ably discusses these themes: The Excitement of Christians of Thessalonica, The Lord's Second Coming, The Conflict Between the Law and the Gospel in Galatia, The First Indication of Gnosticism in Asia Minor, The First Anti-Slavery Petition and The Message to the Gentile Church. 352 pp.

COMMENTARY ON LUKE. In this exhaustive commentary, the author defends the cardinal doctrines of the Christian faith while expounding the text from the original language. Godet uniquely gives a critical analysis and a spiritual application of the text. 584 pp.

COMMENTARY ON JOHN'S GOSPEL. Of this monumental, scholarly and exegetical commentary, Wilbur M. Smith said, "From a theological standpoint and for going to the uttermost depths of the profound teachings of the fourth Gospel, Godet is *THE supreme* work, containing some of the finest pages of christology to be found anywhere." 1130 pp.

COMMENTARY ON ROMANS. This verse-by-verse critical commentary on the Greek text brings a clarity of doctrinal instruction to the student of God's Word, even the beginning Bible scholar will see Scriptural concepts made practical by looking into Godet's clear stream of explanation and exegesis. 544 pp.

COMMENTARY ON FIRST CORINTHIANS. In this commentary of enduring quality, Godet presents a veritable garden of beautiful truth. In addition to the seed thoughts concisely given to inspire further study, the reader reaps a harvest of nourishing spiritual food, for Christian maturity from the Greek roots of the text. 928 pp.